Alfred E. Daniell

London City Churches

Alfred E. Daniell
London City Churches
ISBN/EAN: 9783337262358
Printed in Europe, USA, Canada, Australia, Japan
Cover: Foto ©Lupo / pixelio.de

More available books at **www.hansebooks.com**

LONDON CITY
CHURCHES

LONDON CITY
CHURCHES

BY

A. E. DANIELL

WITH

NUMEROUS ILLUSTRATIONS BY

LEONARD MARTIN

AND

A MAP SHEWING THE POSITION OF

THE CHURCHES

WESTMINSTER

ARCHIBALD CONSTABLE AND CO.

1896

CHISWICK PRESS:—CHARLES WHITTINGHAM AND CO.
TOOKS COURT, CHANCERY LANE, LONDON.

CONTENTS

	PAGE
INTRODUCTION	1

CHURCHES ANTERIOR TO THE FIRE.

All Hallows Barking	15
St. Andrew Undershaft	28
St. Bartholomew the Great, West Smithfield	37
St. Ethelburga, Bishopsgate Street	52
St. Giles, Cripplegate	55
St. Helen, Bishopsgate	73
St. Katherine Cree	94
St. Olave, Hart Street	100

WREN'S CHURCHES.

St. Alban, Wood Street	113
All Hallows, Lombard Street	116
St. Andrew by the Wardrobe	122
St. Andrew, Holborn	126
St. Anne and St. Agnes, Aldersgate	133
St. Augustine, Watling Street	135
St. Benet, Paul's Wharf	139
St. Bride, Fleet Street	142
Christ Church, Newgate Street	150
St. Clement, Eastcheap	159
St. Dunstan in the East	163
St. Edmund the King and Martyr	176
St. George, Botolph Lane	181
St. James, Garlickhithe	183
St. Lawrence Jewry	189
St. Magnus the Martyr	197

Contents.

	PAGE
St. Margaret, Lothbury	205
St. Margaret Pattens	212
St. Martin, Ludgate	216
St. Mary Abchurch	223
St. Mary, Aldermanbury	228
St. Mary Aldermary	232
St. Mary-at-Hill	238
St. Mary-le-Bow	242
St. Michael Bassishaw	252
St. Michael, Cornhill	254
St. Michael Paternoster Royal	259
St. Michael, Wood Street	265
St. Mildred, Bread Street	269
St. Nicholas Cole Abbey	275
St. Peter, Cornhill	280
St. Stephen, Coleman Street	285
St. Stephen, Walbrook	287
St. Swithin by London Stone	294
St. Vedast, Foster Lane	299

CHURCHES SUBSEQUENT TO WREN.

All Hallows on the Wall	307
St. Alphage, London Wall	311
St. Bartholomew the Less	314
St. Botolph, Aldersgate	317
St. Botolph, Aldgate	321
St. Botolph, Bishopsgate	325
St. Dunstan in the West	331
Holy Trinity, Minories	338
St. Katherine Coleman	340
St. Mary Woolnoth	343
St. Peter-le-Poer	348
St. Sepulchre	352

FULL PAGE ILLUSTRATIONS.

	FACE PAGE
ALL HALLOWS BARKING	16
ST. GILES, CRIPPLEGATE	56
ST. HELEN, BISHOPSGATE—NUNS' CHOIR	74
ST. KATHERINE CREE	94
ST. OLAVE, HART STREET	100
ST. BRIDE, FLEET STREET	142
ST. LAWRENCE JEWRY	190
ST. MARGARET, LOTHBURY	206
ST. MARY ABCHURCH	224
ST. MARY-AT-HILL	238
ST. PETER, CORNHILL	280
ST. STEPHEN, WALBROOK	288
ST. SWITHIN BY LONDON STONE	294
ST. VEDAST	300

CITY CHURCHES.

INTRODUCTION.

AMONGST the most interesting objects in the City of London are its parish churches. The architectural beauty of most of them, the rich store of historical memories which they possess, and even their very names, many of which perpetuate topographical and personal incidents which would otherwise have been forgotten, combine to render them worthy of the closest attention.

One of the most striking circumstances in connection with these sacred buildings is the great number of parishes—some of them of extremely small extent—which are contained in the comparatively inconsiderable area of the city. There appears to have been, as London was growing, a constant tendency to break up the large ancient parishes into a number of lesser ones. St. Mary Aldermary, for instance, represents the original church of St. Mary, and out of its parish was taken St. Mary-le-Bow, the later origin of which is indicated by its old name of "New Marie" Church, and, still farther to the north, St. Mary Colechurch, St. Mary Aldermanbury, and St. Mary Staining. On the east were formed the parishes of St. Mary Abchurch, St. Mary Woolchurch, St. Mary Woolnoth, St. Mary Bothaw, and St. Mary-at-Hill, while to the south-west, near the river, were created those of St. Mary Somerset and St.

City Churches.

Mary Mounthaw. To All Hallows, again, there are several dedications, the oldest of which appears to have been All Hallows Barking, and the partition of All Hallows in Upper Thames Street into the two parishes of All Hallows the Great and All Hallows the Less furnishes a striking instance of the excessive subdivision which prevailed. The dates of the foundations of the newer churches, like those of the older, are, with but few exceptions, uncertain. Some of them, as, for example, St. Andrew Hubbard and St. Margaret Moses, are distinguished by the names of benefactors, but whether these were founders or merely rebuilders is not easy to say. St. Lawrence Poultney takes its title from Sir John Poultney, who founded a college of priests there in the reign of Edward III., and the same citizen rebuilt All Hallows the Less, and appropriated it to his college.

Occasionally, however, a contrary course of action was pursued, and parishes were united. When the Priory of Holy Trinity, Christ's Church, Aldgate, was founded by Queen Matilda, the parishes of "St. Mary Magdalene, St. Michael, St. Katherine, and the Blessed Trinity," were made, as Stow tells us, into one parish of the Holy Trinity, though St. Katherine's was afterwards rebuilt and assigned to the parishioners during the episcopate of Bishop Gravesend (1280-1303). About the year 1430 the parish church of St. Augustine in the Wall was assigned to the Brethren of the Papey, "poor impotent priests," and the parishioners were appointed to All Hallows on the Wall. When the Church of the Grey Friars was made parochial by Henry VIII., two parishes, St. Nicholas Shambles and St. Ewin in Newgate Market, were included in the newly-formed parish of Christ Church. Early in Elizabeth's reign the parish of St. Mary at the Axe was united to that of St. Andrew Undershaft.

Introduction. 3

But the whole condition of things in the City of London was changed by the Great Fire of 1666. No less than eighty-six parish churches were either totally consumed or severely damaged. To rebuild all these, in the impoverished state to which the citizens had been reduced by the enormous destruction of property wrought by the conflagration, would have been impossible. In spite of assistance granted to them by Parliament out of the proceeds of a tax on coals, and of the munificent contributions of many individuals, the task of raising sufficient funds for the work was attended with considerable difficulty, and in many cases it was only by parishes combining together that it could be accomplished. Thirty-five churches were not rebuilt, thirty-three of the new edifices being made to serve for two parishes, and one, St. Mary-le-Bow, for three—its original parish, and those of All Hallows, Honey Lane, and St. Pancras, Soper Lane.

Forty-nine churches which had been destroyed were rebuilt by Wren, and he also rebuilt the body of the church of St. Andrew, Holborn, which, though it escaped the flames, had fallen into a state of decay. The reparation of St. Sepulchre's, which was only partly burnt, was most probably not his work, and though he did his best to restore the damaged church of St. Mary Woolnoth, it became necessary to take it down and erect an entirely new church early in the eighteenth century.

Wren had a wonderful capacity for utilizing to their fullest extent the opportunities which the circumstances of each church presented to him. The amount of money at his disposal varied considerably in different parishes, and there was also to be taken into account the diversity of the sites, as some churches occupied conspicuous positions, while others were hemmed in by adjacent houses. His first care was to build solidly and durably in accordance with his own precept, that "Building certainly ought to have the attribute of Eternal." He was most particular as to the quality of the materials which he employed, and he would tolerate no faulty work in the construction. Lack of funds might in some cases debar him from raising a majestic and ornate pile, but his churches were always substantial and well proportioned.

In accordance with the character of the site he judged whether the exterior or the interior would more especially repay his pains. In some buildings the steeple appeared most important, as, for example, St. Mary-le-Bow, St. Magnus, St. Vedast, and St. Michael, Paternoster Royal. In others, as St. Mildred, Bread Street, St. Mary Abchurch, St. Swithin, and St. Stephen, Walbrook, the great merit of the church is to be found in the formation of the interior. In St. Bride's the genius of the architect is singularly displayed both in steeple and interior. The manner in which the various steeples harmonize together, is also, as has been well remarked, a noteworthy feature in Wren's work. As instances of this may be cited the steeples of Christ Church, Newgate Street, and St. Vedast, which serve as preludes to the great steeple of Bow, and the line of towers and spires along the riverside from St. Dunstan's in the East to St. Mary Somerset.

It has sometimes been stated that Wren commenced the practice of building churches without chancels, but this is an egregious error, as will plainly appear from the following considerations.

In most of the mediæval churches remaining in England the chancel was structurally a separate building from the nave, generally with a roof of lower pitch, and it was open to the body of the church by an arch. So common was this arrangement that many persons seem to think that it was an essential condition of a chancel. This, however, is not so. The name implies a portion

Introduction.

screened off, and whether there was a chancel structurally different from the nave, or not, the essential condition was a screen at the entrance to it. In parish churches these were generally of carved oak, and many such screens still remain.

In the City of London, whether from the smallness of many of the buildings, or whether from the fact that by custom the parishioners repaired both nave and chancel, whereas the usage in other parts of the country was for the parish to repair the body of the church and for the rector to repair the chancel, or whether from any other cause, there is no instance that we are aware of to be found either in the remaining pre-Reformation churches or to be derived from any views or descriptions of churches no longer extant, in which any chancel arch appears. The chancel was simply marked off by a screen, and in most of the old churches—All Hallows Barking, St. Andrew Undershaft, St. Olave, Hart Street, St. Giles, Cripplegate, and St. Helen's—the position of this screen is shown either by the existence of the stair turret which led to the rood loft, or by traces showing where the turret formerly stood. There is now no mediæval screen work left in London, but screen work of a later date still marked the separation of nave and chancel in Wren's time, and he adopted the practice he found existing. In two of his churches—All Hallows, Thames Street, and St. Peter's, Cornhill—tall and handsome screens were erected, and in the others there were lower strips of carved open work above the level of the pews; and the distinctions which he made between the chancel and the rest of the church can still be frequently traced, notwithstanding internal alterations. In fact, Wren distinguished his chancels on the same principle, though not in the same method of detail, as chancels had already been distinguished in London.

Twenty-one churches, excluding St. Andrew's, Holborn, escaped the Fire, and one of these, All Hallows Staining, fell down, with the exception of the tower, in 1671, and was rebuilt in 1674-5. Eleven others also became so dilapidated that they had to be rebuilt during the eighteenth century, and a twelfth, St. Dunstan in the West, was re-erected in 1831-3. Eight churches dating from before the Fire, All Hallows Barking, St. Andrew Undershaft, St. Bartholomew the Great, West Smithfield, St. Ethelburga, Bishopsgate, St. Giles, Cripplegate, St. Helen, Bishopsgate, St. Katherine Cree, and St. Olave, Hart Street—all buildings of great interest—still remain.

The number of the churches subsequent to Wren has been reduced from thirteen to eleven by the demolition of St. Martin Outwich and St. James, Duke's Place, and the body of All Hallows Staining also has been pulled down, though the old tower has been spared. The finest of these later churches is St. Mary Woolnoth, the work of Nicholas Hawksmoor; the others are of no great value, the best being St. Botolph, Bishopsgate, and St. Dunstan in the West, although an interest attaches to St. Alphage, London Wall, and St. Bartholomew the Less, the former of which has an ancient porch and the latter its old tower.

The history of St. James, Duke's Place, is a good example of the tendency, first to subdivision, and afterwards to unification of parishes. It was originally built in the precinct of the old Priory of the Holy Trinity, Aldgate, in 1622, because the inhabitants, who had since the Dissolution been parishioners of St. Katherine Cree, wanted a parish church of their own, and in 1874 it was pulled down and its parish again united with that of St. Katherine Cree.

Although the loss of St. James, Duke's Place, St. Martin Outwich, and All Hallows Staining may be contemplated with equanimity, the destruction of Wren's churches is a much more serious

Introduction.

matter, and it makes one both sad and angry to observe the spirit of Vandalism in which they have been dealt with. Fifteen of these beautiful buildings have already been destroyed. First went St. Christopher-le-Stocks to enlarge the Bank of England in 1781; fifty years later St. Michael, Crooked Lane, was swallowed up in the formation of the new London Bridge; St. Bartholomew by the Exchange had to make way for the Sun Fire Office in 1841, and very shortly afterwards St. Benet Fink was demolished on the re-erection of the Royal Exchange. Eleven more of Wren's churches have fallen victims to the Union of City Benefices Act, though happily the handsome tower of St. Mary Somerset has been hitherto suffered to remain. All Hallows, Upper Thames Street, which was shorn of its tower in 1876, is even now being pulled down, and the same fate apparently awaits St. Michael Bassishaw. Several others have also been threatened. There are, however, signs that the public mind is awakening to a sense of the wanton barbarism of these proceedings, and that further devastation will not be allowed to pass unchallenged. At the same time, it behoves all citizens and others who have any appreciation of the beautiful in architecture, or any veneration for the historic monuments of past ages, to use their best endeavours to stem the tide of desecration which is obliterating the memorials of the piety of our ancestors and robbing our city of its noblest ornaments.

The object of the following pages is to present to the public a concise account of each of the churches of the City of London. It is impossible in the present brief and hasty sketch to do anything like justice to the subject; but should any reader be induced to explore for himself these very interesting, but little known buildings, wherein he cannot fail to find ample to reward him for his pains, the object of the writer will have been attained.

City Churches.

PARISH CHURCHES IN THE CITY OF LONDON.

Churches Anterior to the Fire.

1. All Hallows Barking.
2. St. Andrew Undershaft.
3. St. Bartholomew the Great, West Smithfield.
4. St. Ethelburga, Bishopsgate Street.
5. St. Giles, Cripplegate.
6. St. Helen, Bishopsgate.
7. St. Katherine Cree.
8. St. Olave, Hart Street.

Wren's Churches.

1. St. Alban, Wood Street.
2. All Hallows, Lombard Street.
3. St. Andrew by the Wardrobe.
4. St. Andrew, Holborn.
5. St. Anne and St. Agnes, Aldersgate.
6. St. Augustine, Watling Street.
7. St. Benet, Paul's Wharf.
8. St. Bride, Fleet Street.
9. Christ Church, Newgate Street.
10. St. Clement, Eastcheap.
11. St. Dunstan in the East.
12. St. Edmund the King and Martyr.
13. St. George, Botolph Lane.
14. St. James, Garlickhithe.
15. St. Lawrence, Jewry.
16. St. Magnus the Martyr.
17. St. Margaret, Lothbury.
18. St. Margaret Pattens.
19. St. Martin, Ludgate.
20. St. Mary Abchurch.
21. St. Mary, Aldermanbury.
22. St. Mary Aldermary.
23. St. Mary-at-Hill.
24. St. Mary le-Bow.
25. St. Michael Bassishaw.
26. St. Michael, Cornhill.
27. St. Michael, Paternoster Royal.
28. St. Michael, Wood Street.
29. St. Mildred, Bread Street.

Introduction.

WREN'S CHURCHES—continued.

30. St. Nicholas Cole Abbey.
31. St. Peter, Cornhill.
32. St. Stephen, Coleman Street.
33. St. Stephen, Walbrook.
34. St. Swithin by London Stone.
35. St. Vedast, Foster Lane.

CHURCHES SUBSEQUENT TO WREN.

1. All Hallows on the Wall.
2. St. Alphage, London Wall.
3. St. Bartholomew the Less.
4. St. Botolph, Aldersgate.
5. St. Botolph, Aldgate.
6. St. Botolph, Bishopsgate.
7. St. Dunstan in the West.
8. Holy Trinity, Minories.
9. St. Katherine Coleman.
10. St. Mary Woolnoth.
11. St. Peter-le-Poer.
12. St. Sepulchre.

St. Benet, Paul's Wharf, is no longer parochial. It has been used since 1867 for Welsh services, and the church of the parish is St. Nicholas Cole Abbey.

The steeple of St. Dunstan's in the East is Wren's, and one of his most beautiful achievements, but the body of the church, which he rebuilt upon the old walls, having become unsafe, was taken down, and the present body erected between the years 1817-1821.

The tower of the old church of St. Mary-at-Hill escaped the Great Fire. It was replaced by the existing tower about 1780.

St. Sepulchre's was partly destroyed by the Fire, and restored in 1671, but probably not by Wren.

PARISH CHURCHES NOT REBUILT AFTER THE FIRE.

1. All Hallows the Less.
2. All Hallows, Honey Lane.
3. St. Andrew Hubbard.
4. St. Anne, Blackfriars.
5. St. Benet Sherehog.
6. St. Botolph, Billingsgate.
7. St. Faith under St. Paul's.
8. St. Gabriel Fenchurch.
9. St. Gregory by St. Paul's.
10. Holy Trinity the Less.
11. St. John the Baptist upon Walbrook.
12. St. John the Evangelist
13. St. John Zachary.
14. St. Lawrence Poultney.
15. St. Leonard, Eastcheap.
16. St. Leonard, Foster Lane.
17. St. Margaret Moses.
18. St. Margaret, New Fish Street.
19. St. Martin Orgars.
20. St. Martin Pomary.
21. St. Martin Vintry.
22. St. Mary Bothaw.
23. St. Mary Magdalene, Milk Street.
24. St. Mary Mounthaw.
25. St. Mary Colechurch.
26. St. Mary Staining.
27. St. Mary Woolchurch Haw.
28. St. Michael-le-Querne.
29. St. Nicholas Acon.
30. St. Nicholas Olave.
31. St. Olave, Silver Street.
32. St. Pancras, Soper Lane.
33. St. Peter, Paul's Wharf.
34. St. Peter, Westcheap.
35. St. Thomas the Apostle.

WREN'S CHURCHES WHICH HAVE BEEN DESTROYED.

1. All Hallows, Bread Street.
2. All Hallows the Great, Upper Thames Street.
3. St. Antholin, Watling Street.
4. St. Bartholomew by the Exchange.
5. St. Benet Fink.
6. St. Benet Gracechurch.
7. St. Christopher-le-Stocks.
8. St. Dionis Backchurch.
9. St. Mary Magdalene, Old Fish Street.

Introduction.

WREN'S CHURCHES WHICH HAVE BEEN DESTROYED—*continued.*

10. St. Mary Somerset.
11. St. Matthew, Friday Street.
12. St. Michael, Crooked Lane.
13. St. Michael, Queenhithe.
14. St. Mildred, Poultry.
15. St. Olave, Jewry.

The tower of St. Mary Somerset still stands, having been preserved when the church was destroyed.

CHURCHES NOW DESTROYED, WHICH ESCAPED THE FIRE, BUT WERE AFTERWARDS REBUILT.

1. All Hallows Staining.
2. St. James, Duke's Place, Aldgate.
3. St. Martin Outwich.

The tower of All Hallows Staining, which belonged to the old church, has been preserved.

CHURCHES ANTERIOR TO THE FIRE.

ALL HALLOWS BARKING.

At the junction of Tower Street and Seething Lane, and close to Trinity Square and the Mark Lane Station, stands the church of All Hallows Barking, so called from its being an ancient possession of the abbess and convent of Barking in Essex. The date of the foundation of this church is unknown, but we read that as early as the reign of King Stephen the advowson of "Berkingechirche" was given by one Riculphus and Brichtwen his wife to the see of Rochester. Subsequently, but at what date is uncertain, the patronage of All Hallows passed from the Bishop of Rochester to the convent of Barking. It is probable, however, from the designation of "Berkingechirche" being applied to All Hallows in the transfer to the see of Rochester, that this later transfer was but a restoration of original rights, and that it is to the convent of Barking that the primary foundation is due.

The convent of Barking was a religious establishment of great antiquity. It is believed to have been founded by Erkenwald, Bishop of London, at the end of the seventh century. Its wealth was great, and its reputation was high, and All Hallows also received special marks of favour from several English sovereigns. Richard I. added to it a chapel of St. Mary, which stood about one hundred yards to the north of the chancel in the churchyard, which was then of considerable extent. Stow records a tradition that the heart of this warlike monarch was there buried under the high altar; but this appears to be a mere idle tale, as Cœur de Lion gave special instructions for the interment of his heart at Rouen. Edward I. increased the chapel, and presented a statue of "Our Lady of Barking," and Edward IV. interested himself in the establishment of a brotherhood in connection with the chapel by John Tiptoft, Earl of Worcester, Constable of the Tower. This earl was the enlightened patron of Caxton, and a man of far higher scholarly attainments than was common amongst the nobility of that epoch; he was a most zealous partisan of the house of York, and was beheaded in 1470, when Henry VI. was for a brief period restored to his throne by the Earl of Warwick. Richard III. rebuilt the chapel, and established there a college of priests; but both chapel and college were pulled down in 1548, and the site was afterwards utilized for secular buildings. The advowson of All Hallows was on the dissolution of the convent of Barking granted by Henry VIII. to the see of Canterbury, in whose gift it has ever since remained.

The church of All Hallows consists of a nave and chancel, together with north and south aisles. Its total length is 108 feet, its breadth 67 feet, and the height from the ground to the ceiling of the nave is 35 feet. The ceilings of the aisles are at a much lower elevation. The clerestory continues at a uniform level through the whole length of the church. The edifice, as we now see it, bears indubitable marks of two distinct periods of construction, but, contrarily to what is usually the case, the western portion is older than the chancel. In the absence of external evidence on the point, it has been conjectured that the original building only covered the ground now occupied by the nave, and that the church was subsequently enlarged by the addition of the eastern portions.

ALL HALLOWS BARKING.

All Hallows Barking.

The massive pillars at the west end are of Norman character, and form a striking contrast to the slender columns of the eastern arches, which can hardly have been erected before the fifteenth century. The appearance of the chancel was much changed in 1634-5, when the church was repaired at a cost—as recorded by the parish books—of over £1,400. A fresh roof was then put on, and the walls were partially rebuilt. Many of the windows also were renewed, and the church was ornamented after the Tudor fashion. The large east window, however, seems during these alterations to have been left untouched; it is in the late Decorated style, sharply pointed, and the tracery at the head is decidedly handsome.

The fine oak pulpit, which is united in one piece with the reading-desk, was first erected in 1613. The original sounding-board was found too small, and a larger one, which still remains, was substituted in 1638.

In 1649 an explosion of gunpowder at a shop adjoining the churchyard-wall, by which many houses in the vicinity were wrecked and many persons killed, seriously injured the tower, so that in the course of a few years it became unsafe, and had finally to be taken down in 1659, when it was replaced by the present tower, the expense of which was principally defrayed by the voluntary contributions of the parishioners. It is of plain brick, culminating in a turret and weather-vane, and is placed over the west end of the nave, whereas the old tower rose from the west end of the south aisle. The height to the top of the turret is 80 feet.

From the Great Fire of 1666 All Hallows escaped, but in the narrowest possible manner, as Pepys relates in his "Diary," under date September 5th of that year:

"About two in the morning my wife calls me up, and tells me of new cryes of fire, it being come to Barking church, which is at the bottom of our lane.... But going to the fire, I find by the blowing up of houses, and the great help given by the workmen out of the King's yards, sent up by Sir W. Pen, there is a good stop given to it, as well at Marke-lane end as ours; it having only burned the dyall of Barking church, and part of the porch, and was there quenched. I up to the top of Barking steeple, and there saw the saddest sight of desolation that I ever saw."

One of the windows of the north aisle is emblazoned with the arms of Sir Samuel Starling, and below them is an inscription stating it to have been "glassed" in 1666, the year of the "Conflagration of London." Sir Samuel Starling, who lived in Seething Lane, was Lord Mayor in 1669, and was buried at All Hallows in 1674. Beyond this coat-of-arms he has no monument. According to Pepys, he was not a man of a very liberal turn of mind, for during the fire, when the house of his next-door neighbour was in flames, and his own was only saved by the exertions of a number of poor men, he "did give 2^s/6^d among 30 of them."

The well-carved altar-piece with its wreaths and scrolls is recorded to have been presented by Mr. John Richardson in 1685. The font, which stands at the east end of the south aisle, is probably of about the same date. It possesses a wooden cover very elaborately carved, and representing three angels gathering fruit and flowers. There is a tradition that this is the work of Grinling Gibbons, who may possibly have also carved the altar-piece; but at the same time we have no actual proof that he participated at all in the embellishment of All Hallows. The general style of the carving, however, closely resembles his.

During the present century All Hallows has been several times more or less repaired and restored. In 1814 over £5,000 was spent on its renovation. On this occasion a new ceiling was put

All Hallows Barking. 19

up, and the tower was hung with eight bells. More repairs were executed in 1836 and 1860, and a new south porch of no particular merit was added in 1863. In 1870 took place another and somewhat extensive restoration; but in spite of its having been so frequently in the hands of architects and builders, the general appearance of the interior has probably changed but little during the last two centuries and a half. A further restoration is now in progress; the walls of the north aisle and clerestory have been repaired; a new porch, with a chamber above it, has been added, and a new open timber roof has been substituted for the plaster ceiling of the north aisle. The church, thus improved, was reopened in November, 1894; but, when sufficient funds are raised, it is proposed to continue the work by a thorough reparation of the remaining walls, windows, and parapets, and by the construction of open timber roofs for the nave, chancel, and south aisle.

The organ, which still occupies its original situation in the west gallery, is the work of the famous seventeenth-century organ-builder, Renatus Harris, and was erected about 1677. In 1720 it was repaired by Gerard Smith, nephew of Harris's great rival, Father Smith. Since then it has been repaired in 1813 and 1878. Mr. Charles Young was organist here for forty-five years (1713-1758), but an even longer period was spent in the service of the church by one of his successors, Mr. Smethergill, who presided at the organ from 1770 till 1823.

The parish of All Hallows Barking is bounded on the east by the Liberty of the Tower, which is extra-parochial, and this juxtaposition was in the middle ages a fertile source of dispute between the rival authorities of the Crown and the Corporation. Another result of the proximity of the Tower, and one which has now more interest for us, was that All Hallows was frequently used for the interment of the remains of those who perished on the scaffold on Tower Hill. The corpse of John Fisher, Bishop of Rochester—executed on June 22nd, 1535, for denying the king's supremacy in ecclesiastical matters—was first deposited in this church, but was afterwards removed to the chapel of the Tower, the place of sepulture of his friend Sir Thomas More, whose decapitation on a similar charge took place exactly a fortnight after that of the bishop. Here also were buried the remains of that graceful poet and distinguished man, Henry Howard, Earl of Surrey, beheaded on a frivolous charge of high treason, June 19th, 1547, whose bones, however, were removed in 1614 to Framlingham in Suffolk, and there re-interred with all due honour. Almost a hundred years later, All Hallows received the body of Archbishop Laud, who met his death on the block on January 10th, 1645, and here it remained till 1663, when it was transported to a more fitting resting-place at St. John's College, Oxford, of which the hapless prelate had once been president.

Amongst other victims of the axe stated to have been buried at All Hallows, and not subsequently removed, one of the most prominent was Lord Thomas Grey, brother of the Duke of Suffolk, and uncle of Lady Jane Grey. He was deeply involved in the plots of his family, and was beheaded in 1554. In the parish register are also recorded the burials of Sir John Hotham and his son Captain Hotham, executed by order of the Parliament, the son on the 1st, and the father on the 2nd of January, 1644, on an accusation of conspiracy to surrender the important town of Hull, of which Sir John was governor under the Parliament, to King Charles I.

All Hallows contains the best collection of monumental brasses to be met with in any church in London. The most elaborate of these is a beautifully executed Flemish brass, dating from about 1535, to the memory of Andrew Evyngar and Ellyn his wife. It is placed on the floor of the centre of the nave, and has been to some extent defaced by Puritan iconoclasts and thoughtless passengers, and therefore to preserve the delicately worked figures and ornaments from further injury, it is now carefully covered by a mat. Andrew Evyngar, a citizen and salter, is said to have been of Flemish descent, and to have had a house at Antwerp, which is probably the reason why his memorial took the form of a Flemish brass.

In the south aisle of the chancel, not far from the font, is a brass which, though of considerably less artistic merit than that of Evyngar, possesses associations of far greater interest. It is that of William Thynne, Clerk of the Kitchen to Henry VIII., and his wife. The name of William Thynne will ever be held in reverence by all lovers of literature, for to him are due the earliest complete editions of Chaucer, the folio of 1532 and the folio of 1542, of which he was the learned, laborious, and enthusiastic editor. He died on August 10th, 1546, leaving an only son, Francis, who became Lancaster Herald, and appears to have inherited his father's literary tastes, as he wrote some criticisms on a subsequent edition of Chaucer, and assisted Holinshed in the compilation of his "Chronicle." From one of William Thynne's nephews, Sir John Thynne of Longleat, was descended Thomas Thynne, the associate of the Duke of Monmouth, called by Dryden, in "Absalom and Achitophel," "wise Issachar, his wealthy western friend," and celebrated alike for his riches and his tragic end. The present head of the family and owner of Longleat is the Marquis of Bath, who, in 1861, at his own expense, caused William Thynne's brass to be restored.

In the north aisle of the chancel is a well-preserved brass to John Bacon and Joan, his wife. He was a citizen and woolman, and died in 1437. To the west of this is the brass to Thomas Virby, vicar of All Hallows from 1434 to 1453. His effigy has perished, but it is not difficult to decipher the inscription. In the chancel is another brass without effigy, commemorating, as we learn from the epitaph, Thomas Gilbert, citizen and draper of London, and merchant of the Staple of Calais, who died in 1483, and Agnes, his wife, who died in 1489.

In the south aisle, to the west of that of Thynne, are the brasses of John Rusche (died 1498) and Christopher Rawson (died 1518). Rusche's effigy is very well executed, but nothing particular is known about him. He is described in the inscription as a gentleman. The figure of Rawson is flanked by those of his two wives. He was a mercer of London and a merchant of the Staple of Calais, and was appointed Junior Warden of the Mercers' Company in 1516. His father, Richard Rawson, likewise a mercer, of which company he rose to be Senior Warden, was Alderman of the Ward of Farringdon Without, and served the office of Sheriff in 1476. Two of Christopher's brothers, John and Richard, took holy orders. John, who settled in Ireland, became Prior of Kilmainham and a member of the Irish Privy Council, and in 1517 was appointed Lord High Treasurer of Ireland. In 1541 he surrendered his priory to the king, who thereupon granted him a pension for life, and raised him to the Irish peerage under the title of Viscount Clontarf. Richard Rawson was Rector of St. Olave's, Hart Street, Archdeacon of Essex, chaplain and almoner to Henry VIII., and canon of Windsor, where he was buried in St. George's Chapel in 1543. From another brother, Avery, who resided at Avely in Essex, is descended the noble house of Stanhope, through the marriage of his granddaughter, Anne, with Sir Michael Stanhope.

There is also on the floor of the chancel a large brass to Roger James, citizen and brewer, who died in 1591. Brasses had then gone out of fashion, and the workmanship of this specimen is decidedly inferior to that of its predecessors.

Affixed to a pillar in the south aisle is a brass plate with kneeling figures of a father and mother, three sons and four daughters, to the memory of William Armer, Governor of the Pages of Honour under Henry VIII., Edward VI., Mary, and Elizabeth, whose death occurred in 1560. The inscription includes some quaint verses :

> "He that liveth so to this worlde
>   That God is pleased with all,
> He nede not at the judgement daye
>   Fear nothing at all.
> Wherefore in peace lie down with me,
>   And take our rest and slepe ;
> And offer to God, in sacrifice,
>   Our bodies and soules to kepe.
> Unto the day that God shall call
>   Our bodies to rise againe,
> That we with other shall come together
>   To glorify his name."

Armer was a member of the Clothworkers' Company, and in the year 1843 that company paid a tribute of respect to his memory by restoring his monument, as is recorded on a brass plate below.

Towards the western end of the north aisle may be perceived on the floor the unpretentious brass plate of George Snayth, "Auditor," i.e., steward, to Archbishop Laud, who, dying in 1651, requested to be interred in the church where then reposed the body of his beloved master. The epitaph of this faithful servant is as simple as his memorial plate :

"Here lyeth the body of George Snayth Esquire, sometimes Auditor to Will. Lawd late Arch Bpp of Cant. wch George was borne in Durham the 23th of August 1602, and dyed the 17th of February 1651.

Mors Mihi Lucrum."

Two canopied altar-tombs, both of Purbeck marble and both apparently dating from the fifteenth century, stand one in the north and the other in the south chancel aisle. The tomb in the north aisle, which is the larger of the two, is also the more carefully executed. The inscription is gone, and it is not certain to whom it belonged, but it has been surmised that it is the monument of Alderman John Croke, who, at his death in 1477, founded a chantry at All Hallows. The other altar-tomb has also lost its inscription, and the identity of its occupant cannot even be conjectured.

Under a large marble slab now defaced, inserted in the floor of the middle aisle, was interred in 1691 Lady Joanna Kempthorne, widow of Admiral Sir John Kempthorne. Sir John, who predeceased her by twelve years, was a distinguished naval commander, and M.P. for Portsmouth; he is several times mentioned by Pepys. On the pillar of the most eastern arch of the chancel the eye is attracted by a white marble tablet of no great size, but tastefully ornamented. This is the memorial of John Kettlewell, rector of Coleshill in Warwickshire, who after the Revolution chose rather to vacate his living than to take the oath of allegiance to William III. He was a man highly esteemed even by many who differed from him in politics, and Macaulay couples him and

Canon Fitzwilliam, as two Nonjurors who "deserve special mention, less on account of their abilities, than on account of their rare integrity, and of their not less rare candour." "Kettlewell was," adds the same historian, "one of the most active members of his party: he declined no drudgery in the common cause, provided only that it were such drudgery as did not misbecome an honest man." He was not, however, spared many years to continue his advocacy of the divine right of kings and to maintain the doctrine of passive obedience, for he breathed his last on April 12th, 1695, at the early age of forty-two. His epitaph tells of his virtuous character and holiness of life, and bestows on him a glowing eulogy, which in his case, at all events, is not undeserved

On the floor of the south aisle is a stone in memory of Lady Ann Masters (died 1719), the wife of Alderman Sir Harcourt Masters, who in 1717 was one of the sheriffs; and another monument of interest is the very ornate one under the east window of the south aisle, which deserves a word of mention as being from the chisel of Peter Scheemakers, the sculptor of the monuments of Shakespeare, Dryden, and the Dukes of Albemarle and Buckingham, in Westminster Abbey. It was erected in 1741 at the desire and cost of Sir Peter Colleton, in memory of two daughters, a son-in-law, and four grandchildren.

Sir Francis Cherry, merchant vintner and purveyor, who visited Russia in 1588 as the special envoy of Queen Elizabeth, was buried in this church, as the register informs us, on April 14th, 1605, but there is no monument to him now in existence; neither is there any memorial to Sir John Jolles, Lord Mayor 1615, who was interred here in 1621, or to Slingsby Bethell, who was Lord Mayor in 1755, and a member for the City of London in the two last Parliaments of George II., although the parish books of All Hallows record his burial on November 7th, 1758.

Bethell's sword-rest is, however, still preserved, erected in front of the south aisle on the choir-screen, together with those of Sir John Eyles, Lord Mayor 1726, and Sir Thomas Chitty, Lord Mayor 1759, both of whom were at the time of their election to the mayoralty residents in the parish. Sir John Eyles's sword-rest occupies the most southerly position. It bears his own arms, the arms of his company, the Haberdashers, and above these the arms of the City of London and the royal arms of England. Bethell's sword-rest, in the centre, is bedecked with his own arms, the arms of his company, the Fishmongers, and the city and royal arms above; and the same arrangement has been followed in the case of Chitty's sword-rest, which is placed on the north of that of Bethell, and is the most ornate of the three, as Eyles's is the plainest. Sir Thomas Chitty was a salter, and the arms of that company consequently appear. Each of these sword-rests is surmounted by a gilded crown of iron.

At the outbreak of the Civil War the vicarage of All Hallows Barking was held by Dr. Edward Layfield, the son of a sister of Archbishop Laud, by whom he had been appointed to the living. He was a zealous High Churchman and a sturdy Royalist, and in consequence was deprived of his preferments by the Long Parliament, and suffered many privations during the Commonwealth. But he was reinstated at the Restoration, which he survived twenty years, continuing vicar of All Hallows till his death in 1680. He was buried in the chancel, but has no monument.

Dr. George Hickes, who succeeded him, held the living till 1686. Hickes was an eminent scholar, but his special learning lay in a direction then almost altogether uncultivated—the Anglo-

All Hallows Barking.

Saxon and other old Teutonic dialects. He published the results of his studies under the title of "Thesaurus Linguarum," a very erudite work. At the time of the Revolution he was Dean of Worcester, but he resigned his office, and threw in his lot with the Nonjurors, distinguishing himself even amongst these enthusiastic Jacobites by the vehemence and fervour with which he proclaimed the most extreme doctrines of his party. In 1694, on the recommendation of the Nonjuring Archbishop Sancroft, he was appointed by James II. one of those bishops by the creation of whom the Nonjurors endeavoured to perpetuate the episcopal succession in their own body. He died towards the end of 1715 at the age of seventy-three, and his remains were interred in the churchyard of St. Margaret's, Westminster.

In 1783, the archbishopric of Canterbury being then vacant, the Crown, in exercise of its right under such circumstances, appointed to the living the Rev. Samuel Johnes-Knight, who continued to hold it until 1852, when he died, after having been vicar of the parish for nearly seventy years.

In the list of the churchwardens of All Hallows Barking occurs for 1760 and 1761 the name of Brass Crosby, who became Lord Mayor in 1770, and covered himself with glory by the manful conflict which he sustained, in conjunction with his brother aldermen, John Wilkes and Richard Oliver, against the tyranny of the House of Commons, on behalf of the liberty of the press.

In connection with this church another famous name must not be forgotten—that of William Penn, the Quaker, and founder of Pennsylvania, who was baptized at All Hallows Barking on the 23rd October, 1644.

St Andrew Undershaft

The church of St. Andrew Undershaft derives its name from the ancient practice of erecting on May-day a "shaft" or maypole in front of the south door. As the maypole was taller than the steeple, the church acquired its distinguishing title of "undershaft." This custom was discontinued in consequence of a riot in 1517, and the "shaft" itself was finally destroyed as a relic of idolatry in an ebullition of fanaticism during the reign of Edward VI.

St. Andrew's Undershaft is situated at the junction of Leadenhall Street and St. Mary Axe. There is now no church of St. Mary Axe, but there was one originally in this street, dedicated to St. Mary the Virgin, St. Ursula, and the Eleven Thousand Virgins, and called St. Mary-at-Axe, from an axe being the sign of an adjacent house. This church was, however, demolished in 1561, and its parish united with that of St. Andrew Undershaft.

The present church of St. Andrew Undershaft, which occupies the site of a former edifice, the period of the foundation of which is unknown, dates from the early part of the sixteenth century, having been, says Stow, "new built by the parishioners there since the year 1520; every man putting to his helping hand, some

St. Andrew Undershaft.

with their purses, other with their bodies." Sir Stephen Jennings, Lord Mayor in 1508, built at his own expense the whole of the northern and a portion of the southern half of the church. He died in 1523, but William Fitzwilliams, who had been sheriff in 1506, continued the work, and it was finally completed in 1532. It is an imposing church, a late example of the Perpendicular style, consisting of a nave and two side aisles, and surmounted by a tower, rebuilt in 1830, which rises to a height of about 91 feet, and contains six bells. The aisles are lighted by spacious windows, and divided from the nave by clustered columns and obtusely pointed arches, above which is the clerestory, lighted by six windows on each side. The spandrels between the arches were embellished in 1726 with paintings of scriptural subjects at the expense of Henry Tombes, a parishioner, but these are now very much faded. The roof, which is ribbed into compartments, is nearly flat, and is picturesquely studded with stars.

St. Andrew's has undergone considerable restoration during the last thirty years. In 1875 the chancel was reconstructed, and the east window was filled with modern stained glass, representing the Crucifixion. The former glass, on which is painted a very interesting series of five full-length portraits of English sovereigns—Edward VI., Elizabeth, James I., Charles I., and Charles II.—was then transferred to its present location in the west window. Pews formed part of the original design, some being recorded to have been set up by Jennings himself; but pews have now been cleared away and have been replaced by open benches, though specimens of the old woodwork may yet be observed in the high-backed seats of the churchwardens at the west end, and the carved oak pulpit is still retained.

The western organ-gallery was also pulled down at the same time, and the organ, a very fine instrument, built by Renatus Harris, and first opened in 1696, was re-erected at the south of the chancel at an expense of £75. It is a fact worth mentioning that during a period of 116 years only three organists presided at this organ : Mr. Philip Hart, who was appointed in 1720, remained till 1749 ; he was succeeded by Dr. John Morgan, who continued till 1790 ; and then the office was conferred upon Miss Mary Allen, who held it till 1836.

The most interesting monument in the church is that of the great antiquarian and topographer, John Stow, to whom we are indebted for invaluable information concerning mediæval London. It is placed towards the eastern end of the north wall, just beyond the vestry door. The illustrious student is represented sitting at a table, with a book open before him, and holding in his right hand a pen ; while on each side of him is a shelf, and on each shelf a book. The face—as one would expect the face of such a man to be—is refined and intellectual, and marked with the traces of deep and continued thought. Above the effigy rises a canopy, on which is carved the legend :

"Aut scribenda agere, aut legenda scribere."

Beneath the figure is this epitaph :

"Memoriae sacrum
Resurrectionem in Christo hic expectat
Johannes Stowe, civis Londinensis, qui in antiquis monumentis eruendis accuratissima diligentia usus Angliae Annales
et Civitatis Londini Synopsim, bene de sua, bene de postera aetate meritus luculenter scripsit, vitaeque stadio pie et probe decurso obiit aetatis anno 80

St. Andrew Undershaft.

Die 5 Aprilis 1605.
Elizabetha conjunx ut perpetuum sui amoris
testimonium dolens."

The monument is of terra cotta—an uncommon material.

Stow was born in 1525, in the parish of St. Michael, Cornhill, and by trade he was a tailor. But he abandoned the paths of commerce, in which he might easily have attained to opulence, in order to devote himself to those archæological and historical studies by which, as his epitaph truly says, "he merited well of his own generation and well of posterity." Posterity has, indeed, paid him tribute—and it is all posterity can do—by its gratitude and veneration; but his own contemporaries remained grossly insensible to his claims to recognition.

"'Tis strange to me," says Strype, "that the City of London, to which he had done such service and honour in writing such an elaborate and accurate Survey thereof; nor the wealthy Company of Merchant Taylors, of which he was a worthy and creditable member; nor lastly, the State, in grateful remembrance of his diligent and faithful pains in composing an excellent History of the Kingdom, neither of them had allotted him some honorary pension during his life."

The researches by which he acquired such copious and curious knowledge were not carried out without many sacrifices. "It hath cost me," he says himself, "many a weary mile's travel, many a hard-earned penny and pound, and many a cold winter night's study." He was suffering, too, from old age and sickness, "being (by the good pleasure of God) visited with sickness such as my feet (which have borne me many a mile) have of late years refused, once in four or five months, to convey me from my bed to my study." How he was rewarded for the learning, the industry, and the self-denial which produced such priceless results is told in eloquent and feeling words by Isaac Disraeli: "It was in his eightieth year that Stow at length received a public acknowledgment of his services, which will appear to us of a very extraordinary nature. He was so reduced in his circumstances that he petitioned James I. for a licence to collect alms for himself! 'as a recompense for his labours and travel of forty-five years, in setting forth the "Chronicles of England," and eight years taken up in the "Survey of the Cities of London and Westminster," towards his relief now in his old age; having left his former means of living, and only employing himself for the service and good of his country.' Letters patent under the great seal were granted. After no penurious commendations of Stow's labours, he is permitted 'to gather the benevolence of well-disposed people within this realm of England; to ask, gather, and take the alms of all our loving subjects.' These letters-patent were to be published by the clergy from their pulpits; they produced so little, that they were renewed for another twelvemonth; one entire parish in the city contributed seven shillings and sixpence! Such, then, was the patronage received by Stow, to be a licensed beggar throughout the kingdom for one twelvemonth! Such was the public remuneration of a man who had been useful to his nation, but not to himself!"

Stow did not long survive this indignity, dying on April 5th, 1605, "of the stone cholick," says Strype; naïvely adding, "so that it is to be feared the poor man made but little progress in this collection."

Maitland asserts that the contumelious treatment which this great but unappreciated genius received during his lifetime was extended to his corpse after death, stating that neither his distin-

St. Andrew Undershaft. 33

guished services to English literature, " nor any other consideration was sufficient to protect his repository from being spoiled of his injured remains by certain men in the year 1732, who removed his corpse to make way for another."

The remaining monuments in St. Andrew's call up no such memories as does that of Stow; there is one, however—on the same wall, farther west—which is well worthy of attention on account of the beauty of its workmanship. It is that of Sir Hugh Hammersley, Sheriff 1618, Lord Mayor 1627; of whom his epitaph sets forth that he was "Colonel of this City, President of Christ's Hospital, President of the Artillery Garden, Governor of the Company of Russia Merchants and of those of the Levant, free of the Company of Haberdashers and of Merchant Adventurers of Spain, East India, France and Virginia;" also that he "had issue by Dame Mary his wife 15 children," and that he died at the age of seventy-one on October 19th, 1636. Sir Hugh and his wife are represented life-size, kneeling under a canopy, but the most striking part of the monument consists in the excellently sculptured figures of two attendants, standing one on each side of the canopy. The sculptor is stated to have been Thomas Madden, a man of whom little is known, but whom this fine production sufficiently proves to have been possessed of artistic talent of no common order.

On the north side of the chancel is a canopied altar-tomb, in front of which are kneeling figures of Sir Thomas Offley and Joan his wife, together with their three sons. Sir Thomas belonged to the Company of Merchant Taylors; he was Sheriff in 1553, and Lord Mayor in 1556. We learn from his rhyming epitaph that he was a native of Stafford, that he lost his wife in 1578 after fifty-two years of married life, and that he soon afterwards followed her to the grave, having attained the age of eighty-two. "He bequeathed," says Stow, "the one half of all his goods to charitable actions; but the parish received little benefit thereby."

Over the tomb are some quaint moral lines:

> "By me a lykelihood beholde
> How mortal man shall torn to mold,
> When all his pompe and glori vayne
> Shal chaynge to dust and earth agayne;
> Such is his great incertaintye,
> A flower, and type of vanitye."

To the west of the monument of Hammersley is one to Sir Christopher Clitherow, and Mary, his wife. Sir Christopher, who was a benefactor to the parish, was Sheriff in 1625 and Lord Mayor in 1635, and died in 1642. His wife survived him three years. Between the monuments of Hammersley and Stow is an effigy of Dame Alice Byng, kneeling in prayer at a desk and wearing round her neck a large ruff. Her epitaph tells us that she had three husbands, all bachelors and all stationers, and that she died in 1616. She was the daughter of Simon Burton, a citizen and wax-chandler, and a great benefactor to the poor of the parish, who was also buried in this church, in the year 1593, and is commemorated by a brass plate in a frame.

An older and more remarkable brass is that on the east wall of the north aisle to Nicholas Levison and his wife. Levison was a mercer, and sheriff in 1534; he was, as Stow has recorded, a liberal contributor to the work of building the church. Besides the figures of himself and his wife, there appear likewise those of their eighteen children—ten boys and eight girls—all perfectly distinct, and kneeling behind their parents according to sex. Considering that this brass is of no great size, it seems quite a

St. Andrew Undershaft.

triumph of art to have introduced as many as twenty well-defined figures in so small a space. It was restored in 1764 at the expense of the parish, and is in very good preservation.

The north aisle is continued to the extreme west of the church and is terminated by a large window, but the extent of the south aisle—in order to make room for the south porch, which forms the main entrance to the sacred building—is cut short by a wall. On this wall has been placed a handsome brass tablet, bearing the following inscription:

> "To the Glory of God
> And in Memory of
> John alias Hans Holbein,
> Painter to His Majesty King Henry VIII.
> Sometime resident in this parish.
> Born 1491—Died 1543."

Dr. Henry Man, who by an odd coincidence was Bishop of Man, was buried at St. Andrew's in 1556; and here too was interred, but apparently without any monument, Sir William Craven, Sheriff 1600, Lord Mayor 1610, a man of great wealth and a benefactor to the parish, and father of the valiant and chivalrous Earl of Craven, who was himself baptized at St. Andrew's on June 26th, 1608.

Many of the monumental tablets, particularly those on the south wall, have been suffered to become so thickly coated with dirt that they are in their present state totally illegible.

To the north wall, beneath the effigy of Alice Byng, has been recently affixed by Colonel Charles and Caroline Torriano a brass plate in memory of their ancestors, Charles Torriano (1659-1723), a merchant in the City of London, and his wife Rebecca (1667-1754), daughter of Alderman Sir Peter Paravicini; both of whom were buried in the churchyard.

Sir Peter Paravicini was a friend of Pepys, and was one of the four persons who became bail for the Diarist on his arrest in the summer of 1690, on an accusation of furnishing the French Court with information relative to the state of the English Navy—a baseless charge of which he was a few months afterwards honourably acquitted.

Peter Anthony Motteux, a dealer in East Indian produce, who translated Rabelais and "Don Quixote" into English, and enjoyed amongst his contemporaries some reputation as a poet, was buried here in 1718, but he has no monument.

In the vestry are carefully preserved seven remarkable old books, including three copies of Fox's "Acts and Monuments," Sir Walter Raleigh's "History of the World," Erasmus's "Paraphrase of the Books of the New Testament," a volume of Bishop Jewell's works, and a volume of Sermons by William Perkins, a "reverend and judicious Divine," published at Cambridge in the reign of James I. Of these books the "History of the World" and Perkins's Sermons are the only two which are not in the black letter, but they have all been rebound with the exception of two of the copies of the "Acts and Monuments," one of which still retains a fragment of the chain by which it was formerly fastened to a desk at the east end of the south aisle; the other has, however, lost both its cover and chain.

The living of St. Andrew's Undershaft is in the patronage of the Bishop of London, and the rectorship has been attached to the Suffragan Bishopric of Bedford.

ST·BARTHOLOMEW·THE·GREAT·

THE church of St. Bartholomew the Great, West Smithfield, which consists of the choir and transepts of the church of the Priory of St. Bartholomew, is the oldest parochial church now standing in London. It is likewise one of the most interesting ecclesiastical buildings in the metropolis, or indeed in all England; it is interesting on account of the antiquity of its foundation; on account of the legend connected therewith; and on account of the great quantity of original work yet remaining.

The founder of the Priory of St. Bartholomew was Rahere, a courtier of King Henry I., who by reason of his wit and liveliness had acquired the special favour of his sovereign. About the year 1120 Rahere went on a pilgrimage to Rome, and while there he was stricken with a fever; in the course of this illness, it is said, he saw a vision of St. Bartholomew, which so much affected him that he resolved to turn his back upon his former light life, and devote himself for the future to religious and charitable avocations. On his return to England he applied for assistance to the Bishop of London, through whose influence he was enabled to found in 1123 the Hospital and Priory of St. Bartholomew, of which he himself became the first prior.

In 1133 Rahere obtained from Henry I., who took a deep interest in his pious designs, a charter of privileges, which was witnessed by several of the most distinguished men of that period, both lay and ecclesiastical. Ten years later Rahere died, but Augustinian Canons, commonly called "Black" Canons, from their black cloaks and hoods—to which order the founder had belonged—continued to inhabit the priory until the dissolution of monasteries by Henry VIII. In 1546 the king sold the priory to Sir Richard Rich, his attorney-general, with the exception of the choir and transepts of the church, which he granted to the parishioners.

St. Bartholomew's is unfortunately hemmed in by a network of small streets and houses, and the entrance from West Smithfield may easily be missed. It is, however, well worthy of notice, being a pointed Early English arch of considerable elegance, embellished with dog-toothed ornamentation. In monastic times the nave, built in the Early English style, extended to the gateway, which separated the sacred buildings from the outer world; now, after passing through the arch, we go along a narrow passage, across a foot thoroughfare, into the churchyard, whence we gain admission into the church itself by the west door, which is situated at the base of the tower. The exterior was once conspicuous by its fine central tower flanked by two turrets; but these were demolished in 1628, when the present brick tower was built. This tower was somewhat altered early in the present century, but there is nothing very striking about it. It contains, however, five of the oldest bells in London, dating from before 1510, and dedicated respectively to St. Bartholomew, St. Katherine, St. Anne, St. John Baptist, and St. Peter.

The internal length of the church is rather over 130 feet, and its breadth is 57 feet. The organ stands at the west end, and

St. Bartholomew the Great.

eastward from the organ-screen rise the central tower arches, which are in their turn succeeded by five bays, the whole terminating in an apse; while all around runs an ambulatory, which passes behind the altar. On entering, the eye is instantly rivetted on the grand old Norman work, as it stands out in its solid simplicity; particularly beautiful is the prospect of the south aisle, as one gazes through the colonnade of majestic arches. Although subsequent styles of architecture are also represented, the main part of St. Bartholomew's is Norman, and its dignified and venerable aspect equally attracts the admiration of the artist and furnishes food for the reflections of the antiquary and the historian.

The Norman and transitional Norman work was executed by Rahere and his immediate successor, Thomas of St. Osyth, prior from 1143 to 1174. Rahere had presided over the building of the eastern bays of the choir, and the tower was most probably completed before the death of Thomas. During the next half century were added the Early English columns at the south-west, and, in all likelihood, the nave, which was destroyed after the dissolution of monasteries, and the entrance gateway from Smithfield already described. In the Perpendicular style are the clerestory of the choir, above, and in marked contrast with, the Norman triforium, the three side chapels of the north ambulatory, the corbels of the west tower arch, and the Lady Chapel, which was appended at the east of the church. But the most striking innovation introduced during the prevalence of this mode of architecture was the pulling down, early in the fifteenth century, of the upper part of the Norman apse, out of the materials of which a wall was constructed, thus rendering the eastern termination of the church square instead of, as heretofore, round. The chief object of this alteration seems to have been to insert two large east windows filled with stained glass, fragments of the tracery of which have been brought to light in the progress of the restoration of the church, and may be seen carefully preserved in the north triforium. Prior Bolton, who held sway from 1506 to 1532, built in the south triforium a projecting bay window, probably for the purpose of watching the founder's tomb, which is situated on the opposite side. On the middle panel below the window is carved his well-known rebus, a bolt passing through a tun, which also occurs on another piece of his work, the choir vestry door at the south-east.

During the first half of the present century St. Bartholomew's had fallen into a very dilapidated state, and in 1864 the work of restoration was commenced. A portion of the east wall was taken away, and a new apse was erected in exact imitation of the original one, thus restoring to the eastern end of the church its pristine appearance. The architect who designed this important improvement is Mr. Aston Webb, to whom also is due the flat oak ceiling of the tower, erected in 1886, and the restoration of the south transept, to which he has added a central door, first opened for use by the Bishop of London, March 14th, 1891. In fact, all Mr. Webb's work in connection with St. Bartholomew's has been most happily designed and equally happily executed.

The restoration has been carried on at intervals, as far as funds have permitted, up to the present time, and is not yet entirely completed, a large sum being still needed. The encroachments of surrounding buildings have proved a source of much trouble and expense. A portion of a fringe factory projected into the church at the east, and was not finally removed till

St. Bartholomew the Great. 41

1886, when it was purchased at a cost of over £6,000 by the Rev. F. P. Phillips, the patron of the living, who also defrayed the charges of the erection of the new apse, in memory of his uncle, the Rev. John Abbis, for sixty-four years rector of the parish. The north transept was actually occupied by a blacksmith's forge, but this also has been removed, and the north porch, opening out into Cloth Fair, has been completed and adorned with a figure of the patron saint. The wall of the west front, which was built out of the ruins of the nave, when the choir was first used for parochial purposes, has been newly faced with flint and stone. The south side of the stone screen below the great arch at the entrance of the north transept has had to be refaced, although the face on the north side remains in good preservation. A new case for the organ has been supplied by Mr. H. T. Withers in memory of his brother, the late Mr. F. J. Withers, and a new pulpit has been set up out of a legacy from Mrs. Charlotte Hart, who was for forty-one years sextoness, and who bequeathed at her death £600 to the Restoration Fund. The Rev. F. P. Phillips, in addition to his other acts of munificence, has also presented the handsome oak stalls, and the mosaic pavement on which stands the wooden altar, which is itself likewise a gift to the church.

On June 4th, 1893, the new works were inaugurated and dedicated by a special service conducted by the Archbishop of Canterbury, who delivered on the occasion a most interesting sermon upon Rahere's twin foundations, the church and hospital of St. Bartholomew. This service was attended by the Prince and Princess of Wales and many other distinguished personages, and it was hoped that the presence of members of the royal family, and the publicity thus obtained for the work, would be instrumental in procuring a large increase in subscriptions for the restoration. This very natural expectation has unfortunately not as yet been realized. On the contrary, subscriptions have lately shown a decided falling off, as people seem to have taken it into their heads that the royal visit marked the culmination of the whole matter, and that nothing else is left to be done—a most erroneous notion, since about £3,000 is still requisite in order that the Lady Chapel and the crypt may be placed in a thorough state of repair.[1]

The Lady Chapel, which was built early in the fifteenth century, is about 60 feet long by 26 feet wide. Access is gained to it from the main building through a door in the temporary brick east wall of the church, and down a flight of wooden steps. It is in a somewhat ruinous condition, but a portion of the windows in the north wall remain, and on the outside the original buttresses of the south wall are still in existence. Until lately the Lady Chapel was used as a sort of museum for fragments of old work discovered during the repairs, which form a large and interesting collection; but these have now been removed to the north triforium, and it is intended that, as soon as the restoration is completed, the Lady Chapel shall be utilized for parochial purposes.

The crypt is situated beneath the eastern part of the Lady Chapel. It was vaulted by arches of a single span of 22 feet, and lighted by deeply splayed unglazed windows. A considerable portion of it has been excavated, and it will probably be opened some time in the spring of 1895. It has been proposed to devote it to the purposes of a mortuary chapel, now greatly needed in the district—an object which the old crypt would admirably serve.

[1] See note at the end of this chapter.

St. Bartholomew the Great.

There are also some remnants of the cloister still existing, but in a stable, and the entrance door beyond the south transept has been blocked up by the pressure of the adjacent tenements.

St. Bartholomew's contains a number of interesting monuments. The one which pre-eminently attracts attention is naturally that of the founder, which is placed on the north side of the church within the communion rails, in the last bay before that which marked the commencement of the original apse. The tomb is surmounted by the recumbent effigy of the great prior, and overshadowed by a rich vaulted canopy, the work of an artist of the fifteenth century. The effigy itself is, however, considered by the most competent judges to belong to the original monument, and it seems most probable that it was carved under the direction of Rahere's immediate successor, Thomas of St. Osyth. Rahere is represented in the robes of his order, with his head shaved after the monkish fashion; an angel is placed at his feet, and at each side of him kneels a monk. Feeling no doubt that his church and hospital were his truest and noblest monument, the brethren inscribed no pompous eulogy on the gravestone of their departed chief. His epitaph runs simply thus :

"Hic jacet Raherus primus canonicus et primus prior hujus ecclesiae."

Some twenty years back the tomb was opened, and the skeleton of Rahere was found within it, together with a portion of a sandal, which may be seen among other curiosities enclosed in a glass case in the north transept.

Of the more modern monuments that which excites the most interest is the tomb in the south aisle of Sir Walter Mildmay (died 1589) and Mary his wife (died 1576). Sir Walter, who resided in the precincts, was one of Queen Elizabeth's ablest states-

St. Bartholomew the Great. 45

men. He filled, with credit to himself and advantage to the country the offices of Chancellor and Under-Treasurer of the Exchequer, but he is now better remembered as the founder of Emmanuel College, Cambridge. Sir Walter's tomb is constructed in three storeys, crowned by an urn; it is bedecked with marble panelling and gilded mouldings, and bears six shields emblazoned with coats of arms. There are no figures on the tomb, and the Latin inscription after the text, "Death is gain to us," sets simply forth the names of the knight and his lady, the respective dates of their decease, the number of their family, the offices of state which he held, and the fact that he founded Emmanuel College, Cambridge. This careful avoidance of parade and panegyric may be accounted for from the Puritan character of Sir Walter's religious views. The original position of the monument was in the arch opposite the tomb of Rahere; but it was removed in 1865, and placed in its present position further west. In 1870 it was repaired and put generally in order by Mr. H. B. Mildmay, one of Sir Walter's descendants. The Master and Fellows of Emmanuel College subscribed liberally to the restoration fund of St. Bartholomew's, as a tribute of respect to the memory of their illustrious founder.

The remaining monuments commemorate persons of less importance. On the north wall, above the pulpit, and beneath the corbel table of the tower arch, is a figure of Sir Robert Chamberlayne, clothed in his armour, and in an attitude of prayer. Above his head is a canopy supported by four angels, and surmounted by his arms and crest. We learn from a long Latin inscription that this knight was a great traveller, who had visited the Holy Land, and that he perished between Tripoli and Cyprus, in the year 1615, at the age of thirty-five. His memorial, which was composed of white alabaster, is finely executed, but it has been painted black; and a similar fate has befallen the outstretched heads, immediately opposite, of Percival Smalpace and his wife, made out of brown marble, and erected in 1588.

On the south wall, to the west of Prior Bolton's door, but east of the tomb of Sir Walter Mildmay, is a monument to James Rivers, who died in 1641. He was great-grandson to Sir John Rivers, Lord Mayor of London in 1573. The monument consists of a half-length figure, holding a book in one hand and an hour-glass in the other, and covered with a canopy supported by pillars, and ornamented with the arms of the deceased. It is probably the work of Hubert Le Sœur, the sculptor of the statue of Charles I. at Charing Cross. Le Sœur was a French artist, who was settled in England as early as 1630. He lived close by in Bartholomew Close, and is believed to have been buried in the church.

Next to the tomb of Rivers is a half-length figure of Edward Cooke, also sheltered by a canopy, and also holding a volume. This gentleman, we are informed by a Latin inscription, was a learned philosopher and a physician of repute, who died in 1652 at the age of thirty-two. His epitaph concludes with four English lines:

> "Unsluice yor briny floods, what! can ye keepe
> Yo^r eyes from teares & see the marble weepe
> Burst out for shame or if yee find noe vent
> For teares, yet stay, and see the stones relent."

Cooke's monument is composed of a soft kind of marble, known as "weeping marble," from its tendency to break out with drops of moisture. It requires, however, a damp atmosphere to enable it to perform this function. In the old days before the

St. Bartholomew the Great. 47

restoration of the church, when the wet dripped down through the roof so copiously, that one Sunday morning the rector was constrained to put up his umbrella while delivering his sermon, the marble wept abundantly ; but now that the edifice has been rendered watertight, and the pipes of a heating apparatus have been placed just beneath them, " the stones relent " no more.

West of Sir Walter Mildmay's tomb is a tablet bearing a quaint, but touching, and not unpoetical inscription :

> "Captn John Millet Mariner 1660.
>
> Many a storm and tempest past
> Here hee hath quiet anchor cast
> Desirous hither to resort
> Because this Parish was the Port
> Whence his wide soul set forth and where
> His father's bones intrusted are.
>
> The Turkey and the Indian trade ;
> Advantage by his dangers made ;
> Till a convenient fortune found,
> His honesty and labours crown'd.
>
> A just faire dealer he was knowne,
> And his estate was all his owne
> Of which hee had a heart to spare
> To freindshipp and the poore a share.
>
> And when to time his period fell
> Left his kind wife and children well
> Who least his vertues dye unknowne
> Committ his memory to this stone.
>
> Obiit anno aetatis 59 Anno domini 1660 Decembris 12º."

Beyond the side chapels of the north aisle is the sacristy, in the eastern portion of which may be observed a marble tablet, adorned with pillars, and resting on a base carved in the form of six books, to the memory of Thomas Roycroft, honourably known as the printer of the Polyglot Bible, which gives versions of the Scriptures in the Hebrew, Latin, Greek, Chaldean, Arabic, Samaritan, Syriac, Persian, and Ethiopic languages. Roycroft had a printing-press in Bartholomew Close, and was engaged with this great work from 1653 till after the Restoration of Charles II. In 1675 he was elected Master of the Stationers' Company; he died in 1677. The memorial to him was erected by his only son, Samuel Roycroft, who, at his death in 1712, left some funds for the relief of the poor of the parish, which are still annually distributed.

In the south transept is the effigy, removed from the wall of the south aisle, of Mrs. Elizabeth Freshwater, who died in 1617, and is described as the "late wife of Thomas Freshwater of Henbridge, in the County of Essex, Esquire," and the "eldest daughter of John Orme of this Parish, Gentleman, and Mary his wife." She is represented kneeling at a small altar, with her hair arranged after the fashion then in vogue, and her neck encircled with the large ruff characteristic of the period.

In the north aisle a marble tablet records the death of John Whiting, 1681, and Margaret, his wife, 1680. The conclusion of the epitaph is quaint:

> "She first deceased, Hee for a little Tryd
> To live without her, likd it not and dyd."

Another and more ornate tablet, not far from the monument of Sir Robert Chamberlayne, commemorates John Whiting, son of this John and Margaret Whiting, who was an active and highly-esteemed official of the Ordnance Department from the time of Charles II. to that of Queen Anne. At his death, in 1704, he left a sum of money to the parish for educational purposes, which is still applied in accordance with his wishes. The schools which were established under his bequest are situated on the south side of the Lady Chapel, and the foundation stone of the present building was laid by the Duchess of Albany on July 5th, 1888.

East of Prior Bolton's door is a tablet to several members of the Master family, amongst whom is Ann, the wife of Richard Master, " Daughter of Sr James Oxenden of Dean in ye Parish of Wingham in ye County of Kent, by whom the said Richd Master had twelve Sons and eight Daughters. She died Jan. 30th 1705 Aged 99 years and six months and lies interred in this place."

Of her grandson, Streynsham Master, who died in 1724, it is recorded:

" The said Streynsham Master Commanded several ships in ye Royal Navy and did in ye year 1718 particularly distinguish himself in ye Engagement against ye Spaniards on ye Coast of Sicily; by forcing the Spanish Admiral in Chief to surrender to him."

In the north aisle, west of the tablet to John and Margaret Whiting, a very elegant brass has been inserted in the floor, with an inscription stating that it was placed there on St. Bartholomew's Day, 1893, by the old pupils of Witton Grammar School, Northwich, as a memorial to Sir John Deane, the first rector of St. Bartholomew's after the dissolution of monasteries, who founded that school in 1557.

To the western wall of the same aisle is affixed a plain marble tablet inscribed:

" In memory of Mrs. Mary Wheeler
Died October 31st 1844
and of
Mr. Daniel Wheeler
Died 17th July 1834
Aged 84 years

65 years of this parish
this stone is inscribed by
their granddaughter
Charlotte Hart, 1866."

Immediately below is a brass plate:

"In memory of Charlotte Hart
41 years Sextoness of this Church
Born 1815 Died April 3. 1891. She left
a large sum towards the Restoration
Fund of this Church for the erection
of a pulpit and other benefactions."

The font which stands in the south transept is stated by tradition to be the identical font in which were baptized William Hogarth, November 28th, 1697, and his sisters—Mary, November, 1699, and Anne, November, 1701. The great painter continued in after life to take an interest in the neighbourhood where his father had resided, and where he had himself been born. On the rebuilding of St. Bartholomew's Hospital, he gratuitously embellished the grand staircase with six paintings, the subjects of which include Rahere's dream, and Rahere laying the foundation stone, while a sick man is being borne on a bier attended by monks. As an acknowledgment of this act of generosity, Hogarth was created a life-governor of the hospital.

The churchyard contains no tombs of particular interest, but every Good Friday it is the scene of a curious ceremony. After a sermon by the rector twenty-one sixpences are dropped, which are thereupon picked up by an equal number of previously selected women. In the choice of recipients for this bounty the preference is accorded to widows. The origin of the custom and the date at which it first commenced are not certainly known.

St. Bartholomew the Great.

It is said that the twenty-one sixpences were originally derived from a fund left by a lady buried in the nave to pay for masses for her soul, which after the establishment of Protestantism was diverted to this charitable use. This story is not in itself improbable, but the whole matter appears to be involved in obscurity. It is, at all events, certain that the fund, whatever it may have been, has long since disappeared; and the twenty-one sixpences were provided by the churchwardens until a few years ago, when a sum, from the interest of which they are now obtained, was invested by the Rev. J. W. Butterworth.[1]

[1] It is gratifying to learn that during the past twelve months subscriptions to the restoration fund have flowed steadily in, and only £1,300 is now needed. Much progress has been made with the work in the crypt; but it is feared that it is scarcely high enough to enable it to be used, as had been suggested, for a mortuary chapel.

ST·ETHELBURGA· BISHOPSGATE·ST·

IN Bishopsgate Street Within, a little beyond St. Helen's Place, stands a church dedicated to St. Ethelburga, the daughter of Ethelbert, King of Kent, the first Saxon ruler who embraced Christianity, and his queen, Bertha, daughter of Charibert, King of France. Of its foundation and early history we have no record, but from the fact of its being dedicated to St. Ethelburga we may infer that its origin dates from a very remote period. The present church, which in its essence is said to be Early English, appears from its architectural characteristics to have been rebuilt or altered at the close of the fourteenth, or early in the fifteenth, century; but there is no documentary evidence as to the precise date of its erection.

Just as the history of St. Ethelburga's appears to have escaped observation in the past, so the church itself is now very liable to be overlooked. It is extremely small, measuring less than 60 feet by 30, while the height to the centre of the ceiling is under 31 feet, and it is wellnigh crowded out by the pressure of the adjoining houses. Between the shop-windows of Nos. 52 and 53, Bishopsgate Street Within, admission is obtained to the sacred building through an archway, above which the houses

St. Ethelburga, Bishopsgate Street.

meet, and project over it towards the street, concealing everything but the top of the west window and the turret. The authorities, afraid apparently, and not without reason, that passers-by may fail to notice the existence of the church, have resorted to the not too dignified expedient of writing "St. Ethelburga" over the entrance-archway, much in the manner in which tradesmen are wont to inscribe their names above their shops; but its position may be best discovered by casting a glance from the other side of the street, when the turret, rising over the obstructive houses, will strike the eye with a rather picturesque effect.

St. Ethelburga's possesses a south aisle, lighted by four lancet windows, and separated from the main body of the church by four pointed arches, above which is a clerestory containing small windows. There are no traces of a north aisle ever having existed. The roof is divided into compartments, and slopes very slightly at the sides. The walls of the chancel are panelled to a height of over five feet. The organ, which formerly stood in a gallery at the west, has been removed to the south-east. In the north wall, just above the communion rails, is a window larger than those of the south aisle, and there are also two windows at the east—one of which is over the altar, and the other at the extremity of the south aisle—and at the west end an obtusely-pointed window divided into three lights. The arch at the entrance of the nave, which serves to support the tower, is a fine one, and some remnants of handsome carving, probably specimens of sixteenth century work, still adorn the porch. The stone font, also, which bears the Greek inscription, ΝΙΨΟΝ ΑΝΟΜΗΜΑ ΜΗ ΜΟΝΑΝ ΟΨΙΝ ("Cleanse my transgression, not my outward appearance only"), is noticeable for its curiously-designed embellishments; but, taken as a whole, St. Ethelburga's is not a very interesting building. It has undergone several attempts at restoration, but, if one may judge from old engravings, it presented a more pleasing and venerable aspect before it had been quite so much pulled about.

St. Ethelburga's is singularly devoid of historical associations. There are, it is true, some tablets affixed to the walls to the memories of deceased parishioners, but no interest attaches to any of the individuals thus commemorated. In fact, the only two persons of the least celebrity connected with this church appear to be John Larke, a friend of Sir Thomas More, who held the living in Henry VIII.'s time, and was, like Sir Thomas, executed for denying the king's ecclesiastical supremacy; and Luke Milbourn, Dryden's hostile critic, who was rector of St. Ethelburga's from 1704 till his death in 1720.

Pope mentions Milbourn in the "Essay on Criticism," and introduces him in a passage in the second book of the "Dunciad," to which he has appended a sarcastic note:

"Luke Milbourn, a clergyman, the fairest of critics; who, when he wrote against Mr. Dryden's 'Virgil,' did him justice in printing at the same time his own translations of him, which were intolerable."

Before the dissolution of monasteries the patronage of St. Ethelburga's belonged to the prioress and nuns of the neighbouring convent of St. Helen; the living is now in the gift of the Bishop of London.

St. Giles Cripplegate

The church of St. Giles, Cripplegate, stands at the west end of Fore Street in the ward of Cripplegate. Cripplegate, says Stow, was "so called of cripples begging there," a derivation generally accepted till quite recently, but now proved to be erroneous by the researches of Anglo-Saxon scholars, who have discovered that this word is an ancient term for a covered way in a fortification. The church was founded about 1090 by Alfune, who is said to have been a friend of Rahere, and to have been subsequently connected with the Hospital of St. Bartholomew. Matilda, queen of Henry I., who was a woman of exemplary piety, founded a guild of St. Mary and St. Giles in connection with the church. The advowson belonged in 1103 to a certain Aelmund, who in that year, after stipulating for his own incumbency and that he should be succeeded by his son Hugh, presented it to the Dean and Chapter of St. Paul's, by whom it has ever since been retained.

A second church was constructed towards the end of the fourteenth century in place of Alfune's original building, but the interior of this edifice, together with the ancient monuments which it contained, was destroyed by fire in 1545, although the walls, being of extreme thickness, suffered no great injury. The church was at once reconstructed, substantially as we now see it, and has since that time fortunately escaped any serious disaster.

St. Giles's, Cripplegate, is a specimen of the Perpendicular style, including a nave, chancel, and two side-aisles, which are separated from the central portion by clustered columns and pointed arches. The total length from the west door to the eastern end of the chancel is 146 feet, 3 inches; the length of the north aisle is 117 feet, 9 inches, and that of the south aisle is 111 feet, 3 inches. From the floor to the highest point of the roof the height is 42 feet, 8 inches.

Strype's quaint account of the seventeenth century repairs and additions is worth quoting :

"But for the later reparations of this church we begin with the year 1623, in which all the roof over the chancel was on the outside repaired, and in the inside very curiously clouded. To the further grace and ornament of this chancel there was added in the same year the cost of a very fair Table of Commandments; and with these the church (then) was throughout very worthily beautified. In the years of our Lord God 1624 and 1626 the two side galleries were built very fair and spacious. In the year of our Lord 1629 the steeple very much decayed was repaired, all the four spires (standing in four towers at the four corners of it) taken down, with new and very substantial timber work rebuilt; and with the lead new cast, new covered. Every one of these spires enlarged somewhat in the compass, a great deal in height, but most in their stately, eminent, and graceful appearance. In the midst of these, where there was none before

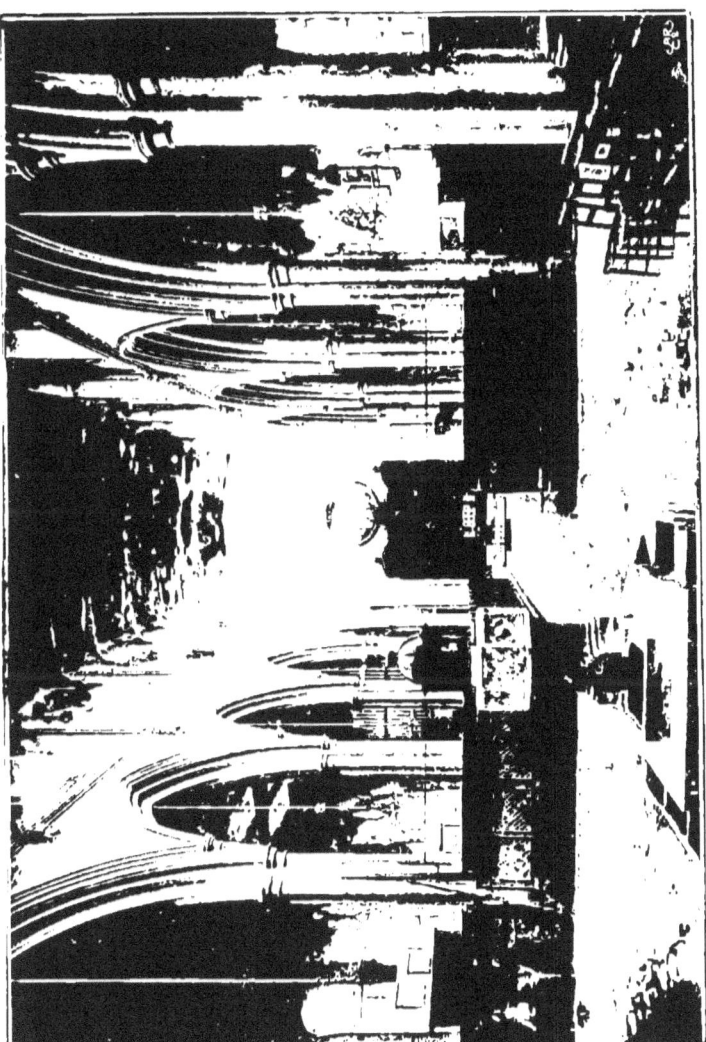

ST. GILES'S, CRIPPLEGATE.

(gracing and being graced by them) was a very fair turret erected; the head of it (which much overpeers those spires) covered with lead, as also the props that support it. This, and the spires, having every one a cross, with very fair vanes upon them. The charge of all this I could not certainly get, and would not uncertainly speak it. But the greatness of the things speak the cost to be great; all being the sole charge of the parishioners."

The steeple, which contains the exceptional number of twelve bells, was raised fifteen feet between the years 1682 and 1684. The height from the pavement below to the parapet of the tower is exactly 104 feet, from the parapet to the cornice of the cupola 16 feet, and thence to the top of the weather-vane 14 feet, 9 inches; thus making a total height from base to summit of 134 feet, 9 inches. The height of each of the four pinnacles, rising from the corners of the parapet, is 12 feet, 9 inches. When the steeple was raised, a new clock was set up, which, proving but an indifferent timekeeper, was taken down and replaced by the present clock, which ever since its erection in 1721 has performed its functions in an eminently satisfactory manner.

In 1704 another restoration was commenced; the church was then re-pewed, and the oak altar-piece was erected. Though it has been slightly altered and repaired, in 1790 and again in the present century, the main features of this noble specimen of early eighteenth century work are still unchanged. It consists of three panels, of which the central one contains a painting of our Lord seated on a throne, while on the smaller side panels are depicted St. Paul and St. Giles.

The beautifully carved pulpit was placed in the church at the same time. It was originally covered with a sounding-board, on which was the figure of a dove. When the sounding-board was taken away, this dove, itself an excellent piece of carving, was attached to the font-cover, where it may now be seen.

The names of the artists to whom are due the altar-piece and pulpit are unknown. The former is said to have been the work of the carver of the representations of Gog and Magog in the Guildhall; the pulpit is commonly, but without any authoritative evidence, attributed to Grinling Gibbons.

At some period not exactly known, but most probably subsequent to this restoration, several of the white marble monuments were varnished over, apparently with the laudable intention of preserving them from injury, but with a result decidedly derogatory to their beauty.

In 1791 the conformation of the church was considerably altered by the insertion of two additional windows on each side of the clerestory—an innovation which occasioned the extension of the roof of the middle aisle, and the consequent curtailment of the chancel. In the same year the east window over the altarpiece was re-glazed with a glory and cherubs, and the king's arms, measuring 6 feet across, were set up over the chancel arch, whence they have since been removed and affixed to the west wall, on which they occupy a conspicuous position.

The latter half of the present century has witnessed a very important and extensive restoration, in commemoration of which there has been set up at the west end of the south wall a slab thus inscribed:

"All glory be to God.
The Restoration of this Church
Commenced in the Year 1858, and carried
On from time to time by
Voluntary Contributions; was in the Year 1869

St. Giles, Cripplegate.

Completed to the Chancel, chiefly at
  The cost of the Parish.
The Revd Philip Parker Gilbert, M.A., Vicar.
William Bassingham } Churchwardens.
Thomas Turner

Also in the Year 1880,
The Church was repaired and further beautified
  At the expense of the Parish.
    James Luke   } Churchwardens."
    Cornelius Gillett

This work included the construction of an open roof, and the substitution of a stone chancel arch, 31 feet 7 inches in height by 17 feet 6 inches in breadth, for the former elliptical plastered arch. The obstructive brickwork at the west end was also removed, when the outline and part of the tracery of the old west window, still bearing the marks of the fire of 1545, were laid open to view. This window, which is very large and handsome, was fittingly restored and reglazed. Many monuments were transferred from the columns to the walls, and the columns were repaired; the pews were cut down, and the galleries taken away. The organ, built by Renatus Harris in 1705, was removed from the west end, and placed at the north of the chancel. It has since been enclosed in a new case, which is, however, hardly worthy of its surroundings. A new font, placed at the west end, has been supplied, and several richly stained memorial windows have been presented, chiefly by parishioners. But the most interesting is that at the west end of the south aisle, comprising "The Shepherds watching their Flocks," "The Nativity," and "The Wise Men coming from the East," with representations of St. Giles and St. Luke on the head lights, inserted at the expense of the neighbouring parish of St. Luke's, Old Street:

"In grateful remembrance of Edward Alleyne, the founder of
Dulwich College."

St. Luke's was originally a part of St. Giles's Cripplegate parish, and was called the "Lordship" portion, *i.e.*, the portion lying outside the City boundaries; but was made into a separate parish in 1732, in consequence of the enormous increase of the population. Alleyne, who acquired most of his wealth in this district, by means of the Fortune Theatre in Golden Lane, Barbican, built for him and Philip Henslowe in 1601, was a munificent benefactor to his poorer neighbours.

The earliest monument now existing is that of Thomas Busby, cooper, the year of whose death was 1575. It is situated on the eastern part of the north wall, and contains a half-length effigy of the old citizen, who is represented with a short, peaked beard, wearing a ruff round his neck, and holding in his right hand a skull, and in his left a pair of gloves. Beneath the figure is an inscription which records his charitable bequest:

> "This Busbie willing to reeleve the Poore with Fire and with Breade
> Did give that howse whearein he dyed, then called ye Queene's Heade.
> Foure full loades of ye best Charcoles he would have bought ech yeare,
> And fortie dosen of wheaten bread, for poore Howseholders heare.
> To see these thinges distributed this Busby put in trust
> The Vicar and Churchwardenes, thinkyng them to be just,
> God grant that poore Howseholders here may thankful be for such,
> So God will move the mindes of moe to doe for them as much,
> And let this good example move such men as God hath blest
> To doe the like before they goe with Busby to there rest.
> Within this Chappell Busbie's bones in Dust awhile must stay
> Till He that made them rayse them up to live with Christ for aye."

A little to the west of Busby's monument is a tablet to another benefactor to the poor, Charles Langley, an "Ale-Brewer," who died in 1602, and whose good deeds are likewise chronicled in verse :

> "If Langlie's life thou liste to knowe reade on and take a viewe
> Of Faith and Hope I will not speake his work shall shew them trew,
> Whoe whilest he lived, wth counsaile grave ye better sorte did guid,
> A stay to weake, a staffe to poore wthout back-bite or pride,
> And when he died he gave his mite all that did him befall
> For ever once a yere to cloath Saint Giles his poore withall.
> All Saintes hee pointed for the day gownes XX redie made
> Wth XX shirts and XX smockes as they may best be hadd,
> A sermon eke he hath ordayned that God may have his praiese
> And others might be wonne thereby to follow Langlie's waies,
> On Vicar and Churchwardens then his truste he hath reposed
> As they will answer him one day when all shall be disclosed,
> Thus beinge deade, yet still he lives, lives never for to dye
> In heaven's blysse, in worlde's fame and so I trust shal I."

To these verses are appended the names of

> "Lancellott Andrewes, Vicar
> John Taylor, Wm. Hewett, Edward Sicklyn, Richard Maye
> Churchwardens."

This was the famous Lancelot Andrewes, who was appointed in 1588 to the vicarage of St. Giles's. He remained here, greatly distinguishing himself by the eloquence of his sermons, till 1605, when he was raised to the episcopal bench.

On the west wall at the end of the north aisle is an unadorned tablet, removed to its present position from the chancel, to the memory of John Fox, the martyrologist, who died in the parish in April, 1587, at the age of seventy years. His epitaph runs thus:

> "Johanni Foxo, Ecclesiae Anglicanae
> Martyrologo fidelissimo, Antiquitatis Historicae
> Indagatori sagacissimo, Evangelicae Veritatis

Propugnatori acerrimo, Thaumaturgo admirabili ;
Qui Martyres Marianos, tanquam Phoenices,
Ex cineribus redivivos praestitit ;
Patri suo omni pietatis officio imprimis colendo,
Samuel Foxus illius primogenitus hoc Monumentum
Posuit, non sine lachrymis.
Obiit Die 18 Mens. April. An. Dom.
1587. jam septuagenarius.
Vita vitae mortalis est spes vitae immortalis."

The following supplementary explanation has been appended :

"Revd John Foxe M.A.
Sometime Vicar of this Parish,
Original Author of the History
of the Christian Martyrs,
Buried in the chancel of the Church."

The statement that Fox was sometime vicar of St. Giles's is, however, incorrect. As he resided in his later years in the parish, in Grub Street, now called Milton Street, he may have assisted the vicar, Robert Crowley, who, like himself, inclined to Puritan opinions, and thus have been informally designated "minister" of St. Giles's ; but the list of vicars does not contain his name, and in fact demonstrates that he could not possibly have held the living. It is well known that, with the exception of a prebend in Salisbury Cathedral, bestowed upon him by Cecil, he declined all preferment, though much was offered him, owing to his conscientious objection to sign the thirty-nine articles.

Beneath the tablet a brass plate has been affixed to the wall, inscribed with an English translation of the Latin epitaph.

Fox is stated to have been buried on the south side of the chancel in the same grave with two brothers Bullen, William, physician to Edward VI., Mary, and Elizabeth, and a learned

St. Giles, Cripplegate.

medical writer, who died in 1576, and Richard, "a faithfull Servant and Preacher of Jesus Christ," who died in 1563.

On account of his strong Protestant views Fox was in 1545 ejected from his fellowship at Brazenose College, Oxford, and afterwards resided as tutor in the house of Sir Thomas Lucy of Charlecote, so well known in connection with Shakespeare's early days, and the original, as some think, of Justice Shallow. It is probable that the Lucy family had their London residence in St. Giles's parish, for Stow mentions as buried here " Thomas Lucie, gentleman, 1447," and there are monuments in the church to Constance Whitney (died 1628), a granddaughter, and Margaret Lucy (died 1634), a great-granddaughter, of Sir Thomas. The monument of the former on the north wall displays a female figure, enveloped in a shroud, rising from a coffin, and extending her hands to receive a crown and chaplet which a cherub on each side is holding out to her: Margaret Lucy is commemorated by a simple, but elegant, tablet of white marble, which was formerly in the chancel, but has now been removed to the wall of the south aisle.

Sir Martin Frobisher was buried at St. Giles's, but, in spite of his gallant services to his queen and country, his body was left to repose in a nameless grave. The year 1888, however, being the tercentenary of the defeat of the Spanish Armada, was felt to be an appropriate period to do honour to the memory of the brave seaman, and a monument was then erected to him by the vestry of St. Giles's on the eastern part of the south wall.

This is, as is befitting for so distinguished a sailor, a very handsome monument. It is composed of Dove, Sienna, Irish green, and Sicilian marbles. In the central portion, which is flanked by pillars, is a representation of a three-masted Elizabethan ship, with Arctic and West Indian scenery in the background, in token of Frobisher's exploits both as an Arctic explorer and on the Spanish Main. Above this centre-piece, and below Sir Martin's arms, which are emblazoned at the top, is a tablet on which are engraved Macaulay's lines :

> "Attend all ye who list to hear our noble England's praise,
> I tell of the thrice famous deeds she wrought in ancient days;
> When that great fleet Invincible against her bore in vain
> The richest spoils of Mexico, the stoutest hearts of Spain."

On the lower part of the monument is another tablet, with this inscription :

> "Within this Church lie the remains of
> Sir Martin Frobisher Knight
> One of the first to explore
> The Arctic Regions and the West Indies,
> Having gained great glory
> By his skill and bravery in the Naval Engagements
> Which terminated in the defeat of the
> Great Spanish Armada, 1588,
> He died of wounds received in action of Brest,
> 22nd November, 1594.
>
> This Monument was erected
> in honour of his memory
> by the
> Vestry of St. Giles, Cripplegate,
> 1888."

On the same wall, farther west, is the monument of John Speed, author of "The Theatre of the Empire of Great Britain," a topographical work, describing the various counties of England and Wales, and "The History of Great Britain under the Conquests of the Romans, Saxons, Danes, and Normans," both published in 1611, and compiler of a set of tables of scriptural genealogy drawn out in the form of pedigrees. He shared Stow's antiquarian

St. Giles, Cripplegate.

tastes, and, like Stow, he was by trade a tailor. His half-length effigy is placed in a sort of closet with representations of open doors on each side. His right hand grasps a book, and his left a skull. On the doors are inscribed the epitaphs of Speed and his wife, which are in Latin, and touchingly and gracefully worded.

The pre-eminent interest attaching to St. Giles's, Cripplegate, lies in the fact that it is the place of sepulture of Milton. His father, John Milton the elder, was buried in the chancel in 1646, and on November 12th, 1674, the remains of the poet himself, who had died on the 8th of that month at his house in Artillery Walk, Bunhill Fields, were interred in the same grave.

Its place is marked by a stone thus inscribed:

> "Near this spot was buried
> John Milton
> Author of Paradise Lost
> Born 1608, Died 1674."

The position of this stone just outside the communion rails is due to the shortening of the chancel when the clerestory was extended in 1791.

There was no monument to the poet till the year 1793, when a bust of him, the work of the elder Bacon, was set up on the north side of the nave at the expense of Mr. Samuel Whitbread. In 1862—during the restoration of the church, which was materially advanced through the general desire to assist in doing honour to the last resting-place of Milton—a cenotaph, designed by the late Edmund Woodthorpe, was erected in the south aisle to the west of the monument of Speed. It stands 12 feet high, and the width at the base is 8 feet. The body of this monument—the material of which is carved Caen stone—is divided into three canopied niches by pillars of coloured marble; in the central niche is placed Bacon's bust of Milton, beneath which, on a marble tablet, is the following inscription:

> "John Milton,
> Author of Paradise Lost,
> Born Dec. 1608.
> Died Nov. 1674.
> His father, John Milton, died March 1646.
> They were both interred in this church.
> Samuel Whitbread posuit, 1793"

Below the inscription the base is ornamented with well-carved representations of the serpent, the apple, and the flaming sword, in allusion to the Fall and the Expulsion from Paradise.

On the west wall is a tablet in memory of William Day, citizen and vintner of London, who died in 1603. He is described as "The Sone of Thomas Daye of Boseham in Sussex, gent., and Elizabeth his Wife," and is stated to have been buried at St. Michael's, Cornhill; but he is here commemorated by reason of his having left a charitable bequest to the poor of St. Giles's. Another citizen and vintner, Roger Mason, who died in the same year as Day, also bequeathed a sum of money for the benefit of the poor of the parish. His widow erected a tablet to his memory on the north side of the chancel arch, which is, however, now concealed by the organ.

Over the north door, which is the principal entrance to the church, is a very finely executed marble monument to Edward Harvist, " Citizen and Brewer of London, Alderman's Deputie of this Parish, and One of his Majesty's Gunners," who died in 1610. It contains figures of himself and his wife Ann, who died in the same year, kneeling at a desk, and is appropriately adorned with representations of cannons. Their epitaph records that they were liberal benefactors to the parish.

A little farther to the east is another well-wrought monument, without effigy, but decorated with pillars, cherubs, and a death's-head, to Robert Cage, who died in 1624, and is designated in his inscription, "Omnium Literarum Homo."

On the same wall is the singular monument to Constance Whitney; beyond which is that of Matthew Palmer (died 1605), and Anne his wife (died 1630), containing figures of themselves and their five children.

Above the Palmer monument projects from the wall a large bracket clock, richly ornamented, and surmounted by a representation of Time. The precise date of its erection is not recorded, but in all probability it is coeval with the altar-piece.

On the same wall, before one reaches the memorials of Langley and Busby, the latter of which is close to the organ, may be noticed a somewhat large and ornate tablet to Edmund Harrison, embroiderer to James I., Charles I., and Charles II., who, as his epitaph states, married after "having lived above 40 yeeres a batchelour," and "had issue 12 sonnes and 9 daughters," and finally "left ye troubles of this world ye 9th day of January 1666, in ye 77 yeare of his age."

On the south side of the chancel arch is a tablet very concisely inscribed:

"Thomas Stagg
Attorney at Law
Vestry Clerk of this Parish
From the 8th day of March 1731
To the 19th day of February 1772
On which day he died.
That is All."

Adjoining this is a beautifully executed monument by Thomas Banks, representing a wife dying in her husband's arms. It was erected to the memory of Mrs. Hand, wife of a vicar of St. Giles's.

At the west end of the north aisle is an elaborate monument to Sir William Staines, Alderman of Cripplegate Ward from 1793 till his death in 1807, Sheriff in 1796, and Lord Mayor in 1800. It includes a bust of Sir William, in his robes, wearing the badge and chain of office of the mayoralty. Above the bust are his arms, and the base of the monument is ornamented by gracefully carved representations of the shield, sword, and mace of the City of London. He was a liberal benefactor to the parish, founding and endowing four almshouses for decayed parishioners.

Adjoining his monument is that of his son, John Staines, who died in 1823, on the upper portion of which are displayed a bible and cross, with a celestial crown above them. Hard by, just to the west of the north door, is a memorial, beautifully adorned with allegorical figures of Faith, Hope, and Charity, to the Rev. John Weybridge, who died in 1835, and his wife Maria, daughter of Sir William Staines, who died in 1842.

Tablets have also been erected commemorative of the Rev. Frederick William Blomberg, D.D., vicar, honourably distinguished for his munificence towards the poor, who died in 1847, in his eighty-sixth year; the Rev. Philip Parker Gilbert, vicar from 1857 to 1886, whose energy and business capacity proved of invaluable service to the work of the restoration of the church; and Mr. George Matthew Felton, a member of the Common Council, who held several important offices under the corporation, and one of the churchwardens of St. Giles's in 1878 and 1879. His active and useful life terminated in 1883.

Over the alderman's seat in the corporation pew, facing the chancel, has been set up a trophy bearing the arms of Sir William

St. Giles, Cripplegate. 69

Staines, Lord Mayor 1800; Sir Matthew Wood, the famous champion of Queen Caroline, twice Lord Mayor, in 1815 and 1816, and a representative of the City of London in no less than ten Parliaments; Alderman Thomas Challis, Lord Mayor 1852; and Alderman Henry Edmund Knight, Lord Mayor 1882; all of whom were aldermen of Cripplegate Ward.

In the middle aisle may be observed two official staffs, bearing the respective dates of 1693 and 1792. The older of the two, which is of massive silver, is surmounted by an elaborately worked model of the Cripple-gate.

It is a little singular that in the identical church to which were consigned the bones of Milton, should have been solemnized the wedding of Oliver Cromwell, with whom he was so closely associated. Cromwell, being then a little over twenty-one years of age, was married at St. Giles's, Cripplegate, on August 22nd, 1620, as stands recorded in the parish register, to Elizabeth, daughter of Sir James Bourchier.

The registers also contain entries relating to another family whose name is linked with Milton's—that of the Egertons, Earls of Bridgewater. It was to the Earl of Bridgewater that Milton presented his "Mask" of "Comus" at Ludlow Castle in 1634. The earl was then President of Wales:

> "And all that track that fronts the falling sun
> A noble peer of mickle trust and power
> Has in his charge, with tempered awe to guide
> An old and haughty nation proud in arms."

Bridgewater House, the residence of the Egertons, stood on the north side of the Barbican. It was originally called Garter House, and is thus described by Stow:

"Next adjoining this is one other great house, called Garter

House, sometime built by Sir Thomas Writhe, or Writhesley, knight, alias Garter principal King of Arms, second son of Sir John, knight, alias Garter, and was uncle to the first Thomas, Earl of Southampton, Knight of the Garter, and Chancellor of England. He built this house, and in the top thereof a chapel, which he dedicated by the name of St. Trinitatis in Alto."

Bridgewater House was burned down in 1687, when two sons of the then earl perished in the flames. Its site was afterwards marked by Bridgewater Square.

Milton himself, who had been living in Aldersgate Street since 1641, removed to a larger house in the Barbican in 1645. In this house his father died, and here he remained till 1647.

Daniel Defoe both was born and died in St. Giles's parish, but was buried in the Bunhill Fields burying-ground.

Several distinguished churchmen, besides Bishop Andrewes, have held the living of St. Giles's, Cripplegate.

His successor, Dr. John Buckeridge, quitted St. Giles's in 1628 on being raised to the see of Ely, and next came Dr. William Fuller, Dean of Ely, who suffered deprivation in 1642, at the outbreak of the Civil War. Dr. Samuel Annesley, who was presented to the vicarage in 1658, surrendered it in 1662 in consequence of the Act of Uniformity. He was not a person of any very particular importance, but his name is interesting for the reason that his daughter married Samuel Wesley, and became the mother of John and Charles Wesley.

The view of St. Giles's from the north is impeded by the Quest House, which stands in front of the north wall. The Quest House formerly served for the meeting-place of the inquest, a body elected to regulate the internal affairs of the ward. The inquest, the powers of which had been gradually curtailed, was abolished in

St. Giles, Cripplegate.

1857, but the Quest House still remains. The vestry meet here in a spacious room, adorned with portraits of Sir Matthew Wood, and the late vicar, the Rev. P. P. Gilbert, and an engraving from a portrait of Sir William Staines, and further embellished by a fine hatchment of the royal arms, and by the arms of Sir Matthew Wood. The upper portion of the house has been ever since 1729 utilized as a lodging for the sexton, and the vestry clerk's office is situated on the ground floor.

The Plague of 1665 raged in its direst form in the parish of St. Giles's. The register testifies to the enormous number of deaths which resulted from it, and the whole of the churchyard was, in consequence of the unparalleled quantity of burials, raised as much as two feet.

The churchyard contains a very interesting relic of antiquity in the shape of a bastion of the old London wall, measuring 36 feet in width, and 12 feet in height from the ground to the top of the battlement. This is the most perfect fragment of the ancient wall now existing. There stands also in the churchyard a handsome fountain, erected by the vestry in the year of her Majesty's jubilee. It is composed of Kentish ragstone, with the basin and pediment of Aberdeen granite, while above the basin, in bronze, executed in bold relief, is displayed the queen's head. On the two towers between which the basin is placed, the following explanatory inscription has been engraved:

"In
Commemoration of
Queen Victoria's
Jubilee
June 21st 1887

Erected by
The Vestry of St. Giles
Cripplegate
Albert Barff M.A. Vicar
John J. Baddeley   } Churchwardens."
Leonard W. Cubitt }

The entrance gateway to the churchyard bears the date 1660

and the names of the churchwardens of that year. The arch, which is very substantially built, has a rounded head, and its spandrels are ornamented with Death's usual adjuncts, the skull and cross-bones, and the hour-glass and scythe.

The adjacent thoroughfare of Well Street, formerly known as Crowder's Well Alley, derived its appellation from Crowder's Well, which once enjoyed a high reputation, as Strype tells us :

"This place is of some note for its well, which gives name to the alley. The water of this well is esteemed very good for sore eyes, to wash them with; and is said to be also very good to drink for several distempers. And some say it is very good for men in drink to take of this water, for it will allay the fumes, and bring them to be sober."

But the fact that the Plague wrought such appalling havoc amongst the inhabitants of the neighbourhood, who were accustomed to drink of its water, seems to point to the conclusion that Crowder's Well did not altogether deserve the commendations bestowed upon it.

Saint Helens Bishopsgate

THE church of St. Helen's, Bishopsgate, is situated just at the back of Bishopsgate Street Within, in the midst of the space known as Great St. Helen's The saint to whom it is dedicated is the Empress Helena, the mother of Constantine, about whose holy exploits several legends are related, and who is traditionally stated to have been the daughter of a British king, although, according to the best authorities, she was a native of Nicomedia in Asia Minor. There is a story, of the truth of which we know nothing, that the original church of St. Helen was founded by Constantine in memory of his mother, but at all events it seems certain that such a church existed in Saxon times, for it is recorded that in the year 1010 Alwyne, Bishop of Helmeham, conveyed the remains of King Edmund the Martyr from Bury St. Edmund's to London, for fear of the Danes, and deposited them in the church of St. Helen, where they were kept for three years.

The history of the present church, however, begins in the latter part of the reign of King John, when, perhaps in the year 1212, William, son of William the Goldsmith, obtained from the Dean and Chapter of St. Paul's, to whom the church belonged, permission to found the Priory of St. Helen for Nuns of the Benedictine Order. This William was an ancestor of Sir William Fitzwilliams, a follower of Cardinal Wolsey and Sheriff of London in 1506, from whom are descended the Earls Fitzwilliam.

In 1308 William de Basinge, Sheriff of London, conferred important benefits on the priory, treating it with such munificence that he was regarded as a second founder. After this the convent grew enormously in wealth, and became one of the richest religious establishments in London, holding much valuable land in different parts of the city. Queen Isabella hired a house in Lombard Street from the convent, and it was from the Prioress Alice Asshfeld that Sir John Crosby in 1466 obtained a lease of the ground on which he erected his magnificent mansion of Crosby Place. It has been estimated that at the dissolution of monasteries the income of the convent was equivalent to £10,000 per annum in our present money. In 1538 the priory was surrendered to Henry VIII., and the church, of which the north aisle adjoining the convent had previously been devoted to the nuns, while the south aisle was occupied by the parishioners, was given in its entirety to parochial uses, the screen, which had been erected to separate the nun's side from the people's side, being removed.

The conventual buildings were bestowed by the king on Sir Richard Williams, the son of a sister of Thomas Cromwell, Earl of Essex, who assumed the name of Cromwell in honour of his uncle, and whose great-grandson was the Protector Oliver; but in 1542 they passed into the possession of the Company of Leathersellers, who used the nuns' refectory as their common hall up to the year 1799, when it was demolished, together with all other visible remnants of the priory, in order to make room for the erection of St. Helen's Place, which is built on the site of the once famous convent.

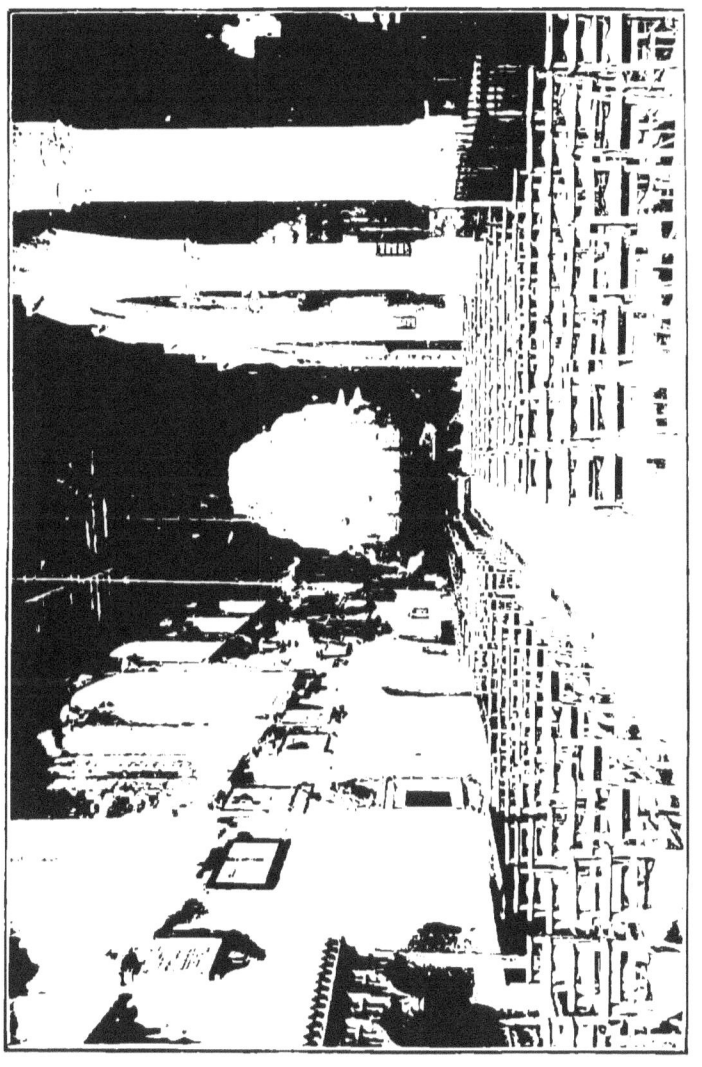

St. Helen's, Bishopsgate.

The double purpose which the church of St. Helen was originally intended to serve accounts for the peculiarity of its construction. It consists of two parallel naves, each 122 feet long; the breadth of the northern or nuns' nave is 26 feet 6 inches, that of the parochial nave 24 feet. The church also contains a south transept, out of which open two eastern chapels, the Chapel of the Holy Ghost, and the Chapel of the Virgin.

In the north wall is an arched doorway which led from the choir into the priory, and also a hagioscope composed of six vertical openings, through which the nuns were enabled to behold the high altar from the cloisters. Two ambries or receptacles for the vessels of the church can likewise be discerned in this wall. All these, together with the arch which divides the nuns' choir from the nave, some portion of the south transept, the lancet window at the west end of the north aisle, and the remains of lancet windows in the north wall, appear to belong to the thirteenth century. The side chapels were added about the middle of the fourteenth, and the rest of the church dates from the fifteenth century. Sir John Crosby, at his death in 1475, bequeathed 500 marks for the repair of the church, which was soon afterwards very considerably altered and transformed. From this period are derived the four central arches of the arcade which divides the north from the south aisle, the clustered columns, the low pitched roof, the east window of the chancel, which has, however, since been altered, and the south windows of the Lady Chapel.

In 1631 it was found necessary to repair the church, and Inigo Jones was called in. The work went on for two years, and was executed at a total cost of £1,300. Its conclusion is commemorated by an inscription over the south door:

"Laus Deo
St. Helena
16 Rep^d 33"

The internal oak porches at the south and west, with their pilasters and carving, were the work of Jones; and pews, communion rails, and an altar-piece after the style then in fashion were set up. The pulpit, a fine piece of seventeenth century work, which still remains, though its position was altered at the last restoration, may also be due to Jones, but it was probably erected a few years earlier. Nothing more of any importance seems to have been done to St. Helen's during this century, with the exception of the erection of the feeble and insignificant turret with which the church is even now crowned.

In 1744 the parishioners subscribed to build a west gallery, and bought a new organ to put in it; this gallery was supported by a screen placed across the church at the second pillar from the west, thus forming a small antechapel. The old roof, being no longer weatherproof, was in 1809 covered with a new exterior slated roof, which involved an outlay of nearly £3,000, and required to be re-slated in 1841.

In 1865 a committee was formed for the purpose of carrying out a thorough restoration, and continued its labours for three years. The west gallery and screen were removed, and the organ transferred to the south transept. The seventeenth century altar-piece, pews, and communion rails were likewise taken away, and the old stalls of the nuns were placed in the chancel. The floor of the nave, which had been raised considerably above its ancient level, was also partially lowered. In 1874 the church of St. Martin Outwich, which stood at the south-east corner of Threadneedle Street, was pulled down, and the parish united with that of

St. Helen's, Bishopsgate.

St. Helen, Bishopsgate. The patrons of St. Martin's were the Merchant Taylors' Company, and a large tablet on the south wall of the Chapel of the Virgin records that the eighteen monuments belonging to that church, of which a complete list with dates is given, "were under the direction and at the cost of the Worshipful Company of Merchant Taylors carefully removed, as far as possible restored, and then placed in this Church of St. Helen;" also that "this work was immediately followed by the Restoration of the two ancient Chapels of the Holy Ghost and the Virgin Mary, which had suffered greatly by decay and neglect, and still more by mutilation. It was done under the auspices and by the munificence of the same Worshipful Company."

This restoration, of which the total cost exceeded £1,500, was completed in 1876.

The most recent repairs at St. Helen's were commenced in 1891. They were rendered absolutely indispensable by the dilapidated state of much of the structure. The walls have been placed in thorough order, the turret has been repaired, and the whole church repaved, the floors of the two parallel naves being lowered to an equality with those of the side-chapels, and thus regaining their original level. Besides these structural renovations, several minor additions and rearrangements have been made, including the erection of a chancel-screen, and of two side-screens, which separate the chancel from the nun's choir and the south transept respectively. The north screen bears the inscription:

"In memory of Sir Andrew Judde, Knight and Skinner, the Gift of the Worshipful Company of Skinners."

That on the south side is inscribed:

"In memory of Sir John Spencer, Knight, Citizen, and

Clothworker, the Gift of the Worshipful Company of Clothworkers."

Over £4,000 was obtained from the Charity Commissioners towards defraying the necessarily heavy expenses of this last important restoration, and the Merchant Taylors' Company continued to interest themselves deeply in the work. The architect employed was Mr. John L. Pearson, R.A. After a year and ten months had been spent in its rehabilitation the church was again opened on June 24th, 1893.

The real attraction of St. Helen's lies not, however, in its fabric. In itself it is a Gothic church, beautiful, no doubt, but of no extraordinary excellence. But it possesses an interest and a charm beyond any other parochial church in the metropolis owing to its unrivalled collection of monuments. It is, indeed, astonishing to find assembled in this comparatively small space so large a number of beautiful and historically noteworthy memorials of the dead, by reason of which St. Helen's has justly acquired its title of "the Westminster Abbey of the City."

On the north wall of the church, beginning from the west, the first monument consists of well-executed figures of a husband and wife and their children, divided according to sex and kneeling on each side of an altar-table. It commemorates Alderman John Robinson, Merchant Taylor and Merchant of the Staple of England, who died in 1599, at the age of seventy, or, as the inscription expresses it, "the glasse of his life held three score and ten yeares, and then ranne out;" and Christian his wife, who "changde her mortall habitation for a heavenly" in 1592. "They spent together," we read, "36 Yeares in holy Wedlock, and were happy besides other worldly blessings in nyne sonnes and seaven daughters."

St. Helen's, Bishopsgate.

Next to the Robinson monument is the tomb of an earlier civic dignitary, Alderman Hugh Pemberton, Merchant Taylor, who was sheriff in 1490 and died in 1500, and Katherine his wife. This is one of the monuments removed from St. Martin Outwich in 1874, and is covered with an ornate canopy. It has been well repaired and cleaned, but the recumbent effigies, which it appears to have originally contained, are no longer in existence.

A little farther east is the memorial of Francis Bancroft, a descendant of Archbishop Bancroft and an officer of the Lord Mayor's Court, who, having amassed, not, it is said, by the most reputable means, a considerable fortune, bequeathed at his death in 1727 over £28,000 to the Company of Drapers in trust for the erection and endowment of almshouses for twenty-four poor old men of that company, and of a school for 100 boys. Bancroft's Almshouses stood in the Mile End Road, but they have now been pulled down, and the fund, which by the judicious care of the trustees has become largely augmented, is now wholly devoted to the purposes of education. The present school, which accommodates 100 boarders and over 200 day-boys, is situated at Woodford in Essex, and was built in 1888.

This Bancroft appears to have been a somewhat eccentric individual. He caused his tomb to be erected in his lifetime, and explained the circumstances in the following inscription:

"The ground whereon this Tomb stands was Purchased of this Parish in MDCCXXIII by Francis Bancroft Esq. for the interrment of himself and friends only (and was Confirm'd to him by a Faculty from the Dean and Chapter of St. Paul's London the same year) and in his Lifetime he erected this tomb, Anno 1726, and settled part of his Estate in London and Middlesex for the Beautifying and keeping the same in Repair for ever."

The tomb was of a square shape, and covered with a lid supplied with hinges, so as to admit of its being opened for the purpose of viewing the corpse, which was embalmed in accordance with the instructions of the deceased. A solemn inspection of the body by the officials of the Drapers' Company took place periodically up till quite recent times, but it became a not too pleasing task, as the art of the embalmer had proved inadequate to arrest the corruption of the remains. At the last restoration this tomb, which was remarkably ugly and extremely in the way, was removed as an eyesore and obstruction to the church, though its position is still marked by a brass strip. Above the spot where it stood a slab has been affixed to the wall, surmounted by Bancroft's arms, and bearing this inscription :

"In memory of Mr. Francis Bancroft who bequeathed the bulk of his property in London and Middlesex on trust to the Worshipful Company of Drapers, to be applied by them in the cause of Charity and Education. He died March XIX 1727, Aged 75."

Almost opposite Bancroft's memorial, in the middle of the church, stands the plain altar-tomb of William Kirwin, of the City of London, Freemason, who died in 1594, his wife Magdalene (died 1592), and their son Benjamin (died 1621). The inscription is partly Latin and partly English, and concludes:

> "Christus mihi vita
> Mors mihi lucrum."

East of Bancroft's slab and on the same wall is an elaborate monument of black marble and alabaster to Martin Bond, Captain of the City Trained Bands at Tilbury in 1588, and subsequently one of the members for the City of London in the Parliaments of

St. Helen's, Bishopsgate. 81

1624 and 1625. He is represented seated at a table in his tent; while outside an attendant is holding his horse, and in front are stationed two sentinels. All the figures are very distinct, and are interesting as clearly showing us the details of the military dress of Queen Elizabeth's time. The monument had been disfigured by several coats of black paint, but these were removed during the restoration of 1865-68, when this elegant piece of sculpture was thoroughly cleaned and repaired at the expense of the Company of Haberdashers, of which Martin Bond had been a member. He died in 1643 at the advanced age of eighty-five, and his highly eulogistic epitaph informs us that:

"His pyety, prudence, courage, and honesty have left behinde him a never dyeing monument."

Slightly to the east of this memorial to Martin Bond, but placed somewhat lower on the wall, is a monument containing kneeling figures, which commemorates the exploits of his father, Alderman William Bond, a merchant adventurer, who was sheriff in 1567, and died in 1576.

William Bond was one of the numerous occupants of Crosby Place, and, says Stow, "increased this house in height with building of a turret on the top thereof."

Further to the east may be observed affixed to the wall a tablet with a Latin inscription, which "Quidam ex amatoribus jurisprudentiae et liberalium artium," as they style themselves, set up in 1877 in honour of the Italian jurist, Albericus Gentilis, author of "De Jure Belli." Albericus Gentilis and his father, Matthew, a physician, came to England about the year 1580, being constrained to quit their native country owing to their Protestant opinions. The learning of Albericus, and the fact that he was an exile for conscience sake, won for him the friendship of many distinguished men, notably Sir Philip Sidney, to whom he dedicated his "De Legationibus." He studied at Oxford, and became Regius Professor of Civil Law in that university. In 1588 he published "De Jure Belli Commentatio Prima," which was followed by "Commentatio Secunda," and "Commentatio Tertia," the whole being finally incorporated in his great work, "De Jure Belli Libri Tres," which appeared in 1598.

The elder Gentilis died in 1602, and was buried in St. Helen's graveyard, and Albericus himself is stated to have been laid beside him on June 21st, 1608. But no stone marks the resting-place either of the father or the son, the very site of their graves is unknown, and it has been reserved for our own generation to pay a fitting tribute to the memory of the great civilian.

Parallel with this tablet is planted on the floor the tomb of Sir Thomas Gresham. It is a large altar-tomb of Sienna marble, with a surmounting slab of black marble, is embellished with a variety of mouldings, and bears the arms of Sir Thomas. This monument was never completed, and the inscription on the top slab is simply copied from the Parish Register:

"Sir Thomas Gresham, knight, buried December 15th, 1579."

It was cleaned and repaired in 1875 at the joint expense of Sir Thomas Gresham's company, the Mercers, and the Gresham Committee. From the north corner of the window above the tomb projects on a bracket Sir Thomas's helmet, which tradition alleges to have been carried before his corpse at the funeral. This window, which marks the eastern termination of the nun's choir, consists of five lights. During the restoration of 1865-68, it was repaired and filled with stained glass representing St. Helen and the Four Evangelists, by the Gresham Committee in memory of Sir Thomas.

St. Helen's, Bishopsgate.

Sir Thomas Gresham, the greatest merchant of his time, who will always be held in grateful remembrance as the founder of the Royal Exchange and of Gresham College, was the owner of a magnificent house in Bishopsgate Street, which, with its gardens, extended into Broad Street. Its site is now marked by Gresham House. He was as famous for his liberality as for his commercial ability, and there is no reason to doubt Stow's statement that he promised to build for the parish a new steeple "in recompense of ground in their church filled up with his monument." He appears, however, to have omitted to make provision in his will for carrying out this project, which is much to be regretted, since St. Helen's, as Stow very justly observes, "is a fair parish church, but wanteth such a steeple as Sir Thomas Gresham promised to have built."

On the corner of the wall, between Gresham's window and the chancel, is a monument to Sir Andrew Judde, who is represented in his armour, kneeling with other figures, both male and female, at a desk. The quaint inscription runs as follows:

"To Russia and Muscoua,
To Spayne, Gynny without fable,
Traveld he by land and sea,
Both mayre of London and Staple.
The Commonwelthe he norished
So worthelie in all his days
That ech state full well him loved
To his perpetuall prayes.

"Three wives he had : one was Mary,
Fower sunes one mayde had he by her,
Annys had none by him truly,
By Dame Mary he had one dowghtier.
Thus in the month of September
A thowsande, five hundred fiftey

> And eight died this worthie stapler
> Worshipynge his posterytye."

Sir Andrew Judde was Sheriff of London in 1544, and Lord Mayor in 1550. He also attained to the dignified position of Lord Deputy and Mayor of the Staple of Calais. He traded in furs, which accounts for his journeys "to Russia and Muscoua," and by this business, at that time an extremely profitable one, he acquired a large fortune. He is still remembered as the founder of the Free Grammar School at Tunbridge, his native town, and he is also the reputed founder of Judd's Almshouses in Great St. Helen's; but it is possible that in the latter good work he was acting less on his own account than as the executor of Dame Elizabeth Holleis, widow of Sir William Holleis, Lord Mayor in 1539. Sir Andrew at his death left the Skinners' Company, of which he was a member, trustees for the accomplishment of his charitable aims. Amongst the property which they were thus called upon to administer was some land in the neighbourhood of St. Pancras, then mere waste ground, but now very valuable; and thus it is that the name of the "worthie stapler" is perpetuated in Judd Street, while memories of his birthplace and his company survive in Tonbridge Street and Skinner Street.

In addition to their erection of a north side screen for the chancel, the Skinners' Company have also repaired Sir Andrew's monument.

Sir William Holleis above referred to, from whom the ducal house of Newcastle traces its descent, died in 1542, and was buried in St. Helen's. Stow mentions that there was a monument to him, and it is stated to have been placed in the middle of the north aisle. Unfortunately not a single vestige of it now exists.

St. Helen's, Bishopsgate.

In the nun's choir there is only one other monument of interest, which is, however, the most curious in the whole church. It is that of Sir Julius Cæsar, and stands between Gresham's monument and the north side-screen of the chancel.

Sir Julius Cæsar, whose full name was Julius Cæsar Adelmare, though he generally preferred to drop the Adelmare and use as a surname Cæsar—in reality part of his Christian name—was the son of Queen Mary's Italian physician, and was born in 1557. After studying at Oxford and Paris, he devoted himself to the law, and was appointed Judge of the Supreme Court of Admiralty under Queen Elizabeth. Under James I. he was admitted a member of the Privy Council, and advanced to the high judicial office of Master of the Rolls, which he retained till his death in 1636. Sir Julius was married three times. His last wife was a niece of Bacon, and he was present at the Earl of Arundel's house at Highgate on the morning of Easter Day, 1626, when the great philosopher breathed his last.

Cæsar's monument is a large altar-tomb of black marble, having the top slab inlaid with white in the form of a deed with appended seal. The Latin inscription, which is composed with due regard to legal formality, may be translated thus:

"To all faithful Christian People to whom this writing may come. Know ye that I Julius Adelmare alias Caesar, Knight, Doctor of Laws, Judge of the Supreme Court of Admiralty of Queen Elizabeth, One of the Masters of Requests to King James, and of his Privy Council, Chancellor of the Exchequer and Master of the Rolls, by this my act and deed confirm with my full consent that, by the Divine aid, I will willingly pay the debt of Nature as soon as it may please God. In witness whereof I have fixed my hand and seal. February 27th, 1634."

Here follows the signature, "Jul. Caesar," and below is another clause, to the effect that :

"He paid this debt, being at the time of his death of the Privy Council of King Charles, also Master of the Rolls: truly pious, particularly learned, a refuge to the poor, abounding in love, most dear to his country, his children, and his friends;" while lower still is written in large letters, "Irrotulatur Caelo" (It is enrolled in Heaven).

The epitaph is finally concluded by a Latin sentence which runs round three sides of the slab at the extreme edge, and records that this monument was erected to his memory by his widow, Lady Ann Cæsar, and that she herself rests here beside him.

The tomb was designed by Cæsar himself, and has for over 250 years remained a standing witness to his zeal for legal forms and ceremonies. It was executed by Nicholas Stone, the master-mason to King Charles I., at a cost, it is said, of £110.

On the north side of the chancel is situated the most magnificent monument in St. Helen's—that of Sir William Pickering. This gallant knight, illustrious as a soldier and a scholar, distinguished himself under Henry VIII., Edward VI., Mary, and Elizabeth, both in military and diplomatic appointments, for which latter service he was particularly adapted, owing to his great linguistic acquirements. He died at his house in St. Mary Axe in 1574, at the age of fifty-eight.

Upon an altar-tomb panelled into compartments, and under a rich marble canopy supported by Corinthian columns, is placed a life-sized recumbent effigy of Sir William, clothed in armour, with trunk breeches, and having a ruff round the neck; the head is uncovered, and the countenance singularly handsome. For sumptuousness of decoration Pickering's tomb is unsurpassed by any monument of the Elizabethan era. The inscription, which is in Latin, records his virtues and accomplishments, and the important services which he so faithfully performed for no less than four sovereigns, and states that this memorial was erected by his executors, Thomas Henneage, the Royal Treasurer, John Astley, Master of the Jewels, Drugo Drury, and Thomas Wotton.

To a neighbouring pillar is affixed a tablet in memory of Sir William Pickering the elder, father of the foregoing, also a brave and worthy soldier, who died in 1542.

On the south side of the chancel, exactly opposite Pickering's monument, is the tomb of Sir John Crosby and Agnes his wife. Sir John was one of the most distinguished citizens of his time, and a devoted supporter of the House of York. He was a member for the City of London in the Parliament of 1467, and the following year he was elected Alderman of Broad Street Ward. On May 21st, 1471, he, being then sheriff, went out with the mayor and aldermen, and a great multitude of Londoners, beyond Islington to meet Edward IV. on his triumphal progress to his capital after the victory of Tewkesbury; and on this occasion he received from the king the honour of knighthood, together with the mayor, John Stockton, and ten other leading citizens.

He was a man of great political ability, and his position of Mayor of the Staple of Calais having given him considerable experience of continental matters, King Edward, who had a just appreciation of his capacity and fidelity, entrusted him with secret and important missions to the Dukes of Burgundy and Brittany. But his active career was cut short by the hand of death in 1475.

Sir John's mansion, Crosby Place, was subsequently the residence of the Duke of Gloster, afterwards King Richard III., and in this connection is familiar to all readers of Shakespeare; and, although after many vicissitudes of fortune it has now been degraded into a restaurant, its remains still stand to keep alive the name of the great citizen its founder.

Upon an altar-tomb, the sides of which are adorned with shields emblazoned with the Crosby arms, are the life-sized recumbent effigies of Sir John and his lady. These figures are very skilfully executed, and have wonderfully escaped mutilation. Sir John has a fine face—the face of a man born to command. He wears a helmet and plate armour, and over his shoulder is thrown his alderman's mantle. In his belt is a dagger, and rings encircle the little finger of his right hand and the third and little fingers of his left. His feet rest upon a lion. Dame Agnes Crosby is clothed in a close-fitting cap, under which her hair is pulled back, a mantle, and a close-bodied gown with tight sleeves. Her head reclines on a cushion, supported by two angels, and at her feet are two little dogs. She was Sir John's first wife, and died in 1466. His second wife survived him.

This handsome monument has been repaired by the Grocers' Company, of which Sir John Crosby was a member.

In its immediate vicinity may be seen fastened to a pillar a piece of curiously carved woodwork, decorated with the city arms and the arms of Sir John Lawrence, Lord Mayor 1664, and culminating in the arms of Charles II., which are supported by two gilded angels, and surmounted by the royal crown. This interesting relic was originally attached to the pew occupied by the Lord Mayor when he attended service at St. Helen's, for the accommodation of the civic sword and mace, but on the removal of the pews it was transferred to its present position.

In the Lady Chapel are the recumbent stone effigies of John

Oteswich and his wife, dating from the beginning of the fifteenth century. He was concerned in the foundation of the church of St. Martin Outwich, as Stow tells us:

"On the south part of which street (Threadneedle Street), beginning at the east, by the well with two buckets, now turned to a pump, is the parish church of St. Martin called Oteswich, of Martin de Oteswich, Nicholas de Oteswich, William Oteswich, and John Oteswich, founders thereof."

In that now demolished church John Oteswich and his wife were buried, says Stow, "under a fair monument on the south side." Their effigies were in 1874 transferred, with the remainder of the St. Martin Outwich monuments, to St. Helen's, and after having been thoroughly cleaned and put in order, were placed upon a plain table in the spot where we now see them.

On a bracket attached to the wall of the same chapel rests a small statue of a woman seated and reading a book. Like so many other products of the sculptor's art, it was formerly disguised by copious applications of black paint. When these were removed, it was found to be composed of alabaster. It is apparently of Italian workmanship, and has been judged to be of a date anterior to the sixteenth century, but as to when it was first set up in the church, and how it was originally acquired, no evidence has ever been discovered.

On the floors of the two chapels may be noticed seven brasses. The names are unknown of the subjects of two of these—a male and female figure dating from about 1400, and a lady of Henry VII.'s time in elaborate robes, probably a member of some religious order. The remaining five are to the respective memories of John Brieux, rector of St. Martin Outwich, 1459;

Nicholas Wotton, rector of St. Martin Outwich, 1483; Thomas Williams, gentleman, and Margaret, his wife, 1495; John Leventhorpe, Keeper of the Chamber to King Henry VII., 1510; and Robert Rochester, Sergeant of the Pantry to King Henry VIII., 1514.

These brasses are all well executed, and have been much admired, especially that of the unknown early sixteenth century lady, the intricacies of whose apparel are very clearly and minutely displayed. Amongst those which are now lost, two are said to have been of considerable beauty; they commemorated Joan (died 1420), daughter of Henry Seamer, and wife of Richard, son of Robert, Lord Poynings; and Thomas Benolte (died 1534), Windsor Herald to King Henry VIII., and his two wives.

On the wall of the south aisle, between the pulpit and the south porch, is a large monument with kneeling figures—one of those removed from St. Martin Outwich—to Alderman Richard Staper and his wife. His epitaph calls him "The Worshipful Richard Staper, elected Alderman of this Cittye ano 1594," and goes on to assert that "hee was the greatest merchant in his tyme, the chiefest actor in discovere of the trades of Turkey and East India." He died about 1608.

To the west of the south porch is the monument of Sir John Spencer, Sheriff 1583, Lord Mayor 1594, commonly called, on account of his immense wealth, "Rich Spencer." He was a native of Waldingfield in Suffolk, and a member of the Clothworkers' Company. He kept his mayoralty at Crosby Place, which he had purchased, and where, says Stow, he "made great reparations." At his death, in 1609, the whole of his vast fortune devolved on his only daughter Elizabeth and her husband William, second Lord Compton, created in 1618 Earl of Northampton.

St. Helen's, Bishopsgate.

Sir John Spencer's monument, which is composed of the purest alabaster, originally stood in the south transept, but during the repairs of 1865-68 it was removed to its present position by the late Marquis of Northampton, who likewise relieved the memorial of his ancestor from the oppression of several utterly superfluous coatings of white paint. Upon the tomb are recumbent life-sized effigies of Sir John and Lady Spencer, with their daughter at their feet, kneeling as if in prayer, beneath a gorgeous arched canopy bedecked with pyramidal ornaments. The inscription is engraved on two panels immediately above the figures. The left-hand panel contains the epitaph proper:

> "Hic situs est Johannes Spencer
> Equis Auratus Civis & Senator
> Londinensis, Ejusdemq. Civitatis
> Practor Anno Dm. MDXCIIII
> Qui ex Alicia Bromfeldia
> Uxore Unicam Reliquit Filiam
> Elizabeth Gulielmo Baroni
> Compton Enuptam. Obiit 3º
> Martii
> Die Anno Salutis MDCIX."

That on the right merely records:

> "Socero Bene Merito
> Gulielmus Baro Compton
> Gener Posuit."

On the south wall, close to the west door, is a tablet to the memory of Dame Abigail Lawrence, who died June 6th, 1682. She was the wife of Sir John Lawrence, who was Lord Mayor in the year of the Plague, and was conspicuous during the whole of that terrible visitation for his courage, his devotion to duty, and his benevolence.

It having been discovered from the parish books of St. Helen's that in 1598 a William Shakespeare, who may have been the great dramatist, though this is not absolutely certain, was a resident in the parish, Mr. Prentice, an American gentleman, has presented a Shakespeare memorial window, which is situated on the north side, a little to the east of the site of Bancroft's tomb. At the west end of the north aisle is a window erected by public subscription, containing full-length figures of ten of the most prominent personages buried at St. Helen's, beginning with Sir John Crosby. Amongst other windows particularly noticeable—besides the one to Sir Thomas Gresham, already mentioned—are the representation of the Crucifixion over the west door, in memory of Alderman William Taylor Copeland, Sheriff 1828, Lord Mayor 1835, for nearly forty years Alderman of the Ward of Bishopsgate; a window in the south wall of the nave, with figures of St. Alban, St. Michael, and St. Edmund, presented by Alderman Colonel Wilson; and one in the same wall, further west, picturing the "Invention of the Cross by St. Helena," erected in memory of his parents John and Susan Williams by the late Mr. William Meade Williams, a painstaking antiquary, who devoted much time and thought to the elucidation of the early history of the church and parish; the east end chancel window, depicting the Ascension, and various incidents in the life of our Lord, the gift of Messrs. Kirkman Daniel and James Stewart Hodgson, in memory of their father, the late Mr. John Hodgson, who was buried in the church; a window in the north aisle over the tomb of Pemberton, of which the subject is Faith, Hope, and Charity, bestowed by Mr. John Macdougall in memory of his father, the late Mr. Alexander Macdougall, who was formerly lay impropriator of the tithes of St. Helen's, and acted towards the church with extreme liberality;

and another in the same wall, more to the east, "Christ healing the lame man," and "Christ receiving little children," inserted in memory of three of his children by the late Rev. J. E. Cox, D.D., for more than twenty years vicar of the parish previous to its incorporation with that of St. Martin Outwich—to whose learning and industry we owe "The Annals of St. Helen's, Bishopsgate, London," a most interesting and valuable work.

There has recently been placed in the church a mural tablet to Dr. Cox, which was unveiled on December 10th, 1894, in presence of the Lord Mayor and Sheriffs, at a Masonic service, the reverend gentleman having been for nine years in succession Grand Chaplain of England.

St Katherine·Cree·

IN the eastern part of Leadenhall Street, on the north side of the way, stands St. Katherine Creechurch, *i.e.*, Christchurch, so called from having been built in the precincts of the Priory of Holy Trinity Christ's Church, Aldgate, founded about the year 1108 by Matilda, queen of Henry I. The parishioners had been accustomed to worship at an altar in the church of the priory, but this practice having been found inconvenient, the church of St. Katherine was erected, as the outcome of an agreement between the prior and convent and the parishioners, effected by Richard de Gravesend, Bishop of London from 1280 to 1303.

The body of the church was rebuilt between the years 1628-1630, the first brick of the new structure being laid on the 23rd June of the former year by the Trained Band Captain Martin Bond, then Alderman's Deputy of Aldgate Ward, who also laid the first stone on the 28th July following. The steeple, however, which, as we learn from Stow, was not built till the beginning of the sixteenth century, was preserved, and is still standing.

The church, having been completed, was consecrated by Laud, at that time Bishop of London, on January 16th, 1631, with a profusion of elaborate and unwonted ceremonies, which drew upon

him the sarcasms of Prynne, and tended to increase the suspicion and dislike with which he was already regarded. In fact, so deep an impression did he create by his genuflections and other observances commonly reputed Popish, that his conduct on this occasion was cited against him at his trial nearly fourteen years later.

It is said—though there is no conclusive evidence on the point —that St. Katherine Cree was designed by Inigo Jones. It is an extremely unconventional building, being a mixture of the Gothic and Classical styles—a bold experiment, which has in this case met with considerable success, as the church is decidedly picturesque, and its very irregularity possesses a certain attraction of its own.

St. Katherine Cree contains two narrow aisles, divided from the nave by Corinthian columns and round arches, which support the clerestory. The ceilings both of the nave and aisles are groined, and on the roof of the nave are displayed the arms of the city and some of the city companies. The total length of the church is 94 feet, its breadth 51 feet, and the height to the ceiling of the nave 37 feet. It is larger than the original church by the inclusion of the space formerly occupied by a cloister, said to have been over seven feet broad, which was situated beyond the north wall of the old structure. At the south-west remains a solitary pillar of the former church, which was left in its original position when the fabric was rebuilt. Its height is said to have been 18 feet, but less than three feet of it now appear above ground, the remainder being beneath the floor, the level of which is thus clearly shown to be considerably higher than that of the ancient floor. The lowness of the floor of the whole church was, indeed, evident in the time of Stow, and did not escape the observation of that sharp-eyed old chronicler, who comments on it thus:

"This church seemeth to be very old; since the building whereof the high street hath been so often raised by pavements that now men are fain to descend into the said church by divers steps, seven in number."

The east window of the chancel is very large. Its upper portion is constructed in the shape of St. Katherine's traditional emblem, the Katherine wheel, and is filled with brightly-stained glass, which is stated by an inscription to have been the gift of Sir Samuel Stainer, Lord Mayor 1713; the glass of the lower part of the window is of recent date. The clerestory and side aisles are lighted by flat-headed windows. The stained glass of the easternmost window in the north wall was presented by Mrs. Pound, the mother of Mr. Alderman Pound, in memory of her deceased husband; and the same lady also provided funds for the enlargement of the organ, which stands in the west gallery. The well-carved pulpit and communion table are of cedar wood, and were both bestowed, as Strype mentions, by John Dyke, a merchant and parishioner. The pews have been reduced in size, but the churchwardens still have high-backed seats at the west; over the corporation seats, facing the chancel, are erected two sword-rests. The font is old, and is placed at the west end of the north aisle.

Through a door in the north wall entrance is gained to the vestry, a considerable portion of which is occupied by a large and handsome table ornamented with carving, and having a brightly-polished top. Beyond the vestry, and opening out of it, is a spacious room, known as St. Katherine's Hall, and used for parochial purposes.

The steeple, which is built of stone, rises at the west end of the church; it was heightened early in the eighteenth century by the

St. Katherine Cree.

superposition upon the old tower of a Tuscan colonnade, supporting a cupola, which is surmounted by a weather-vane. It reaches an altitude of 75 feet.

On the south wall, which abuts on Leadenhall Street, may be discerned between two of the windows a curious old sundial. At the east end of the same wall was formerly a porch, "a very fair gate," Strype calls it, given by William Avenon, citizen and goldsmith, in 1631. This interesting relic of the past stood till quite recently, but it has now been demolished.

St. Katherine Cree is not rich in historical monuments, but it contains—preserved from the old church—the tomb of Sir Nicholas Throckmorton, Chief Butler of England and one of the Chamberlains of the Exchequer, from whom Throgmorton Street takes its name. He was married to a daughter of that Sir Nicholas Carew who was beheaded for complicity in one of the Catholic plots against Henry VIII., and he was himself in imminent danger of experiencing a like fate owing to his connection with Lady Jane Grey; but, although brought to trial on a charge of high treason, he succeeded in saving himself by his skilful defence.

After serving Queen Elizabeth as her ambassador twice in France and twice in Scotland, this distinguished knight died on February 12th, 1570, at the age of fifty-seven. His tomb, surmounted by a canopy beneath which is a recumbent effigy, is placed on the south of the chancel.

There is a tradition referred to by Strype that St. Katherine Cree received the remains of one who is now better remembered than Throckmorton:

"I have been told that Hans Holbein, the great and inimitable painter in King Henry VIII.'s time, was buried in this church; and that the Earl of Arundel, the great patron of learning and arts, would have set up a monument to his memory here, had he but known whereabouts the corpse lay."

Strype, however, does not record this as a fact, but merely as something which he had heard, and Stow, from whom one would have expected some information on the subject, says nothing about it at all. There seems no reason to place much reliance on the story; at the same time there is nothing improbable in it, for Holbein died in the vicinity, and is as likely to have been buried here as anywhere else.

Inserted in the floor in front of the communion table is a brass plate, which marks the site of the burial-place of Sir John Gayer, and was, as the inscription states, placed there in honour of his memory by Mr. Edmund Richard Gayer, of Lincoln's Inn, Barrister-at-law, and others of his descendants, in 1888. Sir John was Sheriff in 1635 and Lord Mayor in 1646. He adhered staunchly to King Charles I., and in consequence suffered imprisonment at the hands of the Parliament. He was concerned in the trade with Turkey and the Levant, and once, when travelling in the Turkish dominions, he encountered in a desert a lion, which did not molest him. In order to show his thankfulness for this providential escape, he bequeathed at his death the sum of £200 to the parish, partly for charitable objects and partly for the establishment of an annual sermon, called the "Lion Sermon," which is still preached every year on October 16th.

There is a rather elegant monument on the south wall to Bartholomew Elmore, who died in 1636, and appears to have been one of the contributors towards the rebuilding of the church; and a bas-relief at the west end to Samuel Thorpe, who died in 1791, demands notice as being by the hand of the elder Bacon; but the remainder of the memorial tablets are not particularly interesting,

St. Katherine Cree.

although they have been supplemented by several from St. James's, Duke's Place, Aldgate, brought hither when that church was pulled down in 1874, and the benefice united with that of St. Katherine Cree.

At the dissolution of monasteries the patronage of St. Katherine Cree, together with the Priory of Holy Trinity, Aldgate, was bestowed by King Henry VIII. on Sir Thomas Audley, whom he subsequently appointed Lord Chancellor and raised to the peerage under the title of Baron Audley of Walden. Stow tells us that Lord Audley "offered the great church of this priory to the parishioners of St. Katherine Christ Church, in exchange for their small parish church, minding to have pulled it down and to have built there towards the street;" but they refused the offer. He thereupon pulled down the priory, and built himself a house on the site, where he died in 1544. He bequeathed the advowson of St. Katherine Cree to the Master and Fellows of Magdalene College, Cambridge. The City Corporation, as patrons of St. James's, Duke's Place, now present to the rectory alternately with Magdalene College.

ST· OLAVE · HART · STREET·

ST. OLAVE'S, Hart Street, is situated at the corner of Hart Street and Seething Lane. It is dedicated to Olaf, an eleventh century Norwegian king, who received the honour of canonization on account of the zeal with which he propagated Christianity amongst his subjects. He was the son of that King Olaf, also a Christian, whose history has been sung by Longfellow. In addition to St. Olave's, Hart Street, the churches of St. Olave, Southwark, St. Olave, Jewry, and St. Olave, Silver Street, the last two of which are no longer in existence, were also dedicated to this Scandinavian saint.

The period of the original foundation of St. Olave's, Hart Street, is unknown; and no allusion to it has been found previous to the year 1319, when an agreement was made between the rector and his neighbours, the brethren of the Crutched Friars. Neither can the precise date be fixed of the erection of the present edifice, although in all probability the greater part of it was constructed during the fifteenth century. Stow tells us that the "principal builders and benefactors" were "Richard and Robert Cely, fellmongers," whose monuments—now totally vanished—he mentions as standing in his time in the church, without, however, assigning a date to them.

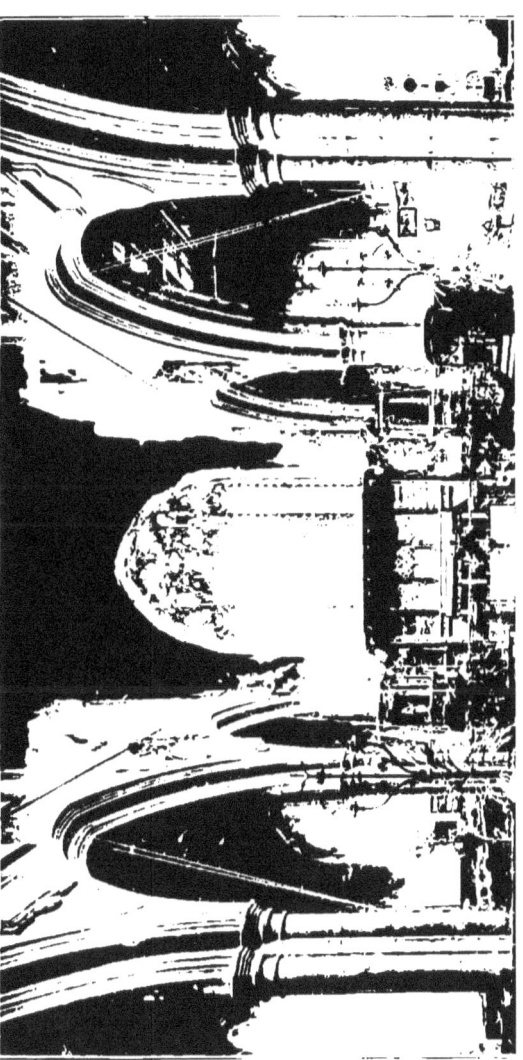

St. Olave, Hart Street.

St. Olave's is not large, but is a handsome church in the Perpendicular style. It possesses a north and a south aisle, separated from the central portion by clustered columns of Purbeck marble and pointed arches, over which is a clerestory with small windows. Each aisle is terminated by a window at the east, and there is above the altar a large central east window, which contains stained glass representations of the Evangelists and Apostles inserted in 1823. This window, the east window of the north aisle, and the west window have heads more sharply pointed, and are apparently of an older date, than the windows in the north and south walls, and the east window of the south aisle.

The church was extensively repaired by the parishioners early in the reign of Charles I. During the present century many alterations have been made, including the removal of the north and south galleries; but the organ-gallery at the west has been spared, and the handsome organ-case, in this prominent position, is a decided ornament to the church. At the restoration of 1863, the brickwork, which had blocked up the base of the tower at the west end of the south aisle, was removed, and the opening thus gained was utilized by the formation of a baptistery, whither the finely-carved font was transferred from its former position at the east end of the north aisle. At the same time the oak roof was re-varnished, and the bosses, with which it is plentifully studded, were re-gilt, and there was erected a new reredos of Caen stone with five panels of alabaster, designed by the late Sir Gilbert Scott. During the years 1870-1871, another reparation was carried out. The pews were then taken away and the chancel transformed. Some interesting relics were also introduced in the shape of carvings from the church of All Hallows Staining, the body of which had been pulled down in 1870, on the union of its parish with that of St. Olave; and the handsome oak pulpit, ascribed to Gibbons, which had belonged to the church of St. Benet Gracechurch, demolished in 1868.

The vestry is a charming little room, and is quite unique, with its ceiling beautifully moulded with angel figures, and its splendid mahogany mantelpiece, on which are depicted Faith, Hope, and Charity.

In St. Olave's are to be seen many interesting monuments, the most ancient of which is a brass to the memory of Sir Richard Haddon, mercer, twice Lord Mayor—in the years 1506 and 1512. It displays the figures of Sir Richard, his two wives, two sons, and three daughters, and although it has suffered considerably from the hand of time, it has fortunately been preserved, and is now affixed to the south wall just to the east of the vestry door.

The altar-tomb of Sir John Radcliffe has perished, but the upper portion of his originally recumbent effigy, clothed in armour, still remains, and has been erected on the east wall of the north aisle, together with the tablet containing his inscription. Dame Anne, his wife, was represented as kneeling beside him on the tomb. Her effigy, which is in a much more perfect condition, now kneels at the south of the altar. Sir John's inscription is in Latin, and states that he was the son of Robert, Earl of Sussex, and died in 1568; Dame Anne, as the English epitaph below her effigy sets forth, survived till 1585. Another Elizabethan worthy is commemorated by a brass plate at the east end of the north aisle, namely, Thomas Morley, clerk of the queen's household at Deptford, who died in 1566.

On the east wall of the south aisle is a tablet, with Latin inscription, to William Turner, who appears to have divided his time between divinity and medicine, as he was at the same period Dean of Wells and physician to the Protector Somerset. Being a staunch Protestant, he found it expedient to quit the country during the reign of Mary, and travelled on the continent in pursuit of knowledge. At the accession of Elizabeth he returned to England, and was restored to his deanery. In the quiet years which he now enjoyed, he was enabled to prepare for the press the results of his botanical studies, and finally in 1568 he published a "Herbal," the earliest work of that nature in English, which he dedicated to the queen in an epistle dated from his house in Crutched Friars. He died in July of the same year.

Immediately below is a small plate inscribed:

"In God is my whole trust.—J. O. 1584.
John Orgene and Ellyne, his Wife.

As I was, so be ye,
As I am, you shall be.
What I gave, that I have,
What I spent, that I had;
Thus I count all my cost,
What I left, that I lost."

Peter Turner, a physician who died in 1614, and son of Dr. William, has a monument with half-length effigy near that of his father.

North of the chancel is a kneeling figure, clothed in armour, representing Peter Chapone, or Caponius, a Florentine gentleman, who died an exile in England in 1582; and two other foreigners, German students who, having come to England in search of knowledge, died here, one in 1618, and the other in 1628, are commemorated by tablets with long Latin inscriptions.

Immediately over the brass of Sir Richard Haddon is an

elaborate monument, with kneeling figures, to Sir James Deane, who died in 1608, and is described as a very charitable person. His inscription gives the names of his three wives, the second of whom was Elizabeth, daughter of Alderman Hugh Offley.

Conspicuously placed to the north of the altar are two well-executed kneeling figures, painted red, and draped in the aldermanic gown; these represent two brothers, Paul and Andrew Bayning, both aldermen, of whom the elder, Paul, served the office of sheriff in 1593. Andrew Bayning died on December 21st, 1610, at the age of sixty-seven; his brother survived him nearly six years, finally passing away, aged seventy-seven, on September 3rd, 1616.

Some quaint lines in honour of both brothers are inscribed on the monument of Paul Bayning:

> "If all great Cities prosperously confess
> That he, by whom their Traffick doth increase,
> Deserves well of them, then th'Adventure's worth
> Of these two, who were Brothers both by Birth
> And Office, prove that they have thankful bin
> For th'Honours which this City plac'd them in;
> And dying old, they by a blest consent
> This Legacy bequeathed, their Monument.
> The happy summ and end of their Affairs
> Provided well both for their Souls and Heirs."

Paul Bayning's son, Sir Paul Bayning, was created in 1627 Viscount Bayning of Sudbury. He died in 1629, and was buried in his father's tomb, above which was erected his coat-of-arms. He left one son, also named Paul, on whose death without male issue in 1638 the viscounty of Bayning of Sudbury became extinct.

The advowson of St. Olave's is said to have anciently belonged

St. Olave, Hart Street.

to the Nevils, and afterwards to Richard and Robert Cely. At a later period it was possessed by the Windsor family, from whom it passed into the hands of Sir Andrew Riccard, who at his death bequeathed it to the parish, appointing five of the senior inhabitants as trustees.

Sir Andrew Riccard, one of the most distinguished merchants of his age, served as sheriff in 1651, and received the honour of knighthood from Charles II. in 1662. He was chairman of the East India Company, and for eighteen years perpetual chairman of the Turkey Company, who at their own expense, as is stated in the inscription, erected in St. Olave's a monument to their "Dictator." This monument, very happily described by Strype as "a stately statue of white marble," stands against the north wall. At the base are engraved two epitaphs, one Latin, the other English, both of which have much the same purport, though the English one is somewhat fuller. Sir Andrew died on September 6th, 1672, at the age of sixty-eight, and was interred in front of the chancel.

But the most interesting person connected with this church is Samuel Pepys, the Diarist, to whose picturesque and vivacious record we are indebted for so much invaluable information as to both public and private life in the years succeeding the Restoration. Residing in a house in Seething Lane adjoining the Navy Office, in which he held the position of Clerk of the Acts, Pepys was a parishioner of St. Olave's, and regularly attended service here, as he notes in his Diary, now and again criticising in his kindly humorous way the preaching of the then rector, Dr. Daniel Mills. In 1673 he was promoted to be Secretary to the Admiralty, and in the same year he was elected M.P. for Castle Rising. In 1684, and again in 1685, he occupied the distinguished position of President of the Royal Society, of which he had been a Fellow since 1665. In James II.'s only parliament he sat for Harwich, but lost his seat at the election for the Convention Parliament of 1688-89. The Revolution also brought about his retirement from official life. His long-standing and close connection with James II., for whom he entertained a warm personal affection, rendered him naturally unwilling to serve under the new dynasty, and he quitted the Admiralty, where he had worked so ably and conscientiously for over a quarter of a century, to spend the evening of his days in well-earned repose. In 1700 he was living in Buckingham Street, Strand, but for the benefit of his health he removed to Clapham, where he died on May 26th, 1703, at the age of seventy-one. His Diary he bequeathed to Magdalene College, Cambridge, at which he had received his education. It covers the period from January, 1660, to May, 1669, when he was obliged to relinquish his task owing to the increasing weakness of his eyes.

Pepys's brother Tom died in 1664, and was buried at St. Olave's in the middle aisle, "just under my mother's pew," as he informs us. In 1669 he lost his wife. She was the daughter of Alexander Marchant, Sieur de St. Michel, a Huguenot belonging to a noble family of Anjou, who, having come over to England in the train of Henrietta Maria, married and settled down in his adopted country.

To the memory of his wife Pepys erected a monument of white marble on the north side of the chancel above the tomb of the Baynings. She is said to have been very beautiful, and beautiful indeed is she represented by her exquisitely sculptured bust, than which it would be hard to find a memorial more charming. Her epitaph is as follows:

St. Olave, Hart Street.

"H. S. E.
Cui
Cunas dedit Somersitia, Octob: 23, 1640
Patrem e praeclara familia   Matrem e nobili Stirpe
  de St Michel   Cliffodorum
  Andegravia   Cumbria
        Elizabetha Pepys,
Samuelis Pepys (Classi Regiae ab Actis) Uxor,
Quae in Caenobio primum, Aulâ dein educata Gallicâ,
Utriusque una claruit virtutibus,
Formâ, Artibus, Linguis, cultissima.
Prolem enixa, quia parem non potuit, nullam,
Huic demum placide cum valedixerat
(Confecto per amoeniora fere Europae itinere)
Potiorem abiit redux lustratura mundum.
        Obiit 10 Novembris,
                  ⎧ Aetatis 29.
        Anno ⎨ Conjugii 15.
                  ⎩ Domini 1669."

The remains of Pepys himself were interred in a vault of his own making, side by side with those of his wife and brother, the funeral service being conducted by the celebrated Nonjuring Divine, Dr. George Hickes. No monument was erected to him; but at length, in our own time, this omission has been supplied. Under the auspices of a committee, formed for this express purpose in 1882, and including amongst its members representatives of the various institutions with which Pepys had been associated, a memorial to the Diarist, designed by Sir A. Blomfield, the cost of which was defrayed by public subscription, was on March 18th, 1884, unveiled by the late James Russell Lowell, then American Minister in this country, in the unavoidable absence, through official duties, of Lord Northbrook, who, as First Lord of the Admiralty, had been justly selected as the most appropriate person to perform the opening ceremony.

This monument is placed on the south wall at the spot formerly occupied by a small gallery reserved for the Navy Office, in which Pepys sat. A medallion of the Diarist—with whose personal appearance we are familiar from several still existing portraits—occupies a sort of shrine, which is beautifully moulded and richly ornamented. Beneath is inscribed:

"Samuel Pepys
born Feb'y 23 1632
died May 26 1703."

On a lower compartment are his family arms, and at the base of the whole are these words:

"Erected by Public
Subscription—1883."

At the south of the chancel is a tablet of black and white marble to Pepys's colleague—whom he often mentions in his Diary—Admiral Sir John Mennis, Comptroller of the Navy and Governor of Dover Castle. Sir John was also something of a poet, and the part-author of "Musarum Deliciæ." He died in 1670. To one of the pillars of the south aisle, at a considerable elevation from the ground, is affixed a very elegant half-length figure of Elizabeth Gore, who died in 1698 at the age of eighteen. Her father, Alderman Sir William Gore, was Sheriff in 1698, and Lord Mayor in 1701.

Dr. Daniel Mills, who was for thirty-two years rector of the parish, and is frequently alluded to by Pepys, was buried at St. Olave's in 1689.

The Plague committed great ravages amongst the parishioners. The names of those who succumbed to this terrible malady are distinguished in the parish registers by the addition of the letter "P." Large numbers of them were buried in the churchyard,

St. Olave, Hart Street.

which is of considerable size, stretching some distance alongside Seething Lane, from which there is an entrance by means of a gateway quaintly decorated with skulls. Through this gateway, as one ascends Seething Lane, a good view is obtained of the brick tower, rising at the south-west end of the church, and conspicuous with its projecting clock and surmounting weather-vane. Within the tower are hung six bells.

In the parish register is entered the baptism in 1591 of Robert Devereux, third Earl of Essex, the commander of the Parliamentary forces at the outbreak of the Civil War. He was the son of the second earl, Elizabeth's ill-starred favourite, and it was not in the church, but in the mansion in Seething Lane, which Essex had inherited from his father-in-law, Walsingham, that the ceremony was performed. Lancelot Andrewes—not yet a bishop—officiated on the occasion.

Sixteen monuments were removed to St. Olave's from All Hallows Staining when that church was demolished. One of these is placed in the baptistery, and the remaining fifteen at the west end of the north aisle; but no special interest attaches to any of them. The authorities of All Hallows do not seem to have always justly appreciated their duty towards ancient memorials of the dead, for Stow, after enumerating the celebrated persons interred in the church, informs us that the monument of "Sir Richard Tate, knight, ambassador to King Henry VIII., buried there 1554," " remaineth yet ; the rest being all pulled down, and swept out of the church, the church wardens were forced to make a large account, 12s. that year for brooms, besides the carriage away of stone and brass, of their own charge."

The body of the church of All Hallows Staining dated from 1674-5, having been then erected in place of the former structure, which, though spared by the Fire, collapsed in 1671. But the tower, which belonged to the original building, has outlasted its more modern appendages, and now stands isolated in the midst of the remnant of the churchyard which has been preserved as a recreation ground. The situation of this garden, approached from Mark Lane by means of Star Alley, and from Fenchurch Street by a passage at the west side of the London Tavern, is quiet and secluded, though so near to the noise and bustle of densely-thronged thoroughfares, and the old tower with its time-worn battlements and venerable aspect forms a striking centre-piece.

WREN'S CHURCHES.

St. Alban·Wood·Street·

ST. ALBAN'S, Wood Street, the only church in the City proper dedicated to the Proto-martyr of Britain, is situated in the Ward of Cripplegate, and stands on the east side of Wood Street, a little to the south of Addle Street. Its history commences in very early times. King Offa, it is said, had a palace in Wood Street, and this church was originally his chapel; at all events, it seems certain that he granted the parish to the Abbey of St. Alban's, which he founded in 793. Paul, the fourteenth Abbot of St. Alban's, exchanged it in 1077 for another advowson with the Abbot of Westminster, and the patronage was exercised till the latter half of the fifteenth century by the Master, Brethren, and Sisters of St. James's Hospital for Lepers in the parish of Westminster, which was "founded," says Stow, "by the citizens of London before any man's memory," and was finally surrendered to Henry VIII., who made his palace of St. James's there. The last presentation to the rectory of St. Alban's by the Hospital was in 1465, after which the advowson passed into the hands of the Provost and Fellows of Eton College, who first presented in 1477, and have ever since continued patrons.

Sir John Cheke, the eminent Greek scholar and tutor of

Edward VI., who died in 1557, was buried at St. Alban's, Wood Street, where a monument was placed to his memory.

The old church, which had become dangerously dilapidated, was pulled down "betwixt Easter and Midsummer," 1632, and rebuilt two years later. Inigo Jones is said to have been the architect of the new church, but his work did not stand long, as the edifice was utterly consumed in the Great Fire.

The church of St. Olave, Silver Street, which had also been destroyed in the Fire, was not rebuilt, and its rectory, which has from early times been in the gift of the Dean and Chapter of St. Paul's, was united with that of St. Alban. It was situated on the south side of Silver Street, at the north-eastern end of Noble Street, and a portion of its churchyard still remains, and is laid out as a recreation ground.

The present church of St. Alban, Wood Street, was built by Wren, who completed it in 1685. It is in the Tudor style of Gothic, having been constructed after the model of the church destroyed by the Fire. It measures 66 feet in length, 59 feet in breadth, and 33 feet in height, and contains two side-aisles, which are divided from the central portion by clustered columns and flat pointed arches. The north aisle is prolonged further to the west than the south aisle. The ceiling of the nave is groined. The church terminates at the east in an apse, whence it is lighted by three stained glass windows. There is a large window at the west over the entrance, which is quite plain, as are also the windows in the north and south walls, and the northern and southern windows of the east wall.

St Alban's has been inordinately altered and modernized. The walls have been stripped of the wainscot of "Norway oak," with which they were panelled to a height of seven and a half feet, although the bases of the columns still remain encased in wood; and the well-carved pulpit, which stands on the south side, is no longer overshadowed by its old sounding-board, described as "a hexagon having round it a fine cornice adorned with cherubim and other embellishments." The old altar-piece surmounted by the royal arms is also gone, and the west gallery has been taken down, and the organ re-erected on the north of the chancel. But the most striking alteration is the formation of the apse above referred to, and the consequent substitution of three smaller windows for the original large east window. In fact, no pains seem to have been spared to render a once interesting and dignified interior as commonplace as possible.

Attached to the north wall are two large monuments of white marble, in memory of Benjamin Harvey, "Major to the Yellow Regiment of Trained Bands," the donor of the font, who died in 1684, and Richard Wynne, a merchant of London and benefactor to the poor of the parish, who died in 1688.

The tower, which rises at the north-west, attains a height of eighty-five feet, and terminates in an open parapet. It is surmounted by eight pinnacles, each seven feet high, thus giving a total altitude of ninety-two feet. The original pinnacles, having become decayed, were replaced by new ones about fifteen years ago. The appearance presented by this tower is graceful and pleasing, and Wren has here evinced more care as to correctness of detail than was usual with him when he essayed to build in the Gothic style.

To the north of the church is a small churchyard, which separates the sacred building from Little Love Lane. Between the churchyard rails on the west side, facing Wood Street, stands a granite fountain with this simple inscription:

"The gift of A. M. Silber, 1875."

ALL HALLOWS, LOMBARD STREET.

THE church of All Hallows, Lombard Street, stands slightly to the north of that thoroughfare, not far from its junction with Gracechurch Street, and just east of Ball Alley. Stow calls it All Hallows "Grasse Church;" "for that the grass market" (still commemorated in the name of Gracechurch Street) "went down that way, when that street was far broader than now it is, being straitened by incroachments."

All Hallows suffered very serious injury by the Great Fire. The parishioners appear to have hoped to be able to patch it up again, for they had the walls coped with straw and lime to arrest further decay, and as late as 1679 hung a bell in the steeple. But the old edifice was damaged beyond the possibility of reparation, and they were compelled to have a new church built, which was completed by Wren in 1694 at a cost of £8,058.

The parish of All Hallows, Lombard Street, was one of the thirteen "Peculiars" of the Archbishop of Canterbury in the City of London. The advowson of the rectory was given in 1053 or 1054 by one Brihtmerus, a citizen of London, to the church of Canterbury, and the patronage remained in the prior and chapter till the dissolution of monasteries, when it was transferred to the Dean and Chapter of Canterbury, who have ever since continued patrons.

Alexander Barclay was instituted as rector in April, 1552, but

All Hallows, Lombard Street.

died within two months afterwards. He had been a priest of Ottery St. Mary in Devonshire, and held at his death, in addition to the rectory of All Hallows, the vicarage of Much Badow in Essex. In his earlier life he was much given to poetry, his most celebrated composition being "The Shyp of Folys (Fools) of the Worlde," which is, however, based upon, and to a certain extent translated from the "Narrenschiff" of Sebastian Brandt, published at Bâle in 1494. He was also the author of "The Castell of Labour," and "The Egloges," and achieved a translation of Sallust's "Jugurtha."

The church of All Hallows is connected with Lombard Street by a passage which is entered through an archway between Nos. 48 and 49. Affixed to the wall on the west side of the passage is a handsomely carved gateway, with this inscription:

> "This ancient gateway
> was erected at the entrance in Lombard Street
> to All Hallows Church soon after the Great
> Fire of London, and was removed to this place
> when the Buildings adjoining in Lombard
> Street were rebuilt in 1865."

The tower, which is of stone and very simple, rises at the south-west. It is divided into three storeys, of which the lowermost displays at its south face a spacious doorway formed by Corinthian columns with entablature and pediment, while the second is pierced by a circular-headed window, and the third by square openings with louvres, each surmounted by a cornice. A cornice and parapet complete the tower, the height of which is about eighty-five feet.

Through the doorway in the tower entrance is gained to the church by means of a porch and vestibule. The interior is constructed on a simple rectangular plan, without aisles, having only one pillar, which rises at the centre of the west gallery between the church and the vestibule. Its length is 84 feet, and its breadth 52 feet, while the height from the pavement to the ceiling is 30 feet. The ceiling is coved at the sides, and is pierced at the centre by a skylight of oblong shape crossed by two bands, which was inserted during the repairs of 1880, as is recorded by an inscription over the churchwardens' seats at the west. There are five windows in the north wall, and four in the south wall, besides one at the west, but there is no east window, although two small windows may be observed in the north and south wall of the recess in which the altar-piece is placed. The deficiency of light at this extremity caused it to be considered advisable to illumine the church from the ceiling. All the windows are filled with stained glass, with the exception of the most western window of the north wall, which has merely a coloured border.

The woodwork of All Hallows is abundant in quantity, and excellent in quality. The walls are panelled with oak to the height of nine feet. The carved oak altar-piece is extremely handsome. It contains four fluted Corinthian columns with entablature and pediment, displays the figure of a pelican, and is surmounted by seven candlesticks, in allusion to the seven golden candlesticks, signifying the seven churches of Asia, which St. John saw in the Revelation. The total cost of this altar-piece is said to have amounted to £186, and a tablet in the vestry-room records the names of the subscribers by whose liberality it was acquired.

The pulpit and sounding-board, which are placed on the north side of the church, are well carved, and there are two fine oak door-cases, one at the north-west, and the other at the south-west. At the upper part of each of these door-cases is a very ingeniously carved representation of a curtain, extending partly across, so as to appear to conceal some of the ornamental openwork. Above the northern door-case stands a wooden figure of Death, about four feet high, and the southern door-case supports a similar figure of Time. The Corporation pew, which is situated at the south-east, and is dominated by two sword-rests, displays some good carving, as do likewise the high-backed seats of the churchwardens, the ends of which are also ornamented with the Lion and Unicorn.

The organ, which is enclosed in a richly gilded case, is now located at the south-east. The marble font, which stands at the west, is beautifully sculptured with cherubim and floral wreaths, and possesses a finely carved cover. Attached to the wall in the vestibule is a frame containing shelves for loaves for distribution to the poor. Over the entrance at the south-west are placed the royal arms.

The church of St. Benet Gracechurch, which stood at the corner of Gracechurch Street and Fenchurch Street, was pulled down in 1867, and its parish united with that of All Hallows, Lombard Street. The rectory had from time immemorial been in the gift of the Dean and Chapter of St. Paul's.

St. Benet Gracechurch was the work of Wren, having been rebuilt by him in 1685, after the destruction of the former church by the Great Fire. It measured 60 feet long by 30 feet wide, and the steeple, which rose at the north-west and consisted of a tower, cupola, and obelisk-shaped spire, attained the height of 149 feet. This church contained much good carving; the pulpit, as has been already mentioned, was removed on its demolition to St. Olave's, Hart Street.

The church of St. Leonard Eastcheap, which was situated on Fish Street Hill, was not rebuilt after the Great Fire, its parish being united with that of St. Benet Gracechurch. Stow speaks of it as "St. Leonard Milke Church, so termed of one William Melker, an especial builder thereof, but commonly called St. Leonard's in Eastcheape, because it standeth at East Cheape corner."

St. Leonard's Eastcheap was one of the Archbishop of Canterbury's thirteen "Peculiars," and in the patronage first of the Prior and Chapter, and afterwards of the Dean and Chapter of Canterbury.

Another "Peculiar" was St. Dionis Backchurch, dedicated to Dionysius the Areopagite, who was one of St. Paul's first converts at Athens, and who, under the name of St. Denis, became the patron saint of France. This church, which was situated at the south-west corner of Lime Street, was called "Backchurch" from its position behind Fenchurch Street, in distinction to St. Gabriel Fenchurch, which, standing in the middle of the street, was sometimes designated "Forechurch."

St. Dionis having been consumed by the Fire, the body of the church was rebuilt by Wren in 1674, and in 1684 he added the tower. The church was divided into a nave and two aisles by Ionic columns, and measured 72 feet in length by 63 feet 9 inches in breadth, while the height of the tower exceeded 100 feet. The east front was ornamented by an Ionic façade. The pulpit was carved by Grinling Gibbons.

St. Dionis was pulled down in 1878, and its parish united with that of All Hallows, Lombard Street, the church of which thus now serves for four parishes. The ten bells of St. Dionis, which were procured in 1727 at a cost of £479 18s., were rehung in the tower of All Hallows.

Among the monuments removed from St. Dionis to All Hallows is an elaborate memorial with a laudatory Latin inscription to Dr. Edward Tyson, who died in 1708. He was a physician of some note and a Fellow of the Royal Society. Garth ridiculed him in "'The Dispensary" under the name of Carus.

Dr. Charles Burney, the author of the "History of Music" and the father of Madame D'Arblay, was appointed organist of St. Dionis Backchurch in 1749, being then twenty-three years old. While here he began to make rapid progress in his profession, but failing health obliged him to quit the metropolis in 1751, and he spent the next nine years at Lynn Regis in Norfolk.

There existed under St. Dionis Backchurch a crypt belonging to the fifteenth century building. This was discovered by Mr. Street, when inspecting the vaults, and is fully described by him in a very interesting letter to "The Builder" of July 24th, 1858. It was, he says, a parallelogram, measuring internally 9 feet 6 inches from north to south, and 13 feet from east to west, and was covered in with a quadripartite vault crossed by diagonal ribs. The height from the floor to the springing of the vault was four feet, and the vault itself rose a similar height. He could find no mark of a window, though there was an opening on the south side which had been walled up. But this he was inclined to believe to have been the original door, as the entrance by which he obtained ingress to the crypt was evidently modern. He also perceived traces of the ancient staircase leading down from the church into the crypt.

St. Andrew by the Wardrobe

THE church of St. Andrew by the Wardrobe stands on the east side of St. Andrew's Hill, and its south front overlooks Queen Victoria Street. It is situated in the Ward of Castle Baynard, and derived its distinguishing title from its proximity to the King's Great Wardrobe, a mansion built by Sir John Beauchamp, Constable of Dover and Warden of the Cinque Ports, and after his death in 1359 purchased from his executors by King Edward III., and used as an office for the keepers of the king's apparel. St. Andrew's Hill was formerly Puddle Dock Hill, and has taken its present name from the church. It runs down into Queen Victoria Street to the west of St. Andrew's, immediately opposite Puddle Dock.

The advowson of the rectory of St. Andrew by the Wardrobe was anciently in the possession of the Fitzwalters, who were hereditary Constables of Baynard's Castle and Standard-bearers of the City of London. It was afterwards divided between the three daughters of Thomas, Lord Berkeley, whose descendants presented alternately. The Crown presented in 1615 and 1629, but in 1663 a presentation was made by the Earl of Leicester, Algernon Sidney's father, as a descendant of one of the former holders; after which the Crown again resumed the patronage. The rectory is now in the gift of the Mercers' Company.

With the parish of St. Andrew by the Wardrobe was united

after the Great Fire that of St. Anne, Blackfriars, of which Stow gives the following account :

"There is a parish of St. Anne within the precinct of the Black Friars, which was pulled down with the Friar's Church by Sir Thomas Carden; but in the reign of Queen Mary, he being forced to find a church to the inhabitants, allowed them a lodging chamber above a stair, which since that time, to wit, in the year 1597, fell down, and was again, by collection therefore made, new built and enlarged in the same year, and was dedicated on the 11th of December."

A portion of the old burying-ground of St. Anne, Blackfriars, may still be seen in Church Entry, Ireland Yard, but, as it is to be let on a building lease, it will not probably remain in existence much longer. William Faithorne, the engraver, who died on May 13th, 1691, at his residence in Printing House Yard, Blackfriars, was buried here.

Vandyck was an inhabitant of St. Anne's parish, and died in it, but was buried in Old St. Paul's. His daughter, Justinian, is recorded to have been baptized at St. Anne's on December 9th, 1641, the very day of her father's death. Sir Samuel Luke, from whom Butler is generally supposed to have drawn Hudibras, was also a parishioner. His marriage in 1624, and the baptisms of several of his children appear in the register.

The church of St. Andrew by the Wardrobe was rebuilt after the Fire at a cost of over £7,000 by Wren, who completed it early in the year 1692. It measures 75 feet in length, 59 feet in breadth, and 38 feet in height, and contains two side-aisles, which are divided from the nave by square pillars encased in wood to the height of the top of the galleries, which they serve to support. The ceiling is divided by bands into panels; the five central compartments contain wreaths of flowers, which produce a very fine effect, and over each column stands out boldly an angel figure. The walls are wainscotted to the height of seven and a half feet. The altarpiece is enclosed by four pilasters with entablature and circular pediment. Above it is a large stained glass window, but the remainder of the windows are plain. The pulpit, which stands on the south side, is well carved, but has been deprived of its sounding-board. The font is placed at the west, and above it the richly gilded case of the organ in the west gallery presents an imposing appearance. The Corporation pews, which are the two easternmost of the central block, are adorned at their entrances by the Lion and Unicorn, each bearing a shield emblazoned with the Union Jack, and to a pillar above the north pew is attached a handsome sword-rest. At the west are high-backed seats for the churchwardens. The eastern portion of each aisle is separated from the chancel by tall iron rails with gate. The church is well lighted, and has a dignified aspect well in keeping with its sacred purpose.

There are pyramidal monuments of white marble to three successive rectors—the Rev. William Romaine, the celebrated preacher, who was instituted in 1766, and died in 1795 at the age of eighty-one; the Rev. William Goode, rector from 1795 till his death in 1816; and the Rev. Isaac Saunders, who died on January 1st, 1836, after holding the living almost twenty years.

Romaine's monument, which is the work of the elder Bacon, stands at the eastern end of the north aisle. It is crowned with a well-executed bust, and on the pyramid is displayed an allegorical figure of Faith, holding on her arm an open Testament, while above her right shoulder is a telescope pointing upwards to a figure of the Saviour. The virtues of the revered divine are set forth in a long inscription beneath.

The monuments to Goode and Saunders are situated at the eastern end of the south aisle. Goode's memorial is by the younger Bacon; on it appears an angel, seated on a sarcophagus, and grasping a Testament, but there is no bust. Saunders's bust, however, like that of Romaine, dominates his pyramid, on which he is represented as being borne aloft by angels to a crown of glory which is sculptured above. Below the angels is displayed an open Bible, and beneath this is his epitaph. The monument was designed by Samuel Manning.

Romaine's widow and Saunders's widow and daughter are also commemorated by tablets. Mrs. Saunders's tablet was erected by a subscription amongst the ladies of the parish.

The exterior of St. Andrew by the Wardrobe is of red brick with stone dressings. The tower rises at the south-west. It is square, and consists of four storeys. In the lowest of these storeys is a small window, and in the second are circular-headed windows; while the third contains the clock, and the highest stage is ornamented with long square-headed openings with louvres. The tower is completed by a cornice and balustrade, and is surmounted by four iron finials and vanes, springing from the summits of the piers, which are carried up the angles of the tower. Its height is about eighty-six feet.

The formation of Queen Victoria Street has been conducive to the better displaying of the beauties of this edifice, which, standing above the level of that thoroughfare, now occupies a very prominent position.

St. Andrew Holborn

THE church of St. Andrew, Holborn, stands between St. Andrew Street and Shoe Lane. Its situation about half-way up Holborn Hill must once have been a prominent one, but the elevation of the road, consequent upon the construction of Holborn Viaduct, has detracted considerably from the effect of the building.

The foundation of this church is lost in the mists of antiquity. Its name occurs as early as the year 971 in a charter of King Edgar, defining the boundaries of the original parish of Westminster. One Gladerinus, a presbyter, appears to have been in possession of the advowson about the beginning of the fourteenth century, and to have bestowed it upon the abbot and monks of Bermondsey, whose property it remained till the dissolution of that convent by Henry VIII.

St. Andrew's was rebuilt during the fifteenth century, but in less than two hundred years it had fallen into a state of dilapidation. The parishioners were already purposing to rebuild it in the reign of Charles I., but the work was long delayed, probably owing to the troubles of the Civil Wars, and it was not till 1686 that Wren, who was busily engaged in re-erecting the churches which had been consumed by the Great Fire, re-constructed this edifice, which, though it had escaped the flames, had wellnigh succumbed to the more gradual devastation wrought by the hand of time. Wren spared the tower, which was in a better condition than the body of the church, but subsequently, in 1704, he refaced it with Portland stone. This tower, which displays some of the original Gothic arches, and rises to a height of 110 feet, constitutes the only existing relic of the old building, the remainder of the church being entirely due to Wren. It stands at the west end, and through a vestibule beneath it access is gained to the interior of the church.

St. Andrew's consists of a nave, chancel, and two side-aisles; it measures 105 feet in length, 63 feet in width, and 43 feet in height from the pavement to the ceiling. The cost of its erection is stated to have been £9,000. The interior is richly decorated, and is much in the same style as, though inferior to, St. James's, Westminster, which Wren had built a few years earlier. The roof of the nave is divided into compartments, painted a soft bluegrey colour, which has a restful effect upon the eye, while the ceilings of the aisles are handsomely gilded. The walls are panelled below the windows, as are also the bases of the columns underneath the galleries. There is a fine altar-piece, and the east window above it is filled with richly stained glass, the work of Joshua Price, inserted in 1718. This window contains two divisions, of which the upper represents the Resurrection of our Lord, and the lower the Last Supper. On either side of it are two large paintings in fresco, now somewhat faded, displaying St. Andrew and St. Peter, and two smaller panels, on which are depicted the Holy Family and the infant St. John. The stained window at the east end of the north gallery bears the date 1687, and this inscription:

"Ex dono Thomae Hodgson de Bramwill in agro Eboracem Militis."
It is emblazoned with the royal arms, and with those of Hodgson. The corresponding window at the end of the south gallery bears the arms of John Thavie, a member of the Armourers' Company, from whom Thavies Inn, Holborn Circus, derives its name. He bequeathed at his death in 1348 some houses belonging to him in Holborn for the repairing of St. Andrew's Church, and this property is still in the possession of the parish.

The pulpit is of oak, finely carved, and is a very prominent object, being elevated on a stone pedestal. The font is placed to the north of the chancel.

The church was repaired in 1851, and again more extensively in 1872, when alterations were made in the churchyard, so as to bring it more into harmony with the changed condition of its surroundings produced by the formation of Holborn Viaduct. The same year (1872) witnessed the disappearance from St. Andrew's of its old organ, an instrument to which was attached an interesting history. The two great organ-builders, Renatus Harris and Father Smith, contended for the honour of supplying an organ for the Temple Church. Each of the rivals constructed an instrument on approval. Blow and Purcell played upon Smith's organ, while Baptiste Draghi, Queen Catherine's organist, performed upon that of Harris. The benchers found the task of judging no easy one, for each builder had his own particular strong point, Harris excelling in reed stops, and Smith in diapason or foundation stops. At length, after they had remained in a state of indecision for nearly a year, they submitted the matter to the arbitration of Judge Jeffreys, who decided in favour of Smith. Harris thereupon constructed two organs out of his rejected instrument, one of which was taken to Dublin, and afterwards

St. Andrew, Holborn.

transferred to a church at Wolverhampton, while the other was set up at St. Andrew's in 1699. The new organ, the work of Messrs. Hill, is a very fine instrument. It occupies the old position in the west gallery, and possesses two sets of pipes, which are arranged one on each side of the entrance arch.

The advowson of St. Andrew's, having come at the dissolution of monasteries into the hands of the crown, was bestowed by Henry VIII. in 1546 on Thomas Wriothesley, Earl of Southampton and Lord Chancellor, whose remains were here interred in 1550, but subsequently removed to Titchfield. It was forfeited to the crown in 1601, when Henry, Earl of Southampton, Shakespeare's patron, shared the condemnation of his friend, the Earl of Essex. His life was, however, spared, and James I. restored him to all his honours and possessions, including the patronage of St. Andrew's. The male line of the Wriothesleys terminated in 1667 in the person of Thomas, Earl of Southampton, the father-in-law of Lord William Russell. The advowson passed to one of his daughters, and subsequently into the family of the Dukes of Buccleugh, in whose possession it still remains.

At the outbreak of the Civil War the rector of St. Andrew's was John Hacket, a man of great coolness and resolution, who was afterwards elevated to the see of Lichfield, and is known as the biographer of Lord Keeper Williams. After the Restoration the living was for some time held by Edward Stillingfleet, who became Bishop of Worcester, and was reckoned one of the most eminent divines of his time. In 1713 the celebrated Dr. Henry Sacheverell received the rectory as a reward for the trial which he had undergone, and the important services which he had thereby rendered to the Tory party, mainly through the instrumentality of Swift, who interested Lord Bolingbroke on his behalf. Sacheverell continued rector till his death in 1724, and was buried in the chancel; the site of his grave was marked by a stone with a simple inscription.

Robert Coke, of Mileham in Norfolk, a bencher of Lincoln's Inn, was buried at St. Andrew's in 1561, and had a monument in the chancel of the old church. He was the father of the eminent lawyer, Sir Edward Coke, who was here married in 1598 to the object of Bacon's ill-requited affection, Lady Elizabeth Hatton, granddaughter of Lord Treasurer Burleigh.

St. Andrew's contains many other interesting associations. It is said, though this does not seem absolutely certain, that John Webster, the dramatist, author, besides other plays, of "The Dutchesse of Malfy" and "The White Devil," was clerk of the parish and was buried in the church. Nathaniel Tomkins was buried here; he was brother-in-law of Edmund Waller, and was hanged at the Holborn end of Fetter Lane on July 5th, 1643, for his complicity in Waller's plot against the Parliament, from the consequences of which the poet himself escaped by his servility and mean betrayal of his associates. The interment is recorded in 1720 of John Hughes, author of "The Siege of Damascus," one of the best of the minor poets of the Queen Anne period; and fifty years later is an entry relating to another and a better remembered poet, Thomas Chatterton,

> "the marvellous boy,
> The sleepless soul that perished in his pride."

He died by his own hand on August 25th, 1770, having not yet completed his eighteenth year, and his remains were consigned to the burying-ground of Shoe Lane Workhouse, the site of which is now occupied by Farringdon Market.

St. Andrew, Holborn.

There is in the church a monumental tablet to John Emery, the comedian, who died July 25th, 1822. Of him the inscription states:

> "Each part he shone in, but excelled in none
> So well as husband, father, friend, and son."

St. Andrew's was the scene of two other famous weddings, besides that of Sir Edward Coke. Here in 1638 John Hutchinson, afterwards colonel in the Parliamentary army, and one of the judges of Charles I., was married to Lucy Apsley, whose "Memoirs" have thrown so much light on the stirring times in which her lot was cast; and here, on Sunday, May 1st, 1808, William Hazlitt was married to Sarah Stoddart, Charles Lamb being best man, and Mary Lamb bridesmaid.

To his experiences on this occasion Lamb alludes in a letter to Southey, bearing date August 9th, 1815:

"I am going to stand godfather; I don't like the business. I cannot muster up decorum for these occasions; I shall certainly disgrace the font. I was at Hazlitt's marriage, and had like to have been turned out several times during the ceremony. Anything awful makes me laugh. I misbehaved once at a funeral. Yet I can read about these ceremonies with pious and proper feelings. The realities of life only seem the mockeries."

At St. Andrew's on January 18th, 1697, was baptized Richard Savage, that unfortunate poet whose sad history has been so touchingly told by his friend, Dr. Johnson; here also was baptized, June 30th, 1757, Henry Addington, Speaker of the House of Commons, and from 1801 to 1804 Prime Minister, on whom Canning has conferred an unenviable immortality:

> "Pitt is to Addington
> As London is to Paddington.

But perhaps the most interesting entry in this connection is one of a somewhat later date:

"Baptized July 31, 1817, Benjamin, said to be about twelve years old, son of Isaac and Maria Disraeli, King's Road, Gentleman. A clergyman named Thimbleby performed the ceremony."

St. Anne & St. Agnes

THE church of St. Anne and St Agnes stands towards the west end of Gresham Street on the north side of the way, in what was formerly known as St. Anne's Lane, between Aldersgate Street on the west and Noble Street on the east. St. Anne and St. Agnes, according to an old tradition, were two sisters who built the church at their own expense. The old edifice was very severely damaged by a conflagration in 1548, and having been reconstructed, perished in the Great Fire of 1666.

The advowson of the rectory belonged originally to the Collegiate Church of St. Martin-le-Grand, and passed with the other appurtenances of that foundation to the Abbot and Convent of Westminster in the reign of Henry VII. Queen Mary bestowed the patronage on the Bishop of London, and it has ever since remained in that see.

The adjacent church of St. John Zachary was also consumed in the Fire, and, as it was not rebuilt, its parish was united with that of St. Anne and St. Agnes. A portion of its old burying-ground is still to be seen on the north side of Gresham Street at the south-east corner of Noble Street. The church was dedicated to St. John the Baptist, and took the name of a twelfth-century priest, its builder or holder, in order to distinguish it from St. John the Baptist upon Walbrook. The advowson of the rectory has been always in the gift of the Dean and Chapter of St. Paul's.

The present church of St. Anne and St. Agnes was completed by Wren in 1681. It is built of brick, and measures 53 feet square, while the height from the pavement to the centre of the ceiling is 35 feet. Within this area another square is formed by four Corinthian columns, standing on high wood-covered bases, and a cruciform appearance is thus produced. The ceiling is coloured a light blue, and is ornamented with fretwork, the effect of which is very pleasing. In the main part it is arched, but over the four quadrangular recesses which are formed at the angles by the entablatures passing from the columns to pilasters attached to the walls, it is flat and of a lower elevation. Of these four quadrangular recesses the north-eastern is occupied by the organ, the south-eastern by a choir-vestry, that at the north-west by the font, and that at the south-west by the entrance door-case.

The church is lighted by a window at the east, which is filled with richly stained glass, and by three windows in the north, and three corresponding windows in the south wall, the central ones being much larger than the others. The walls are panelled with oak to the height of eight and a half feet. The altar-piece, on which a good deal of gilding has been bestowed, contains two fluted pilasters with entablature and pediment. It was originally surmounted by the royal arms, which are now placed below the central window of the north wall. The pulpit stands on the south side. The Corporation seats—the north-easternmost of the central block—are distinguished by a graceful sword-rest.

The tower, which rises at the west, measures 14 feet at the base, and supports a small wooden lantern culminating in a vane shaped like the letter A. The total height to the top of the vane is 95 feet.

St. Augustine

On the north side of Watling Street, at the eastern corner of Old Change, stands a church "dedicated," says Newcourt, "to the Memory, not of St. Augustine, Bishop of Hippo in Africa, that great and famous Father, called by some (and not unworthily) Doctor Doctorum; but rather of St. Augustine the Monk, the first Archbishop of Canterbury."

Stow calls St. Augustine's "a fair church," adding that it had been "lately well repaired." The church was partly rebuilt, and "in every part of it richly and very worthily beautified" in 1630-31, at an expenditure by the parishioners of no less than £1,200. It shared, however, in the general destruction of the Great Fire.

Beneath the choir of Old St. Paul's, and traversed by three rows of massive pillars, was the parish church of St. Faith, therefore called St. Faith "in Cryptis," a title which became corrupted into St. Faith "in the Croudes." There had originally been a church of St. Faith above ground, but that having been pulled down about 1256, when the cathedral was extended towards the east, the parishioners had this subterranean place of worship assigned to them. Also under the choir of the cathedral, but more to the east, was the Jesus Chapel, and thither the parishioners were removed in 1551, "as to a place," says Stow, " more sufficient for largeness and lightsomeness." The inhabitants of St. Faith's parish, he tells us, were "the stationers and others dwelling in Paule's Churchyard, Paternoster Row, and the places near adjoining."

During the Great Fire the booksellers and stationers conveyed their goods to St. Faith's as a place of safety, but their hopes were cruelly disappointed, for the flames penetrated here also and destroyed everything. Pepys was told by a kinsman of his bookseller, Kirton:

"That the goods laid in the churchyard fired through the windows those in St. Fayth's Church; and those coming to the warehouses' doors fired them, and burned all the books and the pillars of the church, so as the roof falling down, broke quite down; which it did not do in the other places of the church, which is alike pillared (which I knew not before); but being not burned, they stood still. He do believe there is above £150,000 of books burned; all the great booksellers almost undone: not only these, but their warehouses under their Hall and under Christchurch, and elsewhere being all burned."

According to Dr. Taswell, then a boy at Westminster School, whose narrative is quoted by Dean Milman, the papers from the books in St. Faith's were carried with the wind as far as Eton.

After the Fire the rectories of St. Augustine and St. Faith, both of which were in the gift of the Dean and Chapter of St. Paul's, were united, and the church of St. Augustine, which was rebuilt by Wren, has since served for both parishes. A portion of the crypt of St. Paul's continued, however, to be used for the interment, not only of the parishioners of St. Faith's, but also of those of St. Augustine's, which possessed no proper burying-ground of its own.

St. Augustine, Watling Street.

The present church of St. Augustine was first opened for divine worship in September, 1683, but the steeple was not finished till 1695. The interior, which measures about 51 feet in length, 45 feet in breadth, and 30 feet in height, is divided into a nave and side-aisles by six Ionic columns and four pilasters. Two of the pilasters are placed against the east, and two against the west wall, and by this means the arches are continued to the extremities of the church. The columns are elevated on remarkably lofty bases. The ceiling of the nave is arched and is pierced by six skylights, three on each side, placed each in a separate panel, and filled with delicately tinted glass; to the west of the skylights it is divided into small panels. The ceilings of the aisles are also arched. There are two windows at the west, and three in the south wall, the easternmost of which is, however, now concealed by the organ. The altar-piece displays four Corinthian columns with entablature and circular pediment. The pulpit, of carved oak, stands at the south-east; the font is placed at the west end of the south aisle. A gallery on the north side still remains, but the west gallery, which formerly contained the organ, has been taken away. The walls were originally panelled to the height of eight feet, but the wainscot has since been considerably cut down.

Over the door at the west end of the south aisle is a marble tablet surmounted by an urn, in memory of Judith, daughter of Robert Booth, citizen of London, the first wife of the eminent lawyer, William Cowper. She died on April 2nd, 1705, before her husband had obtained the Lord Chancellorship and an earldom. This monument was erected by the second Earl Cowper, the Lord Chancellor's son by his second wife, in pursuance of the directions of his father's will.

The steeple of St. Augustine's rises at the south-west, and consists of a tower, lantern, and spire. The tower, which measures 20 feet square at the base, contains three storeys; the lowermost possesses a large window on the western face, fronting Old Change, and a doorway on the southern face, fronting Watling Street; the second is relieved by small circular windows, and the third by square openings with louvres. It is terminated by a rather elaborate cornice and pierced parapet, at the angles of which are placed four tall pinnacles. The lantern, which is very slender, is divided into two stages, and the spire, culminating in a ball, finial, and vane, completes the whole. The total altitude of the steeple is 140 feet.

Dr. John Douglas, who vindicated the reputation of Milton from the calumnies of Lauder, and defended the genuineness of the New Testament miracles against the criticisms of Hume, was rector of St. Augustine and St. Faith from 1764 to 1787. He resigned the living on being advanced to the bishopric of Carlisle. He was translated to Salisbury in 1791, and died in his eighty-sixth year on May 18th, 1807. He was a native of Fifeshire, and after leaving Oxford served for some time as an army chaplain, being present in that capacity at the battle of Fontenoy.

The Rev. Richard Harris Barham, the author of the "Ingoldsby Legends," was rector of St. Augustine and St. Faith from 1842 till his death, June 17th, 1845. He was extremely popular with his parishioners, and they were desirous of petitioning the Dean and Chapter of St. Paul's that his son might be his successor. That gentleman, however, would not consent to their doing so.

St. Benet Paul's Wharf

THE church of St. Benet, Paul's Wharf, stands on Bennet's Hill, having its south front in Upper Thames Street, opposite Paul's Wharf. The old church, described by Stow as "a proper parish church," contained monuments to Sir William Cheney, Chief Justice of the King's Bench, who died in 1442; Doctor Richard Caldwell, President of the College of Physicians, who died in 1585; and Sir Gilbert Dethike, who was Garter King at Arms when Queen Mary granted Derby House, the former residence of the Stanleys, to be the Heralds' College.

But the most illustrious person here buried was Inigo Jones. The great architect died at Somerset House on June 21st, 1652, having almost completed his eightieth year, and on the 26th of that month his body was, in accordance with his instructions, interred beneath the chancel of St. Benet's, hard by the grave in which his parents had been laid to rest over half a century before. A monument of white marble, for which he had set aside £100, was erected to his memory by his executor, John Webb. It stood against the north wall, and bore a Latin inscription, which recorded that Jones was the king's architect, and that he built the Banqueting House at Whitehall, and restored St. Paul's Cathedral. This memorial perished in the Great Fire.

"I could wish," says Peter Cunningham, in his "Life of Inigo Jones," "that Wren, in rebuilding the church, had rebuilt the monument."

The neighbouring church of St. Peter, Paul's Wharf, also called, on account of its small size, St. Peter Parva, was not rebuilt after the Fire, but its burying-ground may still be seen in Upper Thames Street at the bottom of Peter's Hill, and being tastefully planted and laid out, it forms an agreeable relief to the monotony of the warehouses. The parish of St. Peter was united with that of St. Benet.

The present church of St. Benet, Paul's Wharf, was finished by Wren in 1683. It is built of red brick, relieved by stone quoins, and by stone festoons over the windows, of which there are three on the north, three on the south, two at the east, and two at the west. The steeple, which attains a height of 115 feet, is placed at the north-west. It consists of a plain tower, measuring 16 feet square at the base, and completed by a cornice; a lead-covered cupola, pierced with oval openings; and a lantern, which supports a ball and vane. The heavy overhanging roof suits well with the rest of the building, and the whole appearance of St. Benet's is exceedingly picturesque. Placed as it is on the slope leading down to the river-side, it shows to great advantage from the higher ground of Queen Victoria Street.

St. Benet's measures internally 54 feet in length by 50 feet in breadth, being thus almost square, and 36 feet in height. It possesses one aisle, on the north side, which is separated from the nave by two Corinthian columns elevated on lofty bases. The ceiling is divided into panels. There is a north gallery, and also a small west gallery containing the organ, inserted between the tower and the south wall. The walls are wainscotted to the

St. Benet, Paul's Wharf.

height of eight feet. The altar-piece is of oak, and is surmounted by a circular pediment. The pulpit stands on the south side, and the font is located at the north, beneath the gallery. Over the doorway at the north-west are affixed the royal arms.

Owing to its contiguity to the College of Arms and Doctors' Commons, St. Benet's afforded a place of sepulture to a considerable number of heralds and dignitaries of the Ecclesiastical Courts. Amongst the monuments is one to John Charles Brooke, that unfortunate Somerset Herald, who met his death from the pressure of the crowd at the Haymarket Theatre on February 3rd, 1794. William Oldys, "Norroy," the learned author of the "British Librarian" and the "Life of Raleigh," was buried here in August, 1761. His grave is said to be situated at the eastern end of the north aisle, but no memorial marks its site. Mrs. Manley, the author of the "New Atlantis," who died on July 11th, 1724, at Alderman Barber's house on Lambeth Hill, was interred at St. Benet's.

It was in this church that Elias Ashmole, the antiquary, was married to his first wife in 1638.

St. Benet's, the rectory of which was in the gift of the Dean and Chapter of St. Paul's, has ceased to be parochial, its parish having been united with that of St. Nicholas Cole Abbey. It is now devoted to the spiritual needs of the Welsh residents in London, for whom two services are held each Sunday in their native tongue.

THE church of St. Bride, which is situated a little to the south of Fleet Street, slightly west of Ludgate Circus, is dedicated to St. Bridget (of which Bride is a corruption), a Scotch or Irish saint who flourished in the sixth century, and is said to have been buried in County Down in the same grave with St. Patrick and St. Columba. This is the only church in London dedicated to her. The date of the erection of St. Bride's is not known, and no mention of it has been discovered prior to the year 1222.

St. Bride's was situated within the ancient parish of Westminster, the abbot and convent of which possessed the advowson. The benefice was originally a rectory, but somewhere about the beginning of the sixteenth century it was converted into a vicarage, the rectory being appropriated by the Abbot and Convent of Westminster. After the dissolution of monasteries Henry VIII. granted the patronage of St. Bride's to the deanery of Westminster, which he had substituted for the convent. Subsequently he created a bishopric of Westminster, and transferred the patronage to the bishop. Edward VI. abolished the bishopric, and restored the deanery; and Queen Mary re-established the abbot and convent. After her death the abbey was formed by Queen Elizabeth into a collegiate church, and the presentation

St. Bride, Fleet Street.

to the vicarage of St. Bride's has since that time continued to be vested in the Dean and Chapter of Westminster.

St. Bride's, like so many other London churches, was repaired in the reign of Charles I., but was destroyed by the Great Fire of 1666. The only relics of the old church which now survive are the font, a white marble basin supported by a black marble shaft, displaying a sculptured shield which contains the donor's arms, and inscribed, "Deo et ecclesiæ ex Dono Henrici Hothersall A.D. 1615," which stands in the west part of the middle aisle of the present building; and outside the church on the north the entry stone to the vault of the Holdens, which bears the date 1657.

To this family belonged the Mr. Holden who, on June 27th, 1661, supplied Pepys with a "bever," which cost him, as he has recorded, £4 5s.

The present church of St. Bride was built in 1680 by Wren, who added the steeple in 1701. The total cost of the work was not far short of £12,000.

The steeple of St. Bride's, one of Wren's greatest achievements, rose originally to the height of 234 feet. In 1764 it was seriously damaged by lightning, and it became requisite to take down 85 feet of the spire. Sir William Staines, who conducted the repairs, reduced the elevation of the spire by eight feet, so that the total height of the steeple is now 226 feet. But, even in this lowered state, it is still the most lofty of all Wren's steeples (the towering pile of St. Paul's Cathedral of course excepted), being 4 feet 3 inches higher than its nearest rival, that of St. Mary-le-Bow. The height of the tower to the top of the parapet is 120 feet, and thence rises the spire in four octagonal storeys, of which the two lower are Tuscan, the third Ionic, and the fourth Composite, culminating in an obelisk and vane. At the corners of the parapet surmounting the tower, and at the base of the obelisk, vases are introduced to soften the transitions, and the effect of the spire, as it tapers to the summit, after the manner of a pyramid, is exceedingly graceful.

The view of this beautiful steeple from Fleet Street was formerly obstructed by intervening houses, but a fire having occurred in November, 1824, which made a clearance in front of the church, it was resolved to retain the opening thus created—an improvement which was accomplished by the formation in 1825 of St. Bride's Avenue, designed by Mr. J. B. Papworth. The parishioners subscribed liberally towards the expenses of this most desirable alteration, especially Mr. John Blades, of Ludgate Hill, who had served the office of sheriff in 1812. This munificent citizen contributed £6,000, and laid the first stone of the new avenue on November 3rd, 1825.

The interior of St. Bride's is generally considered one of the best specimens of Wren's workmanship. It is entered through a porch within the tower and a vestibule below the organ-gallery, and is divided into a nave and aisles by an arcade of doubled columns on either side. Attached to the columns are pilasters which support the galleries. The roof of the nave is arched, and is crossed by handsomely wrought bands connected at each extremity with the shields which embellish the tops of the columns. Five compartments are thus formed, containing square panels, and harmonizing with the oval windows with which the walls on either side are pierced. The ceilings of the aisles are groined. The length of the church is 111 feet, its breadth 57 feet, and the height from the pavement to the roof of the nave is 41 feet.

The chancel is highly decorated, and the two-storied altar-piece, which culminates in a circular-headed pediment, displays quite a wealth of ornamentation. It is, however, a comparatively recent addition, having been set up from the designs of Mr. Deykes in 1823, in which year the church was extensively repaired. The large east window was formerly filled with a copy of Rubens's celebrated "Descent from the Cross," which hangs in Antwerp Cathedral, executed in 1825 in richly coloured glass by Mr. Muss, at a cost of about £600. But, as it was found to darken the church, it has now been removed, and fresh stained glass of a lighter character inserted. We are still, however, reminded of the old window, as the "Descent from the Cross" has been made the subject of the central compartment of its successor.

St. Bride's, with its panelled walls, its pews, and its galleries overhead, has a peaceful, old-world aspect, which is delightfully soothing when one passes from the turmoil of Fleet Street into the quietude of the sacred building. It is pervaded by an unquestionable charm—but a charm which is rather to be felt than to be described.

The name of John Taylor, alias Cardmaker, vicar of St. Bride's, is included in the roll of Marian martyrs.

The Rev. John Pridden, who was curate of St. Bride's from 1782 to 1797, was a most zealous antiquary, and devoted nearly the whole of his spare time for thirty years to the task of making an epitome of the earlier rolls of Parliament. He died in 1825, and is commemorated by a marble tablet on the north wall of the church.

The vestry-room, which was built in 1797, is situated at the south-west, opening out of the vestibule. In it hangs, over the fireplace, a fine portrait of the Rev. Thomas Dale, who was presented to the vicarage in 1835 by the Crown, in the exercise of its prerogative, his predecessor, Dr. Joseph Allen, having been raised to the episcopal bench. Mr. Dale, finding St. Bride's Church too small for the needs of the parishioners, set himself strenuously to work to remedy this deficiency, and by his unwearied exertions procured the erection of the district church of Holy Trinity, Gough Square, which stands at the junction of Great New Street and Pemberton Row.

Mr. Dale was subsequently appointed to a canonry of St. Paul's, and to the deanery of Rochester. He was a man of considerable learning, and was Professor of the English Language and Literature, first in London University, and afterwards in King's College, London. He was also something of a poet, his best known production being the "Widow of Nain." He died in 1870 at the age of seventy-three.

Wynkyn de Worde, the famous early sixteenth-century printer, resided in Fleet Street, and was buried by his own instructions in St. Bride's Church, before the high-altar of St. Katherine, which probably stood in one of the side-chapels.

Sir Richard Baker, the author of the "Chronicle of the Kings of England," which afforded so much pleasure and instruction to Sir Roger de Coverley, was buried in the south aisle of the old church of St. Bride on February 19th, 1645. He had been a man of affluence and high sheriff of Oxfordshire, but in his later years he fell into pecuniary embarrassments, and died a prisoner in the Fleet.

Richard Lovelace, the cavalier poet, after having spent his whole fortune, and twice suffered imprisonment, in his sovereign's cause, died in extreme poverty in Gunpowder Alley, Shoe Lane,

St. Bride, Fleet Street.

in 1658. He is generally supposed to have been buried at the west end of St. Bride's, but this does not seem absolutely certain.

St. Bride's is, in fact, rather rich in memories of the poets; it was here that Sir John Denham, the bard of "Cooper's Hill," the "strength" of whose verse is praised by Pope, was married to his first wife in 1634; and here were interred the widow and son of Sir William Davenant, the dramatist. This son of Sir William was Dr. Charles Davenant, who enjoyed some celebrity as a political writer, and died in 1714.

At St. Bride's, likewise, was buried Robert Lloyd, the friend of Churchill, and himself a poet of great promise. Like Sir Richard Baker, he was thrown into the Fleet for debt, and died there, on December 15th, 1764, having survived Churchill less than six weeks.

Samuel Richardson, the novelist, and friend of Dr. Johnson and Goldsmith, pursued his business as a printer in Salisbury Court, now Salisbury Square. He died in 1761, and was interred in the middle aisle of St. Bride's. The stone which marks his grave is partially concealed by one of the pews on the south side.

A brass plate on the north wall commemorates the wife and children of John Nichols, who was from 1778 till his death in 1826 editor of the "Gentleman's Magazine." His "Anecdotes" and "Illustrations" contain many curious facts relating to English men of letters during the eighteenth century, and he was also the author of six volumes dealing with the progresses, processions, and festivities of Queen Elizabeth and James I., but the work by which he is best known is "The History and Antiquities of the County of Leicester."

In the porch beneath the tower is a tablet to Alderman Waith-man, with this inscription:

"To the memory of Robert Waithman, Alderman of this Ward, and in five Parliaments one of the Representatives of this great Metropolis. The friend of Liberty in evil times, and of Parliamentary Reform in its adverse days; it was at length his happiness to see that great cause triumphant, of which he had been the intrepid advocate from youth to age."

Waithman, who was elected Sheriff in 1820 and Lord Mayor in 1823, died at the age of sixty-nine in 1833, having lived to become a member of the first reformed Parliament. He belonged to the Company of Framework Knitters, and resided at 103 and 104, Fleet Street, being one of the last eminent citizens to follow the ancient practice of living over his place of business. An obelisk, erected to his memory, stands in Ludgate Circus, opposite his house, and forms a fitting companion to the similar monument on the other side of the way, which was set up in 1775 in honour of John Wilkes, Lord Mayor in that year, who, like Waithman, was Alderman of the Ward of Farringdon Without.

In the vestibule are tablets to Dr. James Molins, physician to Charles II. and James II., who died in 1686, and Isaac Romilly, a London merchant and uncle to Sir Samuel Romilly, who died in 1759.

Milton, after his return from his travels, took up his abode in St. Bride's churchyard, as his nephew Edward Philips records:

"Soon after his return, and visits paid to his father and other friends, he took him a lodging in St. Bride's churchyard, at the house of one Russell, a tailor, where he first undertook the education and instruction of his sister's two sons, the younger whereof had been wholly committed to his charge and care. . . . He made no long stay in his lodgings in St. Bride's churchyard; necessity of having a place to dispose his books in, and other goods fit for the furnishing of a good handsome house, hastening him to take one; and accordingly a pretty garden-house he took in Aldersgate Street at the end of an entry, and therefore the fitter for his turn by the reason of the privacy; besides that there are few streets in London more free from noise than that."

The site of Russell the tailor's house in St. Bride's Churchyard is probably now covered by a portion of the "Punch" office.

Hard by the church was formerly the well of St. Bride, the waters of which were popularly supposed to possess peculiar virtue. Its position is stated to have been identical with that of the pump in the eastern wall of the churchyard overhanging Bride Lane, which lane was, in Strype's time, "of note for the many hatters there inhabiting." From this well is derived the name of Bridewell, which seems to have been a royal residence as early as the reign of Henry III., was a frequent residence of Henry VIII., and was given by Edward VI. to the citizens of London "to be a workhouse for the poor and idle persons of the city."

In Bridewell Place, which was built on the site of the old prison, is situated the present vicarage of St. Bride's, an elegant red-brick building designed by Mr. Basil Champneys.

CHRIST CHURCH, Newgate Street, which stands a little to the north of Newgate Street, and adjoins Christ's Hospital, occupies a portion of the site of the ancient church of the Grey Friars, or Franciscans. Four brethren o that order, then recently established, arrived in London in 1224, and first hired a dwelling in Cornhill from John Travers, who was one of the sheriffs in 1223 and 1224. Their number, however, increasing, and their popularity with the citizens being great, they soon removed to new quarters in the parish of St. Nicholas (wherein was the meat-market called St. Nicholas' Shambles), bestowed upon them by John Ewin, a mercer, who took a deep interest in their work, and himself became a lay brother of the order. A church and monastic buildings were here built for them by the munificence of various wealthy citizens.

Before many years had elapsed a second and more magnificent church was erected for the Franciscans, the choir of which was commenced in 1306 by Queen Margaret, second wife of Edward I. and daughter of Philippe le Hardi, King of France. She contributed largely towards the expenses, and was herself buried in the choir in 1317. The body of the church was built by John, Duke of Brittany and Earl of Richmond, and donations were given by

Christ Church, Newgate Street.

many other distinguished persons, including Queen Isabella, daughter of Philippe le Bel, King of France, and wife of Edward II., and Philippa, Queen of Edward III. This church of the Grey Friars was consecrated in 1325, and was, when completed, one of the finest ecclesiastical edifices in London. It measured 300 feet in length, 89 feet in breadth, and 64 feet 2 inches from the pavement to the roof. It was entirely paved with marble, and the columns were also of the same material. A library, 129 feet in length and 31 in breadth, was subsequently made for the friars by Richard Whittington, who also contributed £400 towards furnishing it with books.

The church of the Grey Friars seems to have been a very favourite place of sepulture. Here, in addition to Queen Margaret, was buried Edward II.'s queen, Isabella, who died in 1358. In the same grave with her was deposited the heart of her hapless husband; and soon afterwards Joan, Queen of Scots, Edward and Isabella's eldest daughter, was laid beside her mother. She was called "Joan of the Tower," from having been born in the Tower of London, and was married to David Bruce, Robert Bruce's son and successor. Here, too, had been buried Queen Isabella's paramour, Roger Mortimer, Earl of March, who was hanged in 1330, when Edward III. assumed the reins of government.

It was computed that altogether 663 "persons of quality" were interred in the Grey Friars' Church, but the monuments met with a sad fate at the dissolution of monasteries.

"All these and five times so many more," says Stow, after enumerating a long catalogue of deceased worthies, "have been buried there, whose monuments are wholly defaced; for there were nine tombs of alabaster and marble, environed with strikes of iron in the choir, and one tomb in the body of the church, also coped with iron, all pulled down, besides seven score gravestones of marble, all sold for fifty pounds, or thereabouts, by Sir Martin Bowes, goldsmith and alderman of London."

Elizabeth Barton, "the Holy Maid of Kent," who was executed at Tyburn in May, 1534, was buried in the church of the Grey Friars. In 1538 the convent surrendered to King Henry VIII. The church then remained shut up for some time; but in 1546 the citizens who had two years previously obtained St. Bartholomew's Hospital, procured from the king the Grey Friars' likewise. "The parishes of St. Nicholas and of St. Ewin, and so much of St. Sepulchre's parish as is within Newgate," says Stow, "were made one parish church in the Grey Friars' Church, and called Christ's Church, founded by Henry VIII." The conventual buildings were destined for charitable purposes. In 1552 Bishop Ridley preached a sermon on the subject; Sir Richard Dobbes, the Lord Mayor, took the matter up warmly, and in this year "began the repairing of the Grey Friars' house for the poor fatherless children; and in the month of November the children were taken into the same, to the number of almost four hundred." On the 26th June of the following year, on the same day on which he granted the charter of Bridewell, only ten days before his death, Edward VI. signed the charter of Christ's Hospital, which occupies the site of the old habitation of the Franciscan Friars.

The old church of the Grey Friars, which had thus become parochial, remained standing till 1666, when it perished in the Great Fire.

Dame Mary Ramsey, widow of Sir Thomas Ramsey, Lord Mayor 1577, was buried at Christ Church, Newgate Street, in 1596. She was a very charitable woman, and a benefactress, amongst other deserving institutions, to Christ's Hospital. A

Christ Church, Newgate Street.

tablet, on which her good deeds are recorded, is to be seen affixed to the east part of the north wall of the present church.

At Christ Church also was interred in 1633, Venetia, the dearly-loved wife of the eccentric, but learned and ingenious Sir Kenelm Digby, the son of Sir Everard Digby of Gunpowder Plot notoriety. Her monument was of black marble, with four inscriptions in copper-gilt, surmounted by her bust, also of copper-gilt. This memorial was destroyed in the Fire, but the bust is said to have been subsequently exposed in a shop in Newgate Street, and finally melted down. Sir Kenelm Digby died on June 11th, 1665, and was interred in the same vault with his wife.

The present church was built by Sir Christopher Wren in 1687, and in 1704 he added the steeple. "This new church," observes Strype, "stands but upon half the ground of the ancient monastical church." Nevertheless, it is an edifice of considerable size; it measures 114 feet in length, and is the widest church in the City, being 81 feet in breadth. The height from the pavement to the roof is 46 feet 7 inches.

Christ Church contains two side-aisles separated from the nave by slender Corinthian columns, the bases of which are encased in wainscot up to their junction with the side galleries. The roof is arched, and is traversed by ornamental bands, similar to those at St. Bride's, and springing like them from the summits of the columns. The spaces intervening between the bands are embellished with representations of flowers. The clerestory possesses twelve windows, six on each side, around which there is a good deal of decoration. The ceilings of the aisles are flat, and are also crossed by bands which stretch from the columns to the tops of pilasters affixed to the walls. The side-galleries are connected by a west gallery, which contains a fine organ in a handsome case. The central east window, which occupies a recess above the altar-piece, is filled with stained glass, representing our Lord blessing little children; it is flanked on each side by a smaller window displaying squares of stained glass of a mosaic pattern. The wall at the sides of these windows is ornamented in the same manner as the clerestory. Above the central window to the highest part of the eastern wall are attached the royal arms.

The font, which stands at the west end of the south aisle, is of white marble bedecked with sculptured angels, flowers, and fruit; its cover is surmounted by a gilt angel. The carvings on the panels of the pulpit, representing the Last Supper and the Four Evangelists, are well executed.

At the east part of the church are attached, both to the north and south walls, shelves to contain loaves for distribution to the poor. At the side of the shelves on the south wall is a tablet thus inscribed:

> "The Bread given here Weekly
> to the Poor of St. Leonard's
> is from a Bequest of
> Sir John Trott and other Benefactors."

A similar tablet on the north wall reads as follows:

> "The Bread here given to the Poor
> is from the Church Rate and the
> Benefactions
> of Mr. Henry Needler, Mr. Roger Harris, and Mr. Thomas Stretchley."

"This church," states an inscription on the front of the organ-gallery, "was repaired and beautified A.D. 1834. The chancel was repaired and beautified by the Governors of St. Bartholomew's Hospital, 1834."

The Governors of St. Bartholomew's Hospital are patrons of the

Christ Church, Newgate Street. 155

vicarage of Christ Church, Newgate Street. After the Great Fire the church of St. Leonard, Foster Lane, was not rebuilt, and the parish was united to that of Christ Church. The incumbent is therefore vicar of Christ Church, Newgate Street, and rector of St. Leonard, Foster Lane. The presentation is made alternately by the Governors of St. Bartholomew's Hospital for Christ Church, and by the Dean and Chapter of Westminster for St. Leonard's.

The steeple of Christ Church attains a height of 153 feet. The base is open on three sides, thus forming a porch at the west of the church. Above the square tower is an octagon, and four arches support a dome, the total height of which is 15 feet. Over this is the lantern, the square colonnade of which rests partly on the dome and partly on the arches. The transitions are softened by vases, which are not, however, placed, as one would rather expect to see them, on the angles, but on the centres of the pediments. Though it can hardly be reckoned one of Wren's finest productions, the steeple of Christ Church is undeniably possessed of considerable beauty.

The two most conspicuous monuments in the church are those of the Rev. Samuel Crowther on the north, and the Rev. Michael Gibbs on the south of the communion table. Each of these monuments is surmounted by a bust of the deceased. Mr. Crowther, who was born in 1769, was a grandson of Samuel Richardson, the novelist. He was a Fellow of New College, Oxford, and was vicar and rector of the united benefice of Christ Church, Newgate Street, and St. Leonard, Foster Lane, from 1800 till his death in 1829. Mr. Gibbs was for forty years vicar and rector. He died on January 19th, 1882, in his seventieth year. He was a Fellow of Gonville and Caius College, Cambridge, and lies buried in the churchyard of Chesterton, Cambridgeshire. The monument in Christ Church was erected to his memory in October, 1882, by the parishioners amongst whom he had so long laboured.

To the south of the chancel is a flat gravestone, on which a coat-of-arms is beautifully carved. The inscription is simple:

> "Here lie the remains of Peter Doré, Esq.
> Norroy King of Arms,
> F.A.S.
> Born 8 January, 1715,
> Died 27 September, 1781."

There are also monuments to the Rev. Joseph Trapp, a translator of Virgil, who died in 1747 after ministering here for twenty-six years; Sir John Bosworth, chamberlain of the City of London (died 1752), and Dame Hester, his wife (died 1749); and John Stock, a painter in the Royal Dockyards, who, at his death in 1781, bequeathed over £13,000 to charitable purposes. Stock's tablet is on the east wall, to the north of Crowther's monument. In accordance with his precise instructions it sets forth the various items of his bequest.

The celebrated Nonconformist divine, Richard Baxter, author of "The Saints' Everlasting Rest," and "A Call to the Unconverted," was buried in the church without any memorial in 1691. His wife had been buried here ten years previously "in the ruins," as he himself says, "in her own mother's grave." Near the pulpit was interred, in 1814, the Rev. James Boyer, headmaster of Christ's Hospital during the school-days of Lamb and Coleridge, with regard to whom Coleridge remarked, "It was lucky the cherubim who took him to heaven were nothing but faces and wings, or he would infallibly have flogged them by the way."

Christ Church, Newgate Street.

The galleries of Christ Church, Newgate Street, are reserved for the accommodation of the Bluecoat Boys. In this church is preached annually on Easter Tuesday the Spital Sermon, which is attended in state by the Lord Mayor, sheriffs, and aldermen. The Spital Sermons were originally preached at the pulpit cross in the "Spital," *i.e.* Spitalfields. This was destroyed during the Civil Wars, and when the sermons were re-established after the Restoration, they were preached at St. Bride's, Fleet Street, until in 1797 the scene was transferred to Christ Church. The Bluecoat Boys, for whom as early as 1594 a gallery was erected by the pulpit cross, have always been present at the Spital Sermon, and on the same day, in accordance with the old custom, pay a visit to the Lord Mayor at the Mansion House.

Many interesting links with the past will be severed when the famous school is removed from its historic quarters, and nowhere will the disruption of old associations be more apparent than at Christ Church, Newgate Street.

ST. CLEMENT, EASTCHEAP.

THE church of St. Clement, Eastcheap, stands on the east side of Clement's Lane. Prior to the dissolution of monasteries the advowson of the benefice was possessed by the abbot and convent of Westminster. Queen Mary, in the first year of her reign, granted it to the see of London, in whose gift the rectory has ever since remained. Stow says that in his time it was a small church, and contained no monuments, except those of Alderman Francis Barnham, sheriff in 1570, who died in 1575, and his son, Benedict Barnham, also an alderman, and sheriff in 1591, who died in 1598.

Alderman Benedict Barnham's daughter, Alice, was married to Sir Francis Bacon at St. Marylebone Church on May 10th, 1606. The idea that the possession of a title would be of assistance to him in his courtship of this lady was one of the reasons which rendered the philosopher anxious to obtain the honour of knighthood, as he explained to his cousin, Robert Cecil, when he implored that statesman to use his influence with King James I. to procure him this coveted distinction.

St. Clement's was destroyed in the Great Fire, when the body of the church of St. Martin Orgar, situated on the east side of Martin's Lane, was also mostly consumed. The rectory of St. Martin was then united with that of St. Clement, and St. Clement's church, which was rebuilt by Wren, serves for both parishes.

St. Martin Orgar derives its name from one Ordgar, who appears to have founded it in the twelfth century, and gave the advowson to the Dean and Chapter of St. Paul's, who have from that time always kept possession of it. Here were buried, as Stow records, Sir William Hewit, Lord Mayor 1559, and "his lady and daughter, wife to Sir Edward Osborne." This is the Osborne who was himself elected to the chief magistracy of the city in 1583, and of whom the story is told that, while he was her father's apprentice, he saved his future wife from drowning by leaping into the river to her assistance from London Bridge. The great-grandson of Sir Edward Osborne and Anna Hewit was Thomas Osborne, created successively Viscount Latimer, Earl of Danby, Marquis of Caermarthen, and Duke of Leeds, the celebrated minister of Charles II. and William III.

The steeple of St. Martin Orgar, which had been repaired in 1630, escaped destruction in the Great Fire, as did also part of the nave, and these remnants of the old church were renovated, and utilized as a place of worship for French Protestants, who continued to meet there till 1820, when the building was pulled down with the exception of the tower. This last relic of the ancient church was, however, removed in 1851, but a fresh tower, which, with its projecting clock, forms a conspicuous object as one descends Martin's Lane, has been erected to mark the site.

The present church of St. Clement, Eastcheap, was built by Wren in 1686. It measures 64 feet in length, 40 feet in breadth, and 34 feet in height. It possesses one aisle on the south side, which is separated from the rest of the church by two columns on high bases. Above the entablature of the columns is a clerestory containing small windows. The ceiling, which is flat, is divided into compartments, the central panel being elaborately orna-

St. Clement, Eastcheap.

mented, and all around it runs a circle adorned with an outer line of fretwork. The walls are wainscotted to the height of 8½ feet, and the handsome oak pulpit and sounding-board, on the north side of the church, are very richly carved, as is also the cover of the marble font, which is placed at the west. The altar-piece is finely executed, and there is some good carving about the doorcases.

The church, though small, is pleasing, but it was "re-arranged" in 1872, and has been rather too much modernized. The removal of the organ from its old position at the west to the south aisle, can hardly be considered an improvement.

The west window is a memorial to Thomas Fuller, the church historian, Bishop Bryan Walton, and Bishop Pearson, and contains figures in stained glass of these three divines, that of Fuller occupying the central position.

Fuller, on his return to London after the surrender of Exeter to the Parliament in 1646, held for a short time the position of lecturer at St. Clement's. Pearson was appointed lecturer at St. Clement's in 1650, and preached here a series of discourses on the Creed, which he afterwards incorporated in his renowned "Exposition," published in 1659, and dedicated to the parishioners of St. Clement's. In 1673, after the death of Wilkins, he succeeded that prelate in the see of Chester, which he occupied till his death in 1686. Walton, the learned compiler of the "Polyglot Bible," was for some time rector of St. Martin Orgar, but he was deprived of the living by the Parliament at the outbreak of the Civil War. At the Restoration he was reinstated, and towards the close of 1660 he was created Bishop of Chester, but died in the following year.

The large east window is flanked by two smaller windows, and that on the southern side, the subject of which is Christ blessing little children, was filled with stained glass in 1872 by the Clothworkers' Company in memory of Samuel Middlemore, clothworker, a parishioner of St. Martin Orgar, who died in 1628, leaving a charitable bequest to the parish, for which he appointed the Company trustees.

Three brass tablets have been affixed, two to the north and one to the south wall, in commemoration of the connection with the united parishes of Pearson, Walton, and Fuller, and likewise of Henry Purcell and Jonathan Battishill, the celebrated musical composers, each of whom was organist at St. Clement's.

The square tower, which rises at the south-west, is of brick with stone dressings, but has been faced with cement. It contains three storeys, above which is a cornice, and is surmounted by a graceful balustrade. The total height is 88 feet.

St. Dunstan's in the East

THE City of London possesses two churches dedicated to St. Dunstan, the great Saxon archbishop, who, in the words of Mr. Green, "stands first in the line of ecclesiastical statesmen who counted among them Lanfranc and Wolsey, and ended in Laud." These two churches are, from their respective positions at the extremities of the city, called St. Dunstan's in the East and St. Dunstan's in the West; the former is situated between Tower Street and Lower Thames Street, at the convergence of St. Dunstan's Hill and Idol Lane, while the latter is placed on the north side of Fleet Street.

The date of the original foundation of St. Dunstan's in the East is not recorded. It was enlarged in 1382, when a south aisle and porch were added at the expense of John, Lord Cobham, a distinguished nobleman and a friend of the poet Gower. He was the builder of Cowling Castle in Kent, and died in 1407. His granddaughter, Joan, married, for her fourth husband, Sir John Oldcastle, the leader of the Lollards.

Stow describes St. Dunstan's as "a fair and large church of an ancient building, and within a large churchyard." It was very extensively repaired, and indeed almost rebuilt, in 1633, at an expenditure of £2,400, but was practically destroyed by the Great Fire, as, although the outer walls remained for the most part standing, the tall lead-covered spire, which was its distinguishing ornament, and the whole of the interior, with its numerous monuments, were utterly consumed.

Amongst the memorials of the dead thus destroyed was that of Sir John Hawkins. This redoubtable seaman, one of the most illustrious of the gallant band of Elizabethan naval heroes, died on an expedition to the West Indies, and his body was committed to the deep; but a monument was erected to his memory by his widow on the north side of the chancel of St. Dunstan's, of which he had for many years been a parishioner.

At St. Dunstan's was buried Alderman James Bacon, fishmonger, sheriff in 1569, who died on June 5th, 1573. He was the third son of Robert Bacon, of Drinkston, in Suffolk, and youngest brother of Sir Nicholas Bacon, the Lord Keeper, and consequently uncle to Francis Bacon. Here also was laid the corpse of Admiral Sir John Lawson, who was mortally wounded in the sea-fight with the Dutch off Lowestoft on June 3rd, 1665.

The patronage of the rectory of St. Dunstan in the East belonged originally to the Prior and Chapter of Canterbury, but was granted by them in 1365 to Archbishop Simon Islip, a relative of whom was rector from 1374 to 1382, and has since that time been always retained by the Archbishops of Canterbury. This parish was one of the thirteen "Peculiars" of the archiepiscopal see of Canterbury in the city of London, *i.e.*, parishes under the direct jurisdiction of the primate. But this ancient usage was abrogated in 1845, in pursuance of the recommendations of the Ecclesiastical Commissioners, by an order in council by which the "Peculiars" were placed under the authority of the Bishop of London.

St. Dunstan in the East. 165

The most famous amongst the rectors of St. Dunstan's in the East was John Morton, who held the living from 1472 till 1474. He became Master of the Rolls and Bishop of Ely under Edward IV., and was one of the executors of that sovereign's will; subsequently, under Henry VII., who owed his crown in a great measure to the wise councils of this sagacious statesman, he was advanced to the archbishopric of Canterbury and the Lord Chancellorship, both which offices he retained till his death. He died on September 15th, 1500, at the advanced age of ninety, and was buried in Canterbury Cathedral.

In the work of re-erecting their church the parishioners were very materially assisted by the munificence of Dame Dyonis Williamson, of Hale's Hall, Norfolk, whose grandfather, Richard Hale, had been buried in the old church. She gave £4,000 towards the expenses of the rebuilding of St. Dunstan's in the East, and besides this act of liberality to a church with which she was particularly connected, she bestowed £2,620 — the largest individual subscription — for the rebuilding of St. Paul's Cathedral, and £2,000 for the rebuilding of the church of St. Mary-le-Bow.

Wren was called in during 1671, and the reconstruction of the church was carried on in accordance with his designs; but the steeple, which is built of stone, and is placed at the west of the church, was not completed till 1699. The steeple of St. Dunstan's is one of Wren's most striking works. The tower, which measures 21 feet square at the base, contains four storeys, of which the lowest displays a doorway, the second and fourth windows, and the third the clock. It is surmounted by four tall pinnacles, one at each angle. From behind these pinnacles spring four arched ribs, which support the lantern and spire, the latter terminating in a ball and vane. The total altitude to the summit of the vane is 180 feet 4 inches.

The appearance presented by this steeple is extremely elegant, and the employment of the four arched ribs to bear the spire renders it quite unique amongst all Sir Christopher's achievements. The steeples of St. Nicholas, Newcastle-upon-Tyne, St. Giles's, Edinburgh, and King's College, Old Aberdeen, are similarly constructed, and from them Wren seems to have derived the plan of the steeple of St. Dunstan's, which, though on a smaller scale, bears a closer resemblance to that of St. Nicholas than to the Scottish examples of this method. There is a tradition that the idea of building a steeple of this kind was first suggested to the great architect by his only daughter, Jane, who did not long survive its completion, dying unmarried at the early age of twenty-six, on December 29th, 1702. The steeple of St. Dunstan's combines the charms of melody with those of outward loveliness, for it possesses eight bells; it can be contemplated to the best advantage from the lower ground at the bottom of St. Dunstan's Hill in Lower Thames Street, whence is obtained an uninterrupted view of this singularly picturesque and beautiful object.

Although this steeple has an almost fragile appearance, it is in reality strongly and very scientifically constructed. When Sir Christopher was told that the terrible hurricane of November, 1703, had damaged all the steeples in London, he replied with calm confidence, "Not St. Dunstan's, I am sure;" and examination proved that his opinion was quite correct.

In reconstructing the church Wren made use of the remaining materials of the old building as far as he could. He did not, however, follow in the interior the Gothic style which he had adopted for the steeple, but divided it into nave and aisles by means of Doric columns. By the year 1810 the fabric had become greatly decayed, and the walls were found to have been forced as much as seven inches out of the perpendicular by the pressure of the roof of the nave. As it was considered hopeless to attempt the reparation of so dilapidated an edifice, the church was pulled down, with the exception of the steeple, and a new church added, the first stone of which was laid by Archbishop Manners Sutton on November 26th, 1817. It was first opened for service on January 14th, 1821. The architect was Mr. David Laing, who a few years before had built the Custom House, and he was assisted by Mr. (afterwards Sir William) Tite, who more than twenty years later rebuilt the Royal Exchange after its destruction by fire.

The present church of St. Dunstan in the East is composed of Portland stone, and is stated to have cost about £36,000. The style is perpendicular Gothic, the object kept in view having been to erect a church in harmony with the steeple. St. Dunstan's measures 115 feet in length, 65 feet 6 inches in breadth, and 40 feet in height, and contains two side-aisles, divided from the central portion by slender clustered columns and pointed arches, above which is the clerestory. From the capitals of the columns rise single shafts to meet the roof of the nave, which is decorated with graceful fan groining, while the ceilings of the aisles are intersected by ribs forming square compartments.

During the excavations which were started as a preliminary step towards the erection of the new building, several relics of the old church which was destroyed in the Great Fire were unearthed, amongst them being the fragments of an east window. These served as a model for the construction of the central east window of the present church, which was closely copied from them, with a view to the reproduction, both in size and characteristics, of the mediæval window. It is divided into two compartments, in the glass of which are typically portrayed the Jewish and Christian dispensations. The Old Covenant, which is the subject of the lower division, is represented by figures of Moses and Aaron, together with the ark and other symbols of the Hebrew worship, while in the upper portion are displayed the figures of our Lord and the Four Evangelists. This happily conceived and executed picture in glass was the work of Mr. John Buckler. At the top of the window appear the royal arms and those of the city of London, and also the arms of Archbishop Manners Sutton, Archbishop Howley, Archbishop Sumner, and Bishop Blomfield.

On each side of the central east window is a smaller window. That on the north contains a copy of Overbeck's painting of Christ blessing little children, and the southern window is filled with a copy of the Adoration of the Wise Men by Paul Veronese. Both were executed by Messrs. Baillie.

To Messrs. Baillie also are due the coats-of-arms of benefactors to the church and parish, which are depicted in the tracery lights of the windows in the north and south walls, each coat-of-arms being accompanied by name and date, and also by a scroll inscribed with an appropriate text of scripture. There are altogether nine windows, five in the south wall and four in the north—the place of a window at the eastern part of the north wall being usurped by the north-east porch, which has a well-groined ceiling—and each of these windows bears two coats-of-arms. The benefactors thus suitably commemorated are: Sir Bartholomew James, 1481; William Sevenoaks, 1426; Matthew Ernest, *alias* Metyngham, 1505; Sir William Heriott, 1506; Henry Herdson, 1555;

St. Dunstan in the East. 169

Sir Richard Champion, 1568; William Haynes, 1590; Mirabelle Bennett, 1632; John Fowke, 1686; Gilbert Keate, 1657; Bernard Hyde, 1674; Viscountess Conway, 1637; Sir Thomas Hunt, 1615; William Bateman, 1648; Dame Dyonis Williamson, 1669; George Hanger, 1607; Sir John Moore, 1702; and Sir William Russell, 1705.

The most eastern window in the south wall, which bears the coats-of-arms of Sir Bartholomew James and William Sevenoaks, has been filled with stained glass in memory of the Rev. Thomas Boyles Murray, who died on September 24th, 1860, after having been rector of St. Dunstan's in the East for twenty-three years. He took a deep interest in the history and antiquities of the church, the "Chronicles" of which—a very lucid and pleasantly written book—he published the year before his death. The remainder of the side windows are plain, with the exception of the coats-of-arms in the tracery lights.

Wren's church was embellished by several fine specimens of wood-carving by Grinling Gibbons, but these disappeared when the edifice was taken down, with one solitary exception—the arms of Archbishop Tenison, Primate from 1695 to 1715, which are now placed over the mantelpiece in the vestry-room. This chamber, which is situated to the north-west of the church, is lighted by a window on the north, on which are emblazoned the arms of Archbishop Sumner. On an oak bracket to the south of the fireplace stands a beautifully executed model of the church as finished by Wren, carved in oak and chestnut. It is 2 feet 7 inches in length, by 1 foot 3 inches in breadth; the height to the top of the spire is 4 feet, and the interior height to the centre of the ceiling is 1 foot 2 inches. The pulpit, reading-desk, and organ are movable, and with such exactitude has this minute work of art been completed that every door is fitted with metal hinges. In a glazed box beneath are kept fifty-seven pieces, mostly in pear-wood, on a larger scale than the complete model, which were apparently designed for another and a bigger model, which was, however, never accomplished. The name of the artist of this *chef-d'œuvre* is unknown. It was purchased at an auction sale some forty years back by a Mr. Leach, a parishioner, who presented it to the church.

On the opposite wall hangs a lithograph of the City of London as it appeared in 1647, after Cornelius Danckers, in which the lofty steeple of the old church of St. Dunstan is a very prominent object. This interesting souvenir was presented in 1832 by Mr. Matthias Prime Lucas, Alderman of the Ward of Tower, in which the parish is situated.

When Wren's church was demolished, St. Dunstan's lost, in addition to Gibbons's carvings, its old organ and marble font. The organ, which was built by Father Smith, and was a very fine instrument, was removed to the abbey church of St. Alban's. It was replaced by a new organ, which stands in the west gallery. The font, however, was by a singular piece of good fortune recovered in 1845—in which year the sacred building was repaired—through the kindness of a Warwickshire clergyman, into whose hands it had fallen, and it now occupies a position at the extreme north-west of the church.

St. Dunstan's in the East contains a considerable number of monuments, and although no person of extraordinary eminence is thus commemorated, they yet form on the whole a very interesting collection.

On the north wall of the chancel is a monument to Sir John Moore, with the following inscription :

St. Dunstan in the East.

"In a vault near this place is deposited the body of
Sir John Moore, Knight, sometime Lord Mayor of London,
One of the Representatives of this City in Parliament,
and President of Christ's Hospital,
Who, for his great and exemplary loyalty to the Crown, was
impowered by King Charles the Second
to bear on a canton one of the Lions of England,
as an augmentation to his Arms.
Who, out of a Christian Zeal for good works,
Founded and Endowed a Free School at Appleby, in Leicestershire,
his native county,
And was a good Benefactor to the Worshipful
Company of Grocers,
to the several Hospitals of this City,
to his own relatives in general, and to this parish.
He departed this life the 2d of June, 1702, aged 82."

Above Sir John's monument is a tablet to his wife, Dame Mary Moore, who died at the age of fifty-eight, on May 16th, 1690, in the thirty-eighth year of their marriage. Both these memorials were cleaned and repaired in 1845 by the Grocers' Company.

The Lion of England with which Sir John Moore was privileged by Charles II. to augment his arms, appears on his monument. He was indeed of great service to that monarch, for he not only accommodated him with large sums of money, but also during his mayoralty, to which he was elected in 1681, directed his whole power and influence to further the policy of the Court.

On this account he has been immortalized by Dryden under the name of Ziloah in the concluding lines of the second part of "Absalom and Achitophel":

"This year did Ziloah rule Jerusalem,
And boldly all sedition's syrtes stem,
Howe'er encumber'd with a viler pair
Than Ziph or Shimei, to assist the chair;

Yet Ziloah's royal labours so prevailed,
That faction at the next election failed ;
When even the common cry did justice sound,
And merit by the multitude was crowned ;
With David then was Israel's peace restored,
Crowds mourned their error, and obeyed their lord."

Sir John Moore was the senior member for the City of London in the only parliament of James II. In addition to his political and municipal celebrity, he is also illustrious as a liberal benefactor to Christ's Hospital, the writing school of which, erected from the designs of Wren in 1694, and capable of holding 500 boys, was built at his sole charge, the cost amounting to £5,000. His statue in marble stands in front of this building, which owes its origin to his generosity, and his portrait is preserved in the Hospital.

The largest monument in St. Dunstan's is one on the south side of the chancel, to Sir William Russell, who died in 1705. It includes a full-length figure of Sir William "in his habit as he lived," wearing a large wig. He is represented as reclining on his left side, and Strype commends the "effigies" as "well resembling him."

His father, Robert Russell, Deputy of the Ward of Tower, who died in 1662, is commemorated by a large tablet on the north wall, erected in place of "ye other demolished in ye late general conflagration."

Another handsome tablet on the north wall was set up by the parishioners in memory of Richard Hale, whose monument had been destroyed in the Fire, as a mark of their gratitude to his granddaughter, Lady Williamson, for her bountiful assistance to them in the rebuilding of the church. The inscription is as follows:

St. Dunstan in the East.

> "Pietati et Charitati Sacrum.
> Hic juxta depositae sunt reliquiae
> Richardi Hale, Armigeri, in Spem
> Beatae Resurrectionis, qui decessit
> An. D. 1620:
> Cujus e filio primogenito, Gulielmo,
> Neptis, Domina Dyonysia Williamson,
> de Hales-Hall in Comit. Norfolc—pro
> Summa pietate et munificentia,
> Ecclesiam hanc incendio deletam,
> impensis MMMM libris, maxima
> ex parte restauravit.
> Exiguum hoc honoris et gratitudinis
> Μνημοσυνον avo posuere P.S.D. Or.
> Tota haec, quam extruxit, sacra moles
> Ipsi erit pro sempiterno monumento.
>
> Tuum erit, Lector, tam illustri exemplo
> Discere, fidem sine operibus mortuam esse.
> Domine, dilexi decorem domus tuae,
> Locum habitationis gloriae tuae."

A third monument replacing one consumed by the flames may be observed in the chancel. It bears a Latin inscription stating it to have been erected in 1674 by Sir Bernard Hyde, of Bore Place, Kent, in memory of his grandparents, Bernard and Anna Hyde (died 1630, 1640), and his parents, Bernard and Hester Hyde (died 1655, 1649).

About the middle of the south wall is a tablet to Alderman Sir Peter Parravicin, or Paravicini, a friend of Pepys, who died on January 29th, 1696, aged fifty-nine, and his daughter, Mary, who died unmarried at the age of fifty-six on May 3rd, 1727.

Dr. John Jortin, author of "Remarks on Ecclesiastical History" and the "Life of Erasmus," was rector of St. Dunstan's from 1751 till his death in 1770. He was buried at Kensington, of which he was also vicar, but there are tablets at St. Dunstan's to some of his family.

In the vestibule at the west is a tablet to Samuel Turner, Alderman of Tower Ward, and Lord Mayor 1768, who died in 1777, and his widow, Elizabeth, who died in 1787. Thomas Turner, their eldest son, who died at Strasburg, while on his travels, in 1771, has also a tablet. Of him it is recorded:

> "He knew no joy but friendship might divide,
> Nor gave his parents grief but when he died."

On the south wall is a tablet to Sir George Buggin, who died in 1825, Jane, his first wife, and Barrington and Ann Buggin, his parents. His second wife, Lady Cecilia Letitia Underwood, daughter of the second Earl of Arran, was afterwards, in 1831, married to the Duke of Sussex, and in 1840 was created Duchess of Inverness.

The most recent memorial which attracts attention is a large monument affixed to the centre of the north wall in memory of one of the heroes of the Indian Mutiny. It bears the following inscription:

> "Sacred
> to the Memory of
> Colonel John Finnis,
> Of the XIth regiment of Bengal Native Infantry,
> Who was killed at Meerut, in the East Indies,
> On the 10th day of May, 1857,
> in the 54th year of his age.
> He was the first victim of the revolt
> in that memorable year,
> in which so many lives were sacrificed.
> He fell
> while endeavouring, with undaunted courage
> to recall a body of mutinous Sepoys
> to order and obedience.

St Dunstan in the East.

> This tablet is erected
> by the Inhabitants of this Parish,
> As a testimony to the worth of
> a brave Soldier and a sincere Christian,
> As a token of sympathy with his bereaved family,
> And as a mark of respect and regard
> for his only surviving brother,
> The Right Honourable
> Thomas Quested Finnis,
> Lord Mayor of the City of London
> in the year 1857,
> And Alderman of the Ward of Tower."

The parochial registers of St. Dunstan's are complete from the year 1558. Frederick Thesiger, who became Lord Chelmsford, and was twice Lord Chancellor, was born at No. 1, Fowke's Buildings, Tower Street, on July 15th, 1794, and baptized here on the 4th September of the same year.

The churchyard, which is very pleasantly shaded with trees, extends to the south of the church; it is raised considerably above the level of St. Dunstan's Hill, from which it is separated by a wall.

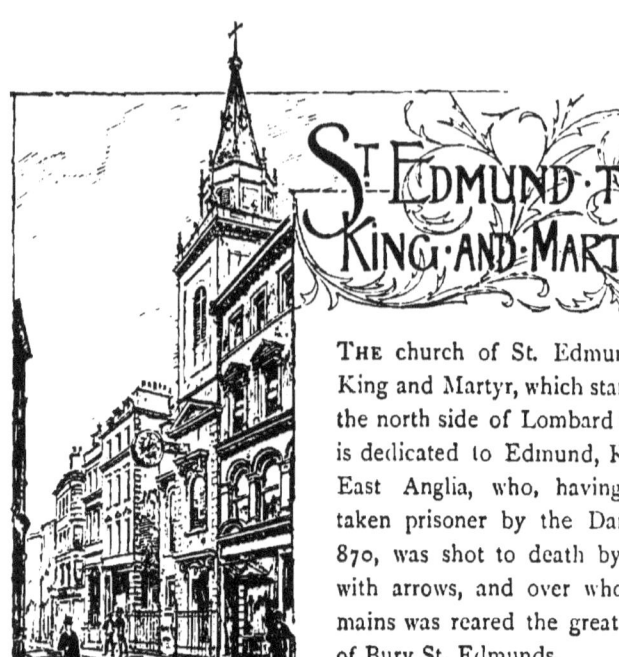

St. Edmund the King and Martyr

THE church of St. Edmund the King and Martyr, which stands on the north side of Lombard Street, is dedicated to Edmund, King of East Anglia, who, having been taken prisoner by the Danes in 870, was shot to death by them with arrows, and over whose remains was reared the great abbey of Bury St. Edmunds.

Like All Hallows, Lombard Street, it was anciently "also called St. Edmund Grasse Church," says Stow, "because the said grass market came down so low." In the old church, which was destroyed in the Great Fire, was a monument to John Shute, a painter-stainer, who, having studied architecture in Italy, published on his return to England "The First and Chiefe Groundes of Architecture," one of the earliest English works dealing with that science. He died in 1563.

The advowson of the rectory of St. Edmund was, prior to the dissolution of monasteries, in the possession of the Prior and Convent of the Holy Trinity, Aldgate, and shortly after that event was bestowed by the Crown on the archiepiscopal see of Canterbury, in whose gift the living has ever since remained.

After the Great Fire the church of St. Nicholas Acon, which stood on the west side of Nicholas Lane, where a portion of its old burying-ground still remains, was not re-erected, and its parish was united with that of St. Edmund. The derivation of the title "Acon" is not with any certainty known; Stow tells us that it was sometimes written "Hacon," "for so have I read it in records," and very possibly Hacon may have been the name of the founder.

The advowson of the rectory of St. Nicholas Acon was given in 1084 by one Godwinus and Turund, his wife, "for the redemption of their souls, and the remission of their sins, and of all Christians," to the Conventual Church of Malmesbury; on the suppression of which it came to the Crown, and has ever since been by it retained. Accordingly, the patronage of the united benefice is alternately exercised by the Crown and the Archbishop of Canterbury.

The parish church of St. Edmund the King and Martyr was completed by Wren in 1690. It measures 59 feet in length, by 40 feet in breadth, and the height from the pavement to the ceiling is 37 feet 9 inches. This church is singular as standing north and south, the altar being placed at the north in a recess measuring 16 feet 8 inches in width, and 12 feet in depth. This unusual arrangement was forced upon Wren by the position of the ground at his disposal. There are no aisles, and the ceiling, which is pierced by a small skylight, is flat at the centre, but coved at the sides. The walls and the bases of the pilasters attached to them are panelled with oak to the height of eight feet. The doorcases at the north-east and north-west, and the pulpit, which stands on the west side, are also of dark oak, and are handsomely carved. The church is lighted on the north by a large stained glass window over the altar, and by two small windows in the sides of the recess, and there are also two tall windows in the north wall, one on each side of the chancel. At the centre of the west wall is a small window, and in the east wall is a larger window, while the south wall is pierced with three windows, which are filled with richly stained glass. The eastern and western windows of the north wall display respectively figures in stained glass of St. Peter and St. Paul, and in the lower division of the central window appear those of St. Edmund and St. Nicholas. In a recess at the south-west, enclosed by rails, is placed a handsome marble font, which is surmounted by a beautifully carved oaken cover.

The church was restored in 1864, and again in 1880. The gallery at the south has been retained, but the organ has been transferred to the north-west. There are high-backed seats at the south for the churchwardens, but the pews have given way to open benches. The most northerly bench on the eastern side is distinguished by an elegant sword-rest.

On the east wall is a marble monument by the elder Bacon, displaying a figure of Hope resting on an urn, in memory of Dr. Jeremiah Milles, Dean of Exeter, rector of the united parishes, and President of the Society of Antiquaries, who died at the age of seventy on February 13th, 1784, and of Edith, his wife, a daughter of Archbishop Potter, who died on June 11th, 1761, aged thirty-five; both of whom were buried here.

Dr. Milles, who was rector of St. Edmund and St. Nicholas Acon for nearly forty years, was a warm advocate of the genuineness of Chatterton's Rowley Poems, of which he published a magnificent quarto edition in 1782, together with a "Preliminary

Dissertation and Commentary," in which he laboured with more zeal than knowledge to establish their authenticity.

Addison was married at St. Edmund's to the Dowager Countess of Warwick and Holland on August 9th, 1716.

The steeple, which rises at the south and faces Lombard Street, consists of a tower, an octagonal lantern, an octagonal spire, and a pedestal supporting a finial and vane. The tower contains three storeys; the lowermost possesses a square-headed doorway, surmounted by a cornice, and opening into a porch which gives access to the church; the second displays a circular-headed window surmounted by a cornice and pediment; and the third a circular-headed window with louvres. The projecting clock, which is so prominent a feature in Lombard Street, is attached to the face of the second storey, just above the cornice of the window. The tower is concluded by a cornice, and a parapet adorned with vases and pineapples. The lantern is ornamented at the angles by flaming urns, in allusion to the Great Fire. The total altitude attained is 136 feet.

On the south wall of the church, to the west of the tower, is an inscription which states that :

> "The Ground
> on each side of the Doorway
> of this Church
> Containing 206 Feet superficial
> is the
> Freehold Property
> of the Parish of St. Edmund
> the King and Martyr."

ST. GEORGE, BOTOLPH LANE.

THE church of St. George, Botolph Lane, the only church in the City of London proper dedicated to the patron saint of England, is situated on the west side of Botolph Lane and the south side of George Lane.

St. George's was consumed in the Great Fire, and was rebuilt of stone by Wren, who completed it in 1674. The church of St. Botolph, Billingsgate, which stood on the south side of Thames Street, opposite the bottom of Botolph Lane, not being re-erected subsequently to the Fire, its parish was united with that of St. George.

The advowson of the rectory of St. George, Botolph Lane, was until the dissolution of monasteries in the possession of the Abbot and Convent of St. Saviour's, Bermondsey, and has since then been retained by the Crown. The rectory of St. Botolph, Billingsgate, has been from old times in the gift of the Dean and Chapter of St. Paul's.

Dr. William Sherlock, whose renunciation of his Jacobite principles and acceptance of the deanery of St. Paul's in 1691, on Tillotson's promotion to the primacy, raised that tremendous ferment among the Nonjurors which is so graphically described by Macaulay, was for over twenty years rector of the united benefice of St. George and St. Botolph. He died in 1707. His son Thomas was successively Bishop of Bangor, Salisbury, and London.

The present church of St. George measures internally 54 feet in length, 36 feet in breadth, and 36 feet in height. It contains two side-aisles, each of which is separated from the nave by two Composite columns standing very far apart. The ceiling of the nave, which is arched and divided into panels, is pierced with four circular openings to admit the light from above, and there are also large windows in each wall. The ceilings of the aisles are flat. The altar-piece is of oak and displays two Corinthian columns with entablature and pediment. The pulpit is well carved; there are two handsome door-cases, and the walls are panelled to the height of about nine feet.

Over the Corporation pew at the south-east is a sword-rest bearing the royal arms, the arms of the City of London, and the arms of Alderman Beckford, and this inscription on a small plate:

"Sacred to the memory of that real Patriot, the Right Hon. William Beckford; twice Lord Mayor of London; whose incessant spirited efforts to serve his Country hastened his dissolution on the 21st of June, 1770, in the time of his Mayoralty, and the 62nd year of his age."

The east front, facing Botolph Lane, with its large central window, flanked by two smaller windows, and its surmounting pediment, presents a picturesque and dignified appearance. The tower, which is placed at the north-west, contains three storeys, of which the lowermost displays a doorway; the second, a circular-headed window with square cornice, and the third, square openings with louvres. It is concluded by a cornice and a parapet, the angles of which are adorned with vases. The total height is about 84 feet.

St. George's, which is in a dilapidated state, is now closed, and in all probability will eventually be demolished.

ST·JAMES·GARLICK·HITHE·

THE church of St. James, Garlickhithe, which stands on the east side of Garlick Hill, between Maiden Lane and Upper Thames Street, was so called, says Stow, "for that of old time, on the bank of the river of Thames, near to this church, garlick was usually sold." He describes it concisely as "a proper church," and adds that it was said to have been rebuilt by Richard Rothing, sheriff in 1326, who was buried here.

At St. James's was also interred Richard Lyons, "a famous merchant of wines and a lapidary." Lyons, who had been sheriff in 1374, the year of Walworth's first mayoralty, was condemned by the Good Parliament in 1376 for conspiring with Lord Latimer, the royal chamberlain, to defraud the Treasury. But the death of the Black Prince, who had been strenuously labouring to put down corruption, saved him from punishment, and he was pardoned and restored to his possessions by the parliament of the following year, which had been packed by John of Gaunt. He remained, however, obnoxious to the people, and during the revolt of 1381 Wat Tyler, who had formerly been his servant in France, caused him to be beheaded.

The Stanleys had a mansion on Paul's Wharf Hill, built by Thomas, Lord Stanley, who married the Lady Margaret, Henry VII.'s mother, and was created Earl of Derby by that sovereign.

In Edward VI.'s reign Edward, the third earl, gave it to the Crown in exchange for some property in Lancashire, and Queen Mary, in 1555, bestowed it on the Heralds for their college.

There were monuments in St. James's to Lady Stanley, Lord Stanley's first wife; to their eldest son, George, in right of his wife Baron Strange, who was a hostage for his father's fidelity to Richard III., and narrowly escaped being beheaded in consequence; and to other members of the family.

The church was extensively repaired, and a new north aisle erected, in 1624, the cost, which exceeded £700, being defrayed by the parishioners. It perished in the Great Fire, and was rebuilt of stone by Wren. The foundation stone of the new edifice, as is recorded on a tablet in the porch, was laid in the year 1676; in 1682 the church was first opened for divine worship, and in 1683 it was entirely completed. The total cost was £5,357 12s. 10d.

The present church of St. James, Garlickhithe, measures 75 feet in length by 45 feet in breadth, while the height from the pavement to the ceiling is 40 feet. It contains two side-aisles, which are separated from the nave by Ionic columns elevated on lofty bases encased in wood. There are six columns on either side, supporting a clerestory, which is interrupted at the centre, half of it being borne by the three eastern, and half by the three western columns, and thus a cruciform appearance is produced. The ceiling of the nave, which is divided into ornamental panels, is flat in the central portion, but coved at the sides. The chancel contains a recess at the east, which has a highly decorated arched ceiling.

The church is lighted by four windows at the east, two being on the north and two on the south of the recess which forms the chancel, and there are also two small windows, one on each side of the altar-piece, in the walls of the recess. The north wall contains three large windows, and a circular window at the centre, but the south wall has a circular window only. All these, together with the windows of the clerestory, are filled with stained glass. In the west wall are four windows, two on the north and two on the south, which are, however, plain.

The altar-piece is of oak, and displays Corinthian columns and entablature. It contains three panels, the subject of the central one being our Lord breaking bread with Cleopas and the other disciple at Emmaus. Above the panels is inscribed, " Holy, Holy, Holy, Lord God Almighty." The altar-piece was originally surmounted by the royal arms, but these have now been removed to the south wall, where with their bright gilding they show out prominently. On the wall above the altar-piece is a large picture of the Ascension, the work of A. Geddes, A.R.A. It was presented to the church in 1815 by Dr. Thomas Burnet, who was at that time curate, and subsequently became rector of the parish.

The walls are panelled with oak to the height of nine feet; the door-cases at the north-east and south-east are handsome, and the pulpit and large sounding-board, which are placed against a pillar on the north side, are well carved. The high-backed seats of the churchwardens at the west likewise display some good carving, and the Corporation pews, the easternmost of the north and south side, are both of them ornamented with elegant sword-rests and with figures of the Lion and Unicorn. The font, which possesses a graceful cover, stands at the north-west. The west gallery is occupied by the organ, a fine instrument in an extremely handsome case, built by Father Smith in 1697.

Though this church has been several times repaired during the present century, it has not, as is too often the case, been totally transformed and modernized. Its beauty is greatly enhanced by the rich and substantial appearance of the woodwork.

The tower rises at the west, and beneath it access is gained to the interior by means of a porch and vestibule. It measures 20 feet square at the base, and contains three storeys, of which the lowest displays a doorway, the middle one a circular window, and the highest, round-headed openings with louvres. It is concluded by a cornice and parapet, with piers at the angles carrying vases. Above the tower, supported by a shallow dome resting on four arches, which is not, however, visible from the outside, is a square lantern, pierced with openings on each of its four faces, and consisting of three stages, through which it gradually tapers to the ball and finial with vane, which complete the entire steeple. The lowest stage of the lantern is beautifully adorned by eight columns, arranged in pairs at each angle, and terminated by urns, which soften the transition. The total altitude of the steeple is about 125 feet. At the junction of the first and second storeys of the tower projects a bracket supporting a clock, above which, facing northwards, is placed a quaint gilded figure of St. James.

The advowson of the rectory of St. James, Garlickhithe, belonged, prior to the dissolution of monasteries, to the abbot and convent of Westminster. Queen Mary gave it to the Bishop of London, and it has since then been retained by that see.

Steele, on attending divine worship here, was deeply impressed by the rector, as he recorded in No. 147 of the "Spectator," August 18th, 1711:

"You must know, sir, I have been a constant frequenter of the service of the Church of England for above these four years last past, and till Sunday was seven-night never discovered, to so great a degree, the excellency of the Common Prayer. When, being at St. James's Garlick-Hill Church, I heard the service read so distinctly, so emphatically, and so fervently, that it was next to an impossibility to be unattentive. My eyes and my thoughts could not wander as usual, but were confined to my prayers. I then considered I addressed myself to the Almighty, and not to a beautiful face. And when I reflected on my former performances of that duty, I found I had run it over as a matter of form, in comparison to the manner in which I then discharged it. My mind was really affected, and fervent wishes accompanied my words. The Confession was read with such a resigned humility, the Absolution with such a comfortable authority, the Thanksgivings with such a religious joy, as made me feel those affections of the mind in a manner I never did before. To remedy therefore the grievance above complained of, I humbly propose that this excellent reader, upon the next and every annual assembly of the clergy of Sion College, and all other conventions, should read prayers before them."

The name of the "excellent reader" was Philip Stubbs. He subsequently became Archdeacon of St. Alban's. The "grievance above complained of" was the bad reading of many of the clergy.

In 1876 the church of St. Michael, Queenhithe, which stood on the north side of Upper Thames Street, opposite to Queenhithe, was demolished, and its parish united with that of St. James, Garlickhithe. St. Michael, Queenhithe, is described by Stow as "a convenient church;" "but all the monuments therein," he continues, "are defaced." It was considerably repaired by the parishioners in 1615, and having been destroyed by the Great Fire, was rebuilt by Wren in 1677.

Wren's church was a plain building without aisles, measuring 71 feet in length by 40 feet in breadth. It was well lighted on either side by a row of windows with circular openings above them. The original altar-piece was painted on canvas, and included representations of Moses and Aaron, for retouching and embellishing which Sir James Thornhill received the thanks of the parish in 1721. They were, however, destroyed by negligence in 1823, when a new altar-piece was set up. Over the doorway at the east were some fine carvings of fruit and flowers, attributed to Gibbons. The tower, which stood at the north-west and attained a height of 135 feet, was remarkable for its gilded vane, made in the form of a ship in full sail, with a hull capable of holding, as was generally said, a bushel of grain, in allusion to the trade in corn, of which Queenhithe was a great centre. This vane may now be seen on the rectory house of the united parishes, which occupies a part of the site of the demolished church.

The patronage of the rectory of St. Michael, Queenhithe, has been from time immemorial in the hands of the Dean and Chapter of St. Paul's.

In the eastern part of Knightrider Street, on the south side of the way, stood the church of the Holy Trinity, also called, in distinction to the great priory at Aldgate, Trinity the Less. The rectory was in the gift of the prior and convent of St. Mary Overy, Southwark, until the dissolution of monasteries, and afterwards the patronage was transferred by the Crown to the Dean and Chapter of Canterbury.

Trinity the Less was rebuilt in 1607-8, but sixty years had not elapsed before the new edifice was consumed in the Great Fire. It was not again re-erected, its parish being united with that of St. Michael, Queenhithe, but its name is still preserved in Great and Little Trinity Lane.

St. Lawrence Jewry

The church of St. Lawrence Jewry is situated on the north side of Gresham Street, to the west of King Street, and to the south-west of the Guildhall. It derives its distinctive title from its having been built in the district of London occupied by the Jews prior to their expulsion from England by Edward I.—an association which is also preserved in the name of "Old Jewry," which formed one of the boundaries of the Hebrew settlement. The living was originally a rectory, but the patronage having been bestowed on Balliol College, Oxford, in 1294, by Hugo de Wickenbroke, Richard de Gravesend, Bishop of London, ordained a vicarage here, on the resignation of the rector, Hugo de Warkenethby, and appropriated the church to the Master and Fellows of Balliol, in whose possession it has since then always remained.

The old church was the burying-place of a considerable number of eminent citizens. Among them were two persons named Richard Rich, father and son, of whom the elder is described as an "esquire of London," and the younger was a member of the Mercers' Company, and sheriff in 1441. This Richard Rich the younger, who died in 1469, was great-grandfather to Richard Rich, who was raised to the peerage as Baron Rich of Leeze, and appointed Lord Chancellor in 1547, and from whom were descended the Earls of Warwick and Holland.

Here also was buried in 1463 Sir Geffrey Bullen, who had been sheriff in 1446, and Lord Mayor in 1457. Sir Geffrey Bullen was a native of Norfolk, and belonged to the Mercers' Company. He married Anne, daughter of Thomas, Lord Hoo and Hastings, and one of his sons, Sir William Bullen, of Blickling, in Norfolk, was the father of Thomas Bullen, Earl of Wiltshire, whose daughter was Anne Bullen, Henry VIII.'s second queen. Sir Geffrey Bullen was thus great-great-grandfather to Queen Elizabeth. Another son of Sir Geffrey, Thomas Bullen, described as an "esquire of Norfolk," was buried beside his father in 1471.

St. Lawrence Jewry received the remains of several other citizens who had held the chief magistracy of London, namely, Geffrey Fieldynge, Lord Mayor 1452; William Purchase or Purchat, Lord Mayor 1497; Sir Richard Gresham, Lord Mayor 1537; Sir Michael Dormer, Lord Mayor 1541; and Sir William Roe, Lord Mayor 1592.

Sir Richard Gresham was the father of Sir Thomas Gresham. He expired in 1548, and was laid by the side of his first wife, Audrey, Sir Thomas's mother, who had already been dead over a quarter of a century. She was the daughter of William Lynn of Southwick, Northamptonshire, and died when her son Thomas was only three years old. Like the Bullens, the Greshams were a Norfolk family.

Dame Alice Avenon was likewise interred here. She was a daughter of Thomas Hutchen, citizen and mercer, and was three times married: firstly, to Hugh Methwold, mercer; secondly, to John Blundell, likewise a mercer; and thirdly, to Sir Alexander

St Lawrence Jewry.

Avenon, who was Lord Mayor in 1569. She was a benefactress to the poor of the parish of St. Lawrence Jewry, for whose succour she, during her second widowhood, endowed a charity, appointing the Mercers' Company trustees. She died at the age of sixty-one, on November 21st, 1574.

In 1666 St. Lawrence Jewry was entirely consumed by the Great Fire.

During this conflagration was also destroyed the parish church of St. Mary Magdalen, Milk Street, which stood on the east side of that street towards the south end, on part of the site occupied by the City of London School, before its recent removal to the Thames Embankment. It was not rebuilt, and the benefice was united with that of St. Lawrence Jewry.

The living of St. Mary Magdalen is a rectory, and was as early as the time of Henry I. in the patronage of the Dean and Chapter of St. Paul's, who have ever since retained the advowson.

The first stone of the new church of St. Lawrence Jewry was laid on April 12th, 1671. It was opened for service in 1677, but was not finally completed till 1680. It was erected at a cost of over £11,870, and is the work of Wren. Its length is 82 feet, its width 71 feet, and the height from the pavement to the ceiling is 39 feet. The church contains only one aisle, which is placed on the north side and is separated from the main body of the building by Corinthian columns. Beyond this aisle, at the extreme north, is a vestibule, and there is another vestibule at the west, between the church and the west door. Above the columns is a richly-worked entablature, which is continued round the church, the place of the columns being supplied on the other sides by pilasters attached to the walls. The ceiling is divided by projecting bands into sunken panels, and the plaster work with which it is adorned is well and carefully executed. At the sides of the ceiling are enriched scrolls, which join the entablature.

The effect of the building is considerably enhanced by the doorways, the organ-case, in a gallery at the west, and the pulpit, standing near the south wall, all of which are of richly carved oak. The font, which is surmounted by a well-carved cover, is placed at the north-west of the church, near to the west wall, a door in which gives ingress to the vestry-room. This is a beautiful little apartment. The walls are entirely encased with dark oak very handsomely carved, and the exquisitely moulded ceiling is covered with a painting by Sir James Thornhill, the subject of which is the Reception of St. Lawrence into Heaven after his martyrdom. Over the chimney-piece hangs an old picture, in which is portrayed the manner of St. Lawrence's death.

To the east of the font, and opposite the vestry-room door, on the projecting wall through an opening in which the north vestibule is reached, is suspended a picture of the Assumption, which is not, however, displayed to advantage in that position, as the light is far from favourable.

Annually on Michaelmas Day the Lord Mayor and Corporation attend service and hear a sermon at St. Lawrence Jewry, before proceeding to the election of a Lord Mayor for the coming year. A large square pew in the centre of the church, on the door of which are displayed the arms of the City of London, is reserved for the Lord Mayor and the other civic dignitaries.

Beneath one of the windows in the south wall is a brass plate, stating that it was filled with stained glass in 1869 by the Mercers' Company, whose arms appear on the plate, in memory of the following illustrious dead buried in the church, whose names with dates are given: Geffrey Fieldynge, Sir Geffrey Bullen,

St. Lawrence Jewry. 193

Richard Rich, Sir Michael Dormer, Sir Richard Gresham, and Alice Blundell.

Below the next window, further east, is a similar plate, bearing the arms of the City of London, which records that this window was inserted by the inhabitants in 1872, in memory of the connection of their parish church with the Corporation of London, and of the connection with chief magistrates of the city of various noble families, whose arms are shown in the margin of the window.

The names of the distinguished citizens and the noble families alluded to are inscribed on the plate. They consist of Sir Thomas Seymour, Lord Mayor in 1526, belonging to the Somerset family; Sir Richard Gresham, from whose younger brother, Sir John Gresham, Lord Mayor in 1547, are descended the Leveson-Gowers of Titsey, a younger branch of the ducal house of Sutherland; John Cowper, Sheriff in 1551, ancestor of the Earls Cowper; Sir Edward Osborne, Lord Mayor in 1583, the great-grandfather of the first Duke of Leeds; Alderman Sir Baptist Hicks, raised to the peerage in 1628 as Viscount Campden, from whom are sprung the Earls of Gainsborough; Sir John Gore, Lord Mayor in 1624, brother to Sir Paul Gore, the ancestor of the Earls of Arran; Sir Nathaniel Herne, Sheriff in 1674, ancestor of the Earls of Jersey; Sir John Shorter, Lord Mayor in 1687, from the marriage of whose daughter Charlotte with Francis Seymour, Lord Conway, are derived the Marquises of Hertford; and Sir Crisp Gascoyne, Lord Mayor in 1752, from whom was descended Frances Mary Gascoyne, wife of the second Marquis of Salisbury, and mother of the present marquis.

There are several other stained glass windows in memory of parishioners and persons connected with the church. The two westernmost windows of the north aisle are still plain. At the east end are two stained glass windows in recesses, one on each side of the altar-piece, and the windows of the clerestory are also stained.

Against the west wall, near the door of the vestry-room, is a monument displaying three busts, in memory of Alderman Sir William Halliday, Sheriff in 1617, who died in 1623; his wife, Susannah, daughter of Sir Henry Roe, Lord Mayor in 1607, who married for her second husband Robert, Earl of Warwick, and died in 1645; and Anne, their daughter, who became the wife of Sir Henry Mildmay, and died in 1656. Sir William had a monument in the old church, which perished in the Fire, and this memorial was erected in 1687 by Dame Margaret Hungerford, as is recorded by an inscription at the base.

At the Restoration the vicarage of St. Lawrence Jewry was held by Dr. Edward Reynolds, who in the course of the year 1660 was elevated to the bishopric of Norwich. He was succeeded by Dr. Seth Ward, a celebrated mathematician and astronomer, who in 1662 became Bishop of Exeter, and was translated to Salisbury in 1667. The next vicar was an even more illustrious man of science, Dr. John Wilkins.

During the Commonwealth Wilkins had been Warden of Wadham College, Oxford, and afterwards Master of Trinity College, Cambridge, at both which places he established societies for the prosecution of scientific research. With Oliver Cromwell he had been closely allied, having married Robina, a sister of the Protector; but the Restoration, though it deprived him of the advantages of family influence, and of his Mastership of Trinity, only served to open a wider field for his energies. He came up to London, and played a leading part in the formation of the

St. Lawrence Jewry.

Royal Society, of which he was himself one of the most distinguished ornaments. He remained at St. Lawrence Jewry till 1668, when he was made Bishop of Chester. He died on November 19th, 1672, at the house of Dr. Tillotson, in Chancery Lane, and was buried under the north wall of the chancel of St. Lawrence.

Tillotson was appointed Tuesday Lecturer at St. Lawrence Jewry not long after Wilkins became vicar. On February 24th, 1664, he was married in this church to Wilkins's stepdaughter, Elizabeth French, the daughter of the Protector's sister by her first husband, Dr. Peter French, canon of Christ Church, Oxford. He continued to hold the lectureship till he was raised to the primacy in 1691. He died on November 22nd, 1694, and was buried at St. Lawrence, his funeral sermon being preached by Bishop Burnet. His monument, on the north wall of the chancel, displays his effigy in bas-relief, flanked by two cherubs, and is thus inscribed :

"P.M.
Reverendissimi et Sanctissimi Praesulis
Johannis Tillotson
Archiepiscopi Cantuariensis
Concionatoris in hac Ecclesia
per Annos XXX celeberrimi,
Qui obiit N° Kal. Decembr. MDCLXXXXIV,
Aetatis suae LXIV.
Hoc posuit Elizabetha
Conjux illius moestissima."

Beneath Tillotson's monument a brass tablet, bearing a Latin inscription, has been affixed to the wall, in memory of Bishop Wilkins.

A little further to the east, on the same wall, is a monument with bust to Dr. Benjamin Whichcote, celebrated for his excellence as a preacher, who succeeded Wilkins at St. Lawrence Jewry, and retained the living till his death in 1683.

The only other monument which calls for comment is a large and elaborate one on the western portion of the south wall to Mrs. Sarah Scott, who died in 1750, leaving £700 to be applied in the service of the parish.

Beneath this memorial is a tablet bearing the following inscription:

"Against this stone is the opening of the vault of the families of the Rawstorns and Robert Baxter, Churchwarden, who set the first foundation-stone of this church, the 12th of April 1671."

The east front of St. Lawrence Jewry, facing King Street, possesses a beautiful façade formed by four Corinthian columns, with richly worked entablature, supporting the pediment. The tower contains three storeys, above which is a square turret supporting a similarly shaped pedestal, on which is placed an octagonal spirelet, surmounted by a ball, and a vane in the form of St. Lawrence's emblem, the gridiron. The total height to the summit of the vane is 160 feet. Within the tower are hung eight bells.

The church was repaired in 1867, and the floor was newly paved, and the exterior roof renewed in 1892.

St. Magnus, London Bridge.

THE church of St. Magnus the Martyr stands on the south side of Thames Street, at the bottom of Fish Street Hill. The particular St. Magnus the Martyr to whom it is dedicated, "for there were divers other martyrs of this name, but none of them of whom such special notice is taken as of this," was, in the opinion of Newcourt, a Christian who "suffered in Cæsarea in Cappadocia in the time of Aurelian the Emperor, Anno Dom. 276, under Alexander the governour."

The old church, which was consumed by the Great Fire, was the place of sepulture of several persons of note in their day, amongst whom may be mentioned Henry Yeuele or de Yeveley, master-mason to Edward III., Richard II., and Henry IV. This skilful workman, who was employed by Richard on his new buildings at Westminster Hall, and constructed the monument of that sovereign's first queen, Anne of Bohemia, in Westminster Abbey, was buried at St. Magnus in 1400 under a monument of his own erection, which was still in existence in the time of Stow.

The church of St. Margaret, New Fish Street, was not rebuilt after the Great Fire, and as it stood close to the spot where the conflagration commenced, its site was utilized for the erection of the Monument by which that momentous event was commemorated.

The rectory of St. Margaret was united with that of St. Magnus. The former had been, before the dissolution of monasteries, in the gift of the abbot and convent of Westminster, and the patronage of the latter had been alternately exercised by the abbot and convent of Westminster and the abbot and convent of Bermondsey. Both advowsons were amongst those given by Queen Mary to the see of London.

The most distinguished name amongst the rectors of St. Magnus is that of Miles Coverdale, the translator of the Scriptures. When he returned from exile after the accession of Elizabeth, his Puritan opinions prevented his re-entering on the bishopric of Exeter, which he had obtained under Edward VI. and lost under Mary. He declined the see of Llandaff, which was offered to him, but accepted the rectory of St. Magnus from Grindal, then Bishop of London, and was instituted on March 3rd, 1563-64. He did not, however, continue here long, as, either influenced by conscientious scruples, or feeling himself rendered by the infirmities of age unequal to the discharge of his duties, he resigned the living in 1566.

John Alcock held the living of St. Margaret, New Fish Street, from 1461 to 1471, resigning it on his elevation to the see of Rochester. From Rochester he was translated to Worcester, and from Worcester to Ely, which last bishopric he obtained in 1486 on Morton's advancement to the primacy. He died in 1500, and was buried in Ely Cathedral. He was a man of importance in the State as well as in the Church—Master of the Rolls, President of Wales, and twice Lord Chancellor; but he is now perhaps best remembered as the founder of Jesus College, Cambridge.

Geoffrey Wrenne, who interests us as belonging to the same family as Sir Christopher, was rector of St. Margaret's from 1512

St. Magnus the Martyr, London Bridge. 199

till his death in 1527. He was also a canon of Windsor, and was buried in the north aisle of St. George's Chapel.

The body of the present church of St. Magnus the Martyr was completed by Wren in 1676, but the steeple was not added till 1705. This steeple, which is placed to the west of the church, is one of the most beautiful of all Wren's works. The stone tower contains three storeys, the lowermost of which is ornamented on the western face by Ionic pilasters, entablature, and pediment. It is terminated by a cornice and pierced parapet, with vases placed in pairs at the angles. Above the tower rises a stone octagonal lantern, crowned by a lead-covered cupola, which, in its turn, is surmounted by a slender lead-covered lantern and spire, culminating in a finial and vane. The total height is 185 feet. The tower contains ten bells.

The most advantageous position from which to contemplate this charming steeple is the southern end of London Bridge. From this side it shows out very prominently, and its effect is enhanced by the proximity of the Monument, which appears just behind the steeple, and unites with it to form a striking and agreeable combination. The view from the top of Fish Street Hill is not so good, as the Monument rises between the spectator and the steeple, and although in reality only seventeen feet higher, appears to dwarf it, in consequence of its situation on more elevated ground.

The ground storey of the tower is open on three sides, like that of Christ Church, Newgate Street. As it was originally built, it was only open on the west side; but during the repairs after the church had sustained some damage by fire in 1760, a passage was made through it from north to south, so as to form a footway to Old London Bridge, which, being about 200 feet to the east

of the present bridge, lay in a direct line with the tower. Wren seems to have foreseen the probability of this communication being required, and had so constructed the arches that no difficulty was experienced in opening them out. Since the formation of the present bridge the footway has of course been no longer needed, and a portion of the carriage road to the old bridge has been acquired as a churchyard and enclosed by a wall.

From the second storey of the tower projects an ornate gilded clock. This was presented in 1709 by Sir Charles Duncombe, Alderman of the Ward of Bridge Within, in which St. Magnus is situated, who was Lord Mayor that year. It is said that he was induced to present a clock to the church from the remembrance of the inconvenience he had once experienced when a boy through not being able to ascertain the time. The cost of the clock was £485 5s. 4d. In 1712 he gave St. Magnus an organ, a very fine instrument, which, though it has been considerably altered, is still in existence. It was built by Abraham Jordan, who announced its opening in the "Spectator" of February 8th, 1712, stating that one of the four sets of keys "is adapted to the art of emitting sounds by swelling the notes, which never was in any organ before."

Sir Charles Duncombe was the ancestor of the Feversham family. His purchase of Helmsley is satirically referred to by Pope:

"And Helmsley, once proud Buckingham's delight,
Slides to a scrivener, or a city knight."

He was a goldsmith, and, like many of the leading goldsmiths of that period, conducted a banking business. His house, "The Grasshopper," in Lombard Street, had been formerly occupied by Sir Thomas Gresham, and stood on the site of the present

No. 68, the bank of Messrs. Martin, on the plates at the entrance of which the old sign of "The Grasshopper" is engraved.

The north front of St. Magnus displays six large circular-headed window-niches, four to the east and two to the west of the doorway, which are, however, all blocked up, with the exception of a small space at the top. They are surmounted by cornices, and a similar aperture over the doorway is crowned by a festoon. The windows in the south wall are glazed throughout, but are without external decorations.

The dimensions of the interior of St. Magnus are 90 feet in length, 59 feet in breadth, and 41 feet in height. It is divided into a nave and side-aisles by slender Ionic columns, standing at considerable distances apart. The ceiling of the nave is arched, and ornamented with fretwork; the ceilings of the aisles are flat. The altar-piece is very handsome. It contains four Corinthian columns, with entablature and pediment, and much carving and gilding has been bestowed upon it. One of its embellishments is a representation of a pelican. The pulpit is also well carved, and the inner door-cases at the west and north are excellently wrought. The walls are panelled to the height of about seven feet.

When the church of St. Bartholomew by the Exchange was demolished in 1840, the remains of Miles Coverdale, who had been there buried, were transferred to St. Magnus on account of his connection with this church as rector. A monument had already been erected in memory of him at St. Magnus, against the east wall, on the south side of the communion-table. It consists of a panel of white marble on a black slab, and beneath carved representations of a bishop's mitre and a bible is the following inscription:

St. Magnus the Martyr, London Bridge.

"To the Memory of Miles Coverdale
Who, convinced that the pure word of God ought to be the
Sole rule of our Faith and guide of our Practice,
Laboured earnestly for its diffusion; and with the
View of affording the means of reading and
Hearing, in their own tongue, the wonderful
Works of God, not only to his own Coun-
trymen, but to the nations that sit in
Darkness, and to every creature
Wheresoever the English lan-
guage might be spoken, spent
Many years of his life
In preparing a trans-
lation of the Scriptures.
On the IV of October, MDXXXV
The first complete English printed Version of
The Bible
Was published under his direction.
The Parishioners of St. Magnus the Martyr
Desirous of acknowledging the mercy of God,
And calling to mind that
Miles Coverdale
Was once Rector of their Parish
Erected this monument to his memory A.D. MDCCCXXXVII.
'How beautiful are the feet of them that preach the Gospel
Of peace, and bring glad tidings of good things.'
Isaiah LII. 7."

The church of St. Michael, Crooked Lane, was pulled down in 1831 to make room for the new London Bridge approaches. Its parish was united with those of St. Magnus and St. Margaret.

St. Michael's, which had been "sometime but a small and homely thing," was rebuilt by John Lovekin, fishmonger, four times Lord Mayor—1348, 1358, 1365, and 1366. He "was buried there in the choir, under a fair tomb, with the images of him and his wife in alabaster."

Sir William Walworth, the stout-hearted mayor who overthrew Wat Tyler, served his apprenticeship to Lovekin. He enlarged the church with a new choir and side chapels, and founded in connection with it a college for a master and nine priests. He was buried in the north chapel, and verses inscribed on his monument recorded his exploits.

The parish of St. Michael, Crooked Lane, was one of the "Peculiars" of the Archbishop of Canterbury. The archbishop now presents to the united benefice alternately with the Bishop of London.

The old church, which had required extensive repairs in the early part of the seventeenth century, perished in the Great Fire. It was rebuilt of stone by Wren, who completed the body of the church in 1688, and the steeple ten years later. The interior, which was without aisles, measured 78 feet in length by 46 feet in breadth. The tower was crowned by four pinnacles, and reached an altitude of about 100 feet; upon it was placed a circular lead-covered lantern in three stages, supporting a cupola surmounted by a lofty vane and cross.

St. Margaret Lothbury.

THE church of St. Margaret Lothbury is situated in the street from which it derives its distinguishing appellation. The benefice is a rectory, the patronage of which belonged in pre-Reformation times to the abbess and convent of Barking, in Essex, but has since the dissolution of monasteries remained in the hands of the Crown.

St. Margaret's was, according to Stow, "newly re-edified and built about the year 1440." Robert Large, mercer, Lord Mayor in that year, who will always be remembered as the master to whom Caxton served his apprenticeship, was a benefactor, for he "gave to the choir of that church one hundred shillings, and twenty pounds for ornaments; more to the vaulting over the water-course of Walbrook by the said church, for the enlarging thereof, two hundred marks."

The church was repaired at the cost of the parishioners in 1621, but was destroyed in the Fire of 1666. It was rebuilt of stone by Wren, who completed it in 1690.

St. Margaret Lothbury measures 66 feet in length by 54 feet in breadth, and the height from the pavement to the ceiling is 36 feet. It consists of a nave, chancel, and one aisle, on the south side, separated from the main body of the church by two Corinthian columns. To the north wall are affixed pilasters, which, supplying the want of columns on that side of the church, serve to support the entablature. The ceiling is flat in the centre, but coved at the sides. It is not decorated. The walls are panelled to a height of about eight feet. The organ stands in a gallery at the west. The south aisle is railed off from the rest of the church, and contains a side-altar at the east; and at its western end, on a marble pavement, stands a remarkably handsome font, attributed to Gibbons, the bowl of which is sculptured with representations of Adam and Eve in Paradise, the Return of the Dove to Noah in the Ark, the Baptism of Christ in Jordan by John, and the Baptism of the Eunuch by Philip. The windows of the clerestory, as well as the lower side-windows and the windows at the west, are stained, but there are no east windows. The niches on each side of the altar-piece are occupied by two flat wooden painted figures of Moses and Aaron, which were brought from the demolished church of St. Christopher, in Threadneedle Street. St. Margaret's has within the last few months received additional ornaments in the magnificent chancel-screen and the pulpit and sounding-board of All Hallows, Upper Thames Street, re-erected here in consequence of the destruction of that sacred edifice. The tower contains three storeys, culminating in a cornice; above it is a lead-covered lantern, upon which is placed an obelisk with finial and vane. The total height of the steeple is 140 feet.

When St. Christopher's was pulled down in 1781 to provide space for the extension of the Bank of England, its parish was united with that of St. Margaret Lothbury. This church was

St. Margaret Lothbury.

known as St. Christopher-le-Stocks, from its proximity to the Stocks Market, which occupied the ground now covered by the Mansion House.

The living of St. Christopher's is a rectory, and is said to have anciently belonged to the Nevil family, but since the fourteenth century it has been in the gift of the see of London.

That illustrious divine, John Pearson, subsequently Bishop of Chester, was instituted as rector on August 17th, 1660, but resigned the living in less than two years.

St. Christopher's was not entirely destroyed by the Fire, but was considerably injured. It was repaired by Wren in 1671, being the first church which he completed, and, exactly a century later, was the first of his churches to be demolished.

The church of St. Bartholomew by the Exchange was pulled down in 1841, and its parish was united with that of St. Margaret Lothbury. It stood at the south-east corner of Bartholomew Lane, facing the Royal Exchange, on the site now occupied by the Sun Fire Office. The advowson of the rectory belonged to Simon Godart or Goddard, a citizen and draper of London, whose son Simon presented in 1337, but afterwards passed into the possession of the Abbey of Graces near the Tower, founded by Edward III. The abbot and convent first presented in 1374. Since the dissolution of monasteries the advowson has been retained by the Crown. The tower of St. Bartholomew's escaped the Fire, but the body of the church was consumed, and rebuilt by Wren in 1679.

Miles Coverdale, the translator of the Scriptures, was buried at St. Bartholomew's in 1568. He was made Bishop of Exeter in 1551, but on the accession of Queen Mary he was deprived of his see, and imprisoned for two years. On his release he left

England, but returned after the accession of Queen Elizabeth. He did not, however, regain his bishopric of Exeter, as his views were of too Puritan a character to find acceptance with the queen, but he was offered in 1563 the see of Llandaff, and on his refusal he was presented by Bishop Grindal to the rectory of St. Magnus, London Bridge, which he resigned in 1566.

His monument, "a fair plated stone on the ground in the chancel," perished in the Fire. On the demolition of St. Bartholomew's, his remains were removed to the church of St. Magnus, where a tablet had already been erected to his memory.

A new church of St. Bartholomew was built in Moor Lane, Cripplegate, by Cockerill in 1849-50, which was intended to be an exact imitation of St. Bartholomew by the Exchange, and to which were transferred the organ, pulpit, and some of the woodwork and masonry of its prototype.

The church of St. Olave Jewry, which was situated on the west side of Old Jewry, was pulled down, and its parish united with that of St. Margaret Lothbury in 1888. The benefice of St. Olave's was originally a rectory, but was converted into a vicarage during the fourteenth century. The earliest known patrons of the living were the Canons of St. Paul's, but towards the close of the twelfth century it passed into the hands of the Prior of Butley in Suffolk. Since the dissolution of that priory under Henry VIII. the advowson has been retained by the Crown.

St. Olave Jewry was anciently called St. Olave Upwell, because, explains Stow, " a well was under the east end of this church, late turned to a pumpe, but decayed."

Robert Large, the Lord Mayor mentioned above, who "gave to that church two hundred pounds," was buried at St. Olave Jewry.

The old church was destroyed in the Great Fire, and the

rebuilding was commenced by Wren in 1673, and finished in 1676. It was restored as recently as 1874, only fourteen years before its demolition. At St. Olave's was buried Alderman John Boydell, Lord Mayor in 1790, the great engraver. He was born in Shropshire in 1719, and died in 1804. A tablet, surmounted by a bust, was erected to his memory by his niece, Mary Nichol, wife of George Nichol, bookseller to George III., who died in 1820, and was laid in the same vault with her uncle. This monument was removed, at the demolition of St. Olave's, to St. Margaret's Lothbury.

After the Great Fire the church of St. Martin Pomary was not rebuilt, and its parish was united with that of St. Olave Jewry. It stood on the east side of Ironmonger Lane, and was therefore sometimes alluded to as St. Martin's, Ironmonger Lane. It was "called Pomary," says Stow, "upon what occasion I certainly know not. It is supposed to be of apples growing where houses are now lately built; for myself have seen large void places there." Modern scholarship bears out in this instance the old antiquary's conjecture.

St. Martin Pomary does not appear to have had any particularly interesting associations. "Monuments in that church," observes Stow, "none to be accounted of." The advowson of the rectory was bestowed by one Ralph Tricket, in the reign of Henry III., on the prior and canons of St. Bartholomew, West Smithfield, and has, since the dissolution of monasteries, remained in the possession of the Crown.

The church of St. Mildred in the Poultry was pulled down in 1872, and its parish united with that of St. Olave Jewry. It was dedicated to a Saxon saint, said to have been a princess of the royal family of Mercia, and was rebuilt on an arch over the Walbrook in 1457.

At St. Mildred's was buried in 1580 Thomas Tusser, who published in 1557 "A Hundreth Good Pointes of Husbandrie," which he expanded in 1573 into "Five Hundreth Pointes of Good Husbandrie." His monument perished in the Fire.

After the Fire the church was rebuilt by Wren in 1676. On its demolition in 1872 the pulpit and some of the wood-carvings were erected in St. Paul's, Goswell Road, a new church which was built and endowed out of the sum obtained by the sale of St. Mildred's, the total amount of which was £50,200.

"The Wedding," which forms the subject of one of the "Last Essays of Elia," took place at St. Mildred's, and Lamb seems to have found the character of "father" to the daughter of Admiral Burney as difficult to sustain with becoming gravity as that of "best-man" to Hazlitt.

"I do not know what business I have to be present in solemn places. I cannot divest me of an unseasonable disposition to levity upon the most awful occasions. I was never cut out for a public functionary. Ceremony and I have long shaken hands; but I could not resist the importunities of the young lady's father, whose gout unhappily confined him at home, to act as parent on this occasion, and give away the bride. Something ludicrous occurred to me at this most serious of all moments—a sense of my unfitness to have the disposal, even in imagination, of the sweet young creature beside me. I fear I was betrayed to some lightness, for the awful eye of the parson—and the rector's eye of St. Mildred's in the Poultry is no trifle of a rebuke—was upon me in an instant, souring my incipient jest to the tristful severities of a funeral."

The rectory of St. Mildred was, prior to the dissolution of monasteries, in the gift of the prior and convent of St. Mary

Overy, Southwark, but has since that event continued in the possession of the Crown.

After the Great Fire the church of St. Mary Colechurch was not rebuilt, and its parish was united with that of St. Mildred in the Poultry. It was situated at the south end of Old Jewry, and, according to Stow, was "named of one Cole that built it;" but Mr. Loftie tells us that it "probably stood in that part of the market where coal or charcoal was sold."

St. Mary Colechurch was appropriated to the master and brethren of the Hospital of St. Thomas of Acon, i.e., Thomas à Becket, who received that title, it is said, from the belief that he miraculously intervened to procure the capture of Acre by the Crusaders. The hospital was founded by Thomas Fitztheobald, Baron of Helles in Tipperary, and Agnes his wife, sister to Thomas à Becket, about twenty years after the great archbishop's tragic death; "they gave to the master and brethren," says Stow, "the lands with the appurtenances that sometimes were Gilbart Becket's, father to the said Thomas, in the which he was born, there to make a church."

The site of the Hospital of St. Thomas of Acon, and thus of Becket's birthplace, between Ironmonger Lane and Old Jewry, is now occupied by the Mercers' Hall and Chapel, the Hospital, together with the advowson of St. Mary Colechurch, having been purchased by that company from Henry VIII., through the instrumentality of Sir Richard Gresham.

The church of St. Margaret Lothbury thus serves, besides its own original parish, for six other parishes, those of St. Christopher, St. Bartholomew by the Exchange, St. Olave Jewry, St. Martin Pomary, St. Mildred in the Poultry, and St. Mary Colechurch.

St. Margaret Pattens.

THE church of St. Margaret Pattens stands on the north side of Eastcheap, at the south-eastern corner of Rood Lane, in which pattens were once made and sold. It was rebuilt, as Stow tells us, in the reign of Henry VIII., and between the years 1614 and 1632 it appears to have been extensively repaired and embellished, but it does not seem to have possessed any noteworthy monuments, or to have been otherwise a particularly interesting building, so that we have no great cause to regret its destruction by the Fire of 1666.

The advowson of St. Margaret Pattens belonged anciently to the Nevil family, but in 1408 it came into the possession of Richard Whittington and other citizens, who three years later bestowed it on the mayor and commonalty of London. The rectory has from that time continued in the gift of the Lord Mayor and Corporation.

St. Margaret Pattens.

With the parish of St. Margaret Pattens was united after the Fire that of St. Gabriel Fenchurch, the rectory of which—in pre-Reformation days appertaining to the important priory of Holy Trinity, Aldgate—is now in the gift of the Lord Chancellor.

St. Gabriel Fenchurch—so called from the swampy nature of the ground on which it was built—stood in the midst of Fenchurch Street, which thence takes its name.

The present church of St. Margaret Pattens was completed by Wren in 1687. It consists of a nave, chancel, and north aisle, and measures 66 feet in length, 52 feet in breadth, and 32 feet in height from the pavement to the ceiling. The ceiling is flat in the central part, and is encircled by an ornamental cornice, beyond which it slopes down to the walls. The columns on the north side, which separate the aisle from the nave, and also serve to support a north gallery, are encased in wood to the height of the top of the gallery. Upon them rests an entablature, which is continued round the church by pilasters affixed to the walls. The building is well lighted, having a large east window, with a smaller window on each side of it, three spacious windows in the south wall, and throughout the whole church a series of circular windows above. There are also two large windows on the north side, but these do not admit much light, owing to the juxtaposition of the gallery and stairway. The altar-piece is adorned with some excellent carvings, and on its upper part is placed a small picture, beautifully executed, representing angels ministering to our Lord, which is said to be the work of Carlo Maratti (1625-1713), a Roman painter. The pulpit—of oak, and solid and substantial in appearance—is placed near the south wall. The font is situated at the north-west, and the organ, enclosed in a handsome case, occupies

the west gallery. On the front of this gallery are prominently dis-
p'ayed the royal arms, which are brightly gilded.

The church, as an inscription on the organ-gallery records, was reseated in 1880, but two high official pews at the west are still retained. At the south end of the southern pew is a large carved figure of a lion, and at the northern end of the north pew is a corresponding figure of a unicorn. The sword-rest at the opposite end of the latter pew is extremely handsome.

The north aisle is terminated by some finely carved woodwork, against which is placed a side-altar, surmounted by figures of the Virgin and Child, very recently erected, in memory, as a Latin inscription on the north wall explains, of Thomas Wagstaffe, one of the ablest of the Nonjurors, who was appointed to the rectory in 1684, and deprived in 1690, owing to his refusal to take the oath of allegiance to the new sovereigns.

A later rector, Dr. Thomas Birch, was a very industrious man of letters. He was author of "The General Dictionary, Historical and Critical," "Memoirs of the Reign of Queen Elizabeth from 1581 till her death," and a "History of the Royal Society," of which he was secretary. He was also the biographer of Henry, Prince of Wales, the eldest son of James I., of Archbishop Tillotson, and of Robert Boyle, the natural philosopher, and edited Spenser's "Faery Queen," the works of Sir Walter Raleigh, Bacon's "Letters and Speeches," and the prose writings of Milton. He died in 1766, after having been rector for nearly nineteen years, and was buried in the chancel of the church.

Birch was succeeded by another literary rector, Peter Whalley, who held the living till his death in 1791. Whalley, who was for eight years head-master of Christ's Hospital, edited the works of Ben Jonson, and also published "An Enquiry into the Learning of Shakespeare, with Remarks on several Passages of his Plays," and "A Vindication of the Evidences and Authenticity of the Gospels from the Objections of the late Lord Bolingbroke, in his Letters on the Study of History."

On the north side of the church, against a pillar, is a monument erected in memory of his parents by Sir Peter Vandeput in 1686. Sir Peter, who was a merchant of Flemish extraction, and had been sheriff in 1684, gave £100 to be laid out for the use of the poor of the parish. On the south wall is a large and elaborate monument to Sir Peter Delmé, Lord Mayor in 1723, who died on September 4th, 1728. It is the work of Johan Michael Rysbrack, a native of Antwerp, and a sculptor of considerable merit.

The tower of St. Margaret Pattens is terminated by a cornice and a balustrade, at the corners of which are placed four pinnacles; above the tower rises a lofty lead-covered spire, culminating in a ball and vane. This spire, which attains an altitude of 200 feet, is taller than any of Wren's other lead-covered spires and lanterns, and amongst all his church steeples comes third in order of height, being only exceeded by the stone steeples of St. Bride and St. Mary-le-Bow. An excellent view of it from the south can be obtained by ascending the lane called St. Mary-at-Hill, which runs into Eastcheap exactly opposite St. Margaret Pattens.

St. Martins Ludgate

THE church of St. Martin, Ludgate, stands on the north side of Ludgate Hill, to the east of Old Bailey, and to the west of Stationer's Hall Court.

An apocryphal legend assigning a British origin to this church is quoted by Weever from "my old author, Robert of Gloucester," but leaving tradition, and coming down to later times, we learn from Stow that St. Martin's was rebuilt in the reign of Henry VI., "for in the year 1437 John Michael, Mayor, and the Commonalty granted to William Downe, parson of St. Martin's at Ludgate, a parcel of ground, containing in length twenty-eight feet and in breadth four feet, to set and build their steeple upon."

In St. Martin's was a monument to William Sevenoake, Lord Mayor in 1418, about whom Lambarde in his "Perambulation of Kent" relates a legend, while describing the town of Sevenoaks, or Sennocke, as he prefers to call it.

"About the latter ende of the reigne of King Edwarde the thirde," says he, "there was found (lying in the streetes at Sennocke) a poore childe, whose Parents were unknowne, and he (for the same cause) named after the place where he was taken up, William Sennocke.

St. Martin, Ludgate.

"This Orphan was by the helpe of some charitable persons brought up and nourtured in such wise, that being made an Apprentice to a Grocer in London, he arose by degrees (in course of time) to be Maior, and chiefe magistrate of that Citie.

"At which time, calling to his minde the goodnes of Almightie God, and the favour of the Townesmen, extended towardes him, he determined to make an everlasting monument of his thankfull minde for the same.

"And therefore, of his owne charge, builded both an Hospitall for reliefe of the poore, and a Free Schoole for the education of youthe within this Towne: endowing the one and the other, with competent yeerely living (as the daies then suffered) towards their sustentation and maintenance."

Though Sevenoake undoubtedly took his name from his native town, Lambarde's pretty story hardly agrees with the account which Stow gives of him:

"This William Sevenoke, son to William Rumsched of Sevenoke in Kent, was by his father bound an apprentice with Hugh de Bois, citizen and ferrer (farrier) of London, for a term of years, which being expired in the year 1394, the 18th of Richard II., John Hadley being Mayor of London, and Stephen Spilman Chamberlain of the Guildhall, he alleged that his master had used the trade or mystery of a grocer, and not of a ferrer, and therefore required to be made free of the Grocers' Company, which was granted. This William Sevenoke founded in the town of Sevenoke a free school and almshouses for the poor."

St. Martin's was repaired at the cost of the parishioners in 1623, but was destroyed in the Great Fire. It was rebuilt of stone by Wren, and completed in 1684.

The tower rises at the centre of the south front of the church, facing Ludgate Hill. It measures 22 feet square at the base, and contains three storeys; the first of which displays a doorway formed by Corinthian columns with entablature and pediment; the second, a window with cornice, and a panel above; and the highest, circular-headed openings filled in with louvres and surmounted by ornamental work. Two large carved scrolls connect the tower with the parapet which crowns the side walls of the church. The tower is concluded by an enriched cornice; then comes a narrower stone stage, from which springs a lead-covered octagonal cupola, supporting a lantern, the base of which is encircled by a balcony. A tapering spire, with ball, finial, and vane, completes the steeple, the height of which is 158 feet.

The south front of the church presents three windows and three doors, there being a window and a door on each side of those in the tower. The side windows are capped with cornices similar to that over the central window. The eastern and western extremities of the parapet are decorated with pineapples.

The general aspect of the exterior is pleasing, and the steeple in particular is exceedingly graceful, but the effect is rather marred by the pressure of the adjoining houses.

The interior of St. Martin's, which is reached through a vestibule, is noticeable as being both broader and higher than it is long. Its total width is 66 feet, and height 59 feet, while its length is only 57 feet. The appearance is rendered cruciform by the introduction of four Composite columns, standing on lofty bases, which, together with pilasters affixed to the walls, support entablatures at the angles of the church. By reason of the excessive breadth the cross thus produced is in the form of the long-armed Greek cross, instead of the more usual Latin cross.

The ceiling is lowered in the quadrangular corners enclosed by the entablatures of the columns.

The church possesses some good woodwork. The oak altar-piece contains four pilasters with entablature and pediment; the pulpit is well carved; the walls are panelled; and there are handsome inner door-cases at the south-east and south-west.

The font, which is of white marble, was presented by Thomas Morley, a native of the parish, in 1673. It stands in the recess at the north-west, and bears the inscription, ΝΙΨΟΝ 'ΑΝΟ-ΜΗΜΑ ΜΗ ΜΟΝΑΝ ΟΨΙΝ ("Cleanse my transgression, not my outward part only"), which has been already observed on that of St. Ethelburga, Bishopsgate Street. This sentence, which was engraved on several fonts both in England and on the continent, appears to have first attracted the early Greek Church from the fact that it reads the same backwards as forwards.

The advowson of the rectory of St. Martin, Ludgate, was, till the dissolution of monasteries, in the possession of the abbot and convent of Westminster. It was bestowed by Queen Mary on the see of London.

Samuel Purchas, who was presented to the rectory about 1614, was a diligent and enthusiastic collector and writer of voyages and travels. His knowledge and industry in these fields gained him the title of the "English Ptolemy." His principal works were "Purchas his Pilgrimage, or Relations of the World and the Religions observed in all Ages," first published in 1613, and "Hakluytus Posthumus, or Purchas his Pilgrimes, containing a History of the World, in Sea Voyages and Land Travels by Englishmen and others." This latter work, in which he made use of Hakluyt's unpublished MSS., appeared in 1625, and was followed in 1626 by a fourth and greatly enlarged edition of the

"Pilgrimage." The expenses of publication unfortunately plunged this meritorious author into pecuniary embarrassment. The king promised him a deanery, but he died in September, 1626, before this promise could be fulfilled.

The church of St. Mary Magdalene, Old Fish Street, was situated on the north side of Knightrider Street at the south-west corner of Old Change. It was destroyed in the Great Fire, and rebuilt by Wren in 1685.

One curious relic, which fortunately escaped the flames, was preserved and re-erected in the new church. This was, to use Strype's words, "a brass plate fixed up near the font, where is the representation of an old man in a gown, and the year of our Lord, viz., 1586, set over him, and these verses:

"'In God the Lord put all your Truste,
   Repente your formar wicked Waies;
Elizabethe our Queen moste juste,
   Blesse her, O Lord, in all her Daies.
So Lord encrease good Counselers
   And Preachers of his holie Worde;
Mislike of all Papistes' desiers,
   Oh Lord, cut them off with thy Sworde.

"'How small soever the Gifte shal bee,
Thanke God for him who gave it thee.
XII Penie Loaves to xii poor foulkes
Geve every Sabbath Day for aye.'"

The figure is supposed to be that of Thomas Berry, a fishmonger, who "gave a messuage in Southwark, called the Red Cross, with its appurtenances" to the poor of the parish, subject to a small annual payment to the towns of Walton and Bootle in Lancashire.

With the parish of St. Mary Magdalene was united after the

St. Martin, Ludgate.

Fire that of St. Gregory by St. Paul's. The benefice of St. Mary Magdalene was a rectory in the gift of the Dean and Chapter of St. Paul's, and the church of St. Gregory belonged to them, and was served by a curate whom they appointed.

St. Gregory's was situated close to the south-west wall of the old cathedral, thus giving occasion to Fuller's quaint description of St. Paul's as "truly the mother church, having one babe in her body," *i.e.* St. Faith's, "and another in her arms," *i.e.* St. Gregory's.

When Inigo Jones was making his portico to St. Paul's, he began to pull St. Gregory's down, viewing it in the light of an obstruction. Before, however, he had demolished more than half of it, Parliament met, and the parishioners, who were much aggrieved by his proceedings, petitioned that he might be restrained from doing further damage, complaining bitterly of the arbitrary manner in which he treated them. Jones was accordingly summoned to the bar of the House of Lords, and prohibited from continuing the work of destruction, while the stones which he had brought to London to use in the reparation of St. Paul's were given to the parishioners to rebuild their church with.

At St. Gregory's was buried Alison, wife of George Heriot, James I.'s goldsmith, the "Jingling Geordie" of "The Fortunes of Nigel." She died on April 16th, 1612, before she had completed her twentieth year, and was commemorated by "a very goodly monument in the south ile of the quire uppermost," with a long Latin inscription, partly prose and partly verse, in which her husband styles himself, "Georgius Heriot, Armiger, Regis, Reginæ, Principum Henrici et Caroli Gemmarius."

Dr. John Hewet, minister of St. Gregory's, was beheaded June

8th, 1658, on a charge of conspiring against the Commonwealth, together with Sir Harry Slingsby, a Yorkshireman of good family, who had been returned as a member to the Long Parliament, but had from the outset of the war adhered to the king. A full account of the matter is given by Clarendon, who describes Hewet as "an eminent preacher in London, and very orthodox, to whose church those of the king's party frequently resorted, and few but those;" and Sir Harry as "a gentleman of a good understanding, but of a very melancholic nature, and of very few words."

St. Mary Magdalene, as rebuilt by Wren, was a plain building without aisles. The east and south fronts, each of which displayed a row of circular-headed windows, surmounted by a continued cornice, were, however, picturesque. The steeple, which was placed at the north-west, consisted of a tower and stone lantern, but only attained a height of 86 feet. The church was seriously damaged by a fire in December, 1886, and was thereupon pulled down to save the expense of repairing it. The rectory was united with that of St. Martin, Ludgate.

The Rev. Richard Harris Barham, the author of the "Ingoldsby Legends," was rector of St. Mary Magdalene and St. Gregory from 1824 till 1842, when he removed to the neighbouring benefice of St. Augustine and St. Faith. He desired, however, to be buried in his earlier church, as several of his children had already been interred there, and his remains were accordingly laid in the rector's vault of St. Mary Magdalene on June 21st, 1845.

ST. MARY ABCHURCH.

ST. MARY ABCHURCH stands in Abchurch Yard, which opens out of Abchurch Lane on the west side, just before its southern termination in Cannon Street. Abchurch Yard was originally the burying-ground of the church, and its boundaries are still marked by posts. The name signifies "Up-church," and is accounted for by the position of the edifice on rising ground.

The advowson of the rectory belonged in ancient times to the prior and convent of St. Mary Overy, Southwark, but about the middle of the fifteenth century it came into the possession of the master and chaplains of the college of Corpus Christi, founded in connection with the church of St. Lawrence Poultney by Sir John Poultney, four times Lord Mayor—in 1330, 1331, 1333, and 1336. Poultney's College surrendered to Edward VI., and Queen Elizabeth, in the tenth year of her reign, was induced by Archbishop Parker, who had been educated at Corpus Christi College, Cambridge, to bestow the advowson of St. Mary Abchurch upon the master and fellows of that college, in whose gift the living has since continued.

The neighbouring church of St. Lawrence Poultney, which stood on Lawrence Poultney, or, as it is now written, Pountney Hill, just south of Cannon Street, was not rebuilt after the Fire, and its parish was united to that of St. Mary Abchurch. St. Lawrence was called Poultney after Sir John Poultney, and the

St. Mary Abchurch.

master and chaplains of his college, which adjoined the church, were the patrons of the living. After the reign of Queen Mary it was served by a curate, and in 1717 the right of presentation to the curacy was purchased from the parishioners by Corpus Christi College, Cambridge.

A portion of the old churchyard of St. Lawrence Poultney even now exists at the south of Lawrence Pountney Hill, above the entrance to Duck's Foot Lane, extending eastwards to Lawrence Pountney Lane. The refreshing verdure of the trees and plants which spring from its soil, and the cooling breezes from the river, combine to render this ancient landmark one of the most agreeable spots in the whole city.

St. Mary Abchurch was rebuilt by Wren in 1686 at a cost of a little under £5,000. It is almost square, measuring 63 feet in length and 60 feet in breadth, and is surmounted by a cupola, which rises from a cornice, and is supported by pendentives attached to the walls. This cupola is embellished with paintings by Sir James Thornhill, and is pierced a little above the base by four circular lights. It attains at its apex an elevation of 51 feet. The altar-piece is enclosed by four Corinthian columns, with entablature and pediment, and displays above the centre a gilded figure of a pelican with outspread wings. It is adorned with some beautifully carved festoons of fruit and flowers, which are amongst the finest works of Gibbons. The pulpit, which is of carved oak, and is overshadowed by a large sounding-board, is placed on the north side of the church, and the font, which is surmounted by a carved oak cover ornamented with figures of the four evangelists, stands in a recess at the south-west beneath the gallery. This gallery occupies the space between the tower and the south wall, and a portion of it holds the organ, the handsome case of which shows prominently from its position between two pillars.

On each side of the altar-piece is a stained glass window, and above these are two smaller circular windows. In the centre of the south wall is a large window containing representations of the Last Supper and the Ascension, the latter of which occupies the upper portion. There are also in this wall two smaller windows, one east and the other west of the central window, and two circular windows above. The north wall has no windows, but the west wall possesses a large window in the centre, with a smaller window to the south, above which is a circular window. This last is the only one visible from the interior, as the other two are blocked by the gallery and stairway. The two westernmost of the central block of pews display, at the ends opening into the middle aisle, figures of the lion and unicorn bearing shields emblazoned with the City arms, and the high Corporation pews at the extreme west, close to the gallery, are dominated by two elegantly wrought sword-rests. Against the north and south wall stands a row of high pews, the upper parts of which are well carved, and over the door-case at the north-west appears another gilded pelican with extended wings.

Against the eastern wall, obstructing the view of the south-east window, is a large monument to Sir Patience Ward, a zealous Whig, who was elected to the mayoralty in 1680, and was senior member for the City of London in the Convention Parliament of 1688-89. He died on July 10th, 1696.

Not far from this memorial, against the south wall of the chancel, is a highly ornate monument to Edward Sherwood, of the parish of St. Lawrence Poultney, who died in January, 1690.

St. Mary Abchurch is built of red brick with Portland stone

dressings. The tower consists of four storeys, the first of which displays a round-headed door, surmounted by a square cornice; the second, a round-headed window; the third, a circular window; and the fourth, a round-headed window with louvres. The tower is finished by a cornice, and upon it is placed a cupola, above which are a lantern and lead-covered spire, terminated by a ball and vane. The height to the summit of the spire is about 140 feet.

St Mary the Virgin Aldermanbury

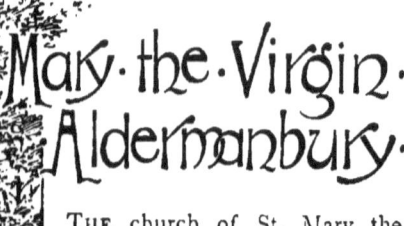

THE church of St. Mary the Virgin, Aldermanbury, is situated in the thoroughfare of that name, to the north-east of Love Lane. This church, the patronage of which was originally in the hands of the Dean and Chapter of St. Paul's, was appropriated by them in 1332 to the neighbouring Hospital of St. Mary the Virgin, then newly founded by William Elsing. After the surrender of that establishment to Henry VIII. the advowson was granted to the parishioners, by whom the vicar is still appointed.

In the old church were buried a considerable number of citizens of repute, and also two persons who, though of a less exalted rank, are far more interesting to posterity, namely, Henry Condell and John Heminge, the fellow-actors of Shakespeare, whom he remembered in his will, and the editors of the folio of 1623, which constitutes the first collected edition of his plays.

Milton's second wife, Katherine Woodcocke, was a parishioner of St. Mary, Aldermanbury. His marriage with her on November 12th, 1656, is entered in the register.

The celebrated Presbyterian divine, and joint-author of "Smectymnuus," Edmund Calamy, was appointed minister of St. Mary, Aldermanbury, in 1639, and remained there all through the Civil

St. Mary the Virgin, Aldermanbury.

War and the Commonwealth. He warmly favoured the Restoration of Charles II., and in acknowledgment of his services was offered the bishopric of Coventry and Lichfield. This he declined, and after the passing of the Act of Uniformity he decided to throw in his lot with the Nonconformists, and gave up his living, which the parishioners then offered to Tillotson, who, however, refused it. Calamy still continued to reside in the parish, and to attend the church. He died at the age of sixty-six on October 29th, 1666, from the shock, it is said, produced on his mind by the devastation wrought by the Great Fire, and was buried beneath the ruined edifice with which he had been so long connected, and where almost a quarter of a century earlier the body of his wife had been laid.

One of his sons, Dr. Benjamin Calamy, was minister of St. Mary, Aldermanbury, from 1677 to 1683, when he obtained the benefice of St. Lawrence Jewry. Unlike his father, he was a zealous High Churchman. He had a great reputation as a preacher, and would probably have obtained high preferment had his life been prolonged. He died in 1686, and was buried at St. Lawrence Jewry. His funeral sermon was preached by Sherlock.

Dr. Edmund Calamy, a grandson of the distinguished Presbyterian, and himself a leading Nonconformist minister, was buried at St. Mary, Aldermanbury, on June 9th, 1732. He was a voluminous author, and his biographies of the ministers ejected in consequence of the Act of Uniformity and "Historical Account" of his own life contain much interesting matter.

The present church of St. Mary, Aldermanbury, was completed by Wren in 1677. It is built of stone. It measures internally 72 feet in length, 45 feet in breadth, and 38 feet in height, and includes two side-aisles, each of which is divided from the main body by six Composite columns. The south wall contains four large windows to the east of the south-west doorway, a small circular window over the doorway, and another large window still further west. The north wall is pierced with corresponding windows, except that there is no window at the extreme northwest. The easternmost window in this wall, being blocked by the present position of the organ, has been boarded over. The eastern wall has a central window, and two small circular windows, and at the west are two small windows. The ceiling of the nave is arched; in the space between the three eastern and the three western columns it is pierced on either side, a little above its junction with the entablature, by a semicircular window. The ceilings of the aisles are flat.

The church has been excessively re-arranged and modernized, and now presents anything but a venerable aspect. The pulpit, reredos, and seats are all new, and the west gallery has been removed, and the organ transferred to the north of the chancel, thereby utterly concealing, as has been already pointed out, one of the handsome windows. The font stands at the south-west. The royal arms, which are brightly gilded, and were originally placed over the altar-piece, are now affixed to the west wall.

Against the west part of the north wall is a large white marble monument, displaying two busts in niches, in memory of two brothers, Richard and John Chandler, who died in 1691 and 1686 respectively. On the east wall, south of the altar, is a beautiful piece of sculpture in white marble, the work of an Italian artist, representing a female figure seated on a gun, while above her rises a broken column. This is the memorial of Lieutenant John Smith, a gallant young naval officer, who was

St. Mary the Virgin, Aldermanbury.

drowned off Staten Island, at the age of twenty-four, on September 7th, 1782.

The remains of Judge Jeffreys, which had been interred in the Tower after his death there on April 19th, 1689, were removed to St. Mary, Aldermanbury, and deposited in a vault beneath the communion-table, on November 2nd, 1693. While Common Serjeant and Recorder of the City of London, Jeffreys had been a prominent inhabitant of the parish. His son, the second and last Baron Jeffreys, and several others of his children, were also buried here.

Externally St. Mary, Aldermanbury, is an imposing structure, and from the south and east an uninterrupted view of it is gained. The east front possesses a handsome cornice and pediment, and is embellished with large carved scrolls at the sides of the central window. Over the entrance doorway at the south-west may be noticed a carving of the Virgin and Child. The tower rises at the west; it is completed by a cornice and a pierced parapet, the angles of which carry pedestals. Upon the tower is placed a square turret in two stages, the lower containing clock-faces, and the upper one being pierced with large circular-headed openings; and the whole is concluded by a concave roof tapering to a point, and crowned by a finial and vane. The height is about 90 feet.

To the south of the church is a pleasant churchyard, which is furnished with seats, and opened to the public for several hours daily. A drinking-fountain has been erected between the churchyard rails. It is thus inscribed:

" November 1890.
The gift of Robert Rogers Esq[ro]
Deputy of the Ward to the Parish of
St. Mary the Virgin, Aldermanbury."

ST. MARY ALDERMARY

THE church of St. Mary Aldermary is situated on the north side of Queen Victoria Street, at the corner of Bow Lane. It dates from a very remote period, being, as Stow explains, "called Aldemarie church, because the same was very old, and elder than any church of St. Marie in the City." Sir Henry Keble, grocer, Lord Mayor in 1510, commenced to rebuild it in that year, and dying in 1518, before the work was finished, bequeathed £1,000 towards its completion.

An earlier benefactor was Richard Chaucer, vintner, who "gave to that church," Stow tells us, "his tenement and tavern, with the appurtenance, in the Royal Street, the corner of Kerion Lane, and was there buried 1348." Stow calls this Richard Chaucer "father to Geffrey Chaucer the poet, as may be supposed." But this is mere conjecture, as nothing certain is known with regard to Chaucer's parentage.

It was at St. Mary Aldermary that Milton was married to his third wife, Elizabeth Minshull, on February 24th, 1663.

Little more than a century after its erection the steeple had become "greatly decayed and perished;" and two parishioners, William Rodoway and Richard Pierson, both of whom died in the year 1626, bequeathed respectively £300 and 200 marks towards the expenses of its reconstruction. The new steeple was completed three years afterwards at a cost of £1,000, and in 1632 the body of the church was extensively repaired by the parishioners.

St. Mary Aldermary.

In 1666 the church was destroyed by the Great Fire, with the exception of the tower, which escaped the ravages of the flames.

The Great Fire also consumed the church of St. Thomas the Apostle in Knightrider Street, which was not rebuilt, its parish being united with that of St. Mary Aldermary.

The advowson of the rectory of St. Mary Aldermary originally belonged to the prior and chapter of Canterbury, but Archbishop Arundel, in the year 1400, gave them the advowson of the living of Westwell, in Kent, in exchange for it; and the patronage has ever since remained in the hands of the primate. One of the rectors of St. Mary Aldermary, Henry Gold, came to a tragic end, being executed at Tyburn in 1534, together with Elizabeth Barton, "the Holy Maid of Kent," two monks, and two friars. He was buried in the church. The rectory of St. Thomas the Apostle has been from time immemorial in the gift of the Dean and Chapter of St. Paul's.

The present church of St. Mary Aldermary was built by Wren in 1681 and 1682. A legacy of £5,000 had been left by a Mr. Henry Rogers for the rebuilding of a church, and his widow and executrix consented to apply it for the reconstruction of St. Mary Aldermary; she stipulated, however, that the new church should be an exact imitation of Keble's church, and the architect was thus compelled to follow a system widely differing from his ordinary methods, and although some of its details are somewhat incorrect, he has reproduced a handsome edifice in the Tudor style of architecture.

St. Mary Aldermary consists of a nave, chancel, and two side-aisles, which are separated from the central portion by clustered columns and very slightly pointed arches. It measures 100 feet in length, 63 feet in breadth, and about 45 feet in height. The ceilings both of the nave and aisles are conspicuous for their elaborate fan-groining, and the deeply-indented circular panels of the ceiling of the nave, each ornamented at its centre with a flower, are very happily designed and executed. The spandrels of the arches are adorned with foliage, and shields containing the arms of the archiepiscopal see of Canterbury, and those of Henry Rogers. The north side of the chancel is prolonged to a greater extent than the south side, which gives the church rather a curious appearance. The large east and west windows still retain the old stained glass, and in the former are emblazoned the arms of Henry Rogers. These windows are constructed in two heights, and divided into five lights.

St. Mary Aldermary was very much restored in 1876-7, so that its present aspect is new rather than venerable. There is a new screen of carved oak at the west, dividing the church from the lobby; there are new seats and new stalls; the organ has been removed from its old western position and re-erected at the north of the chancel. A new pavement covers the floor, and new stained glass has been inserted in the side windows. A new reredos has likewise been substituted for the old altar-piece presented by Dame Jane Smith, widow of Alderman Sir John Smith, who was sheriff in 1669, and was interred in the church in 1673. The old pulpit has, however, been preserved, and also the old font, placed in the lobby at the extreme north-west, which bears a Latin inscription stating it to have been given by Dutton Seaman, a parishioner, in 1682.

The monuments are of no particular interest. On a black marble tablet over the west door is a Latin inscription recording the munificence of Henry Rogers.

The tower, though not actually destroyed in the Fire, was so

St. Mary Aldermary.

much injured that it required considerable repair, and the upper portion was entirely rebuilt about the year 1701. It contains four storeys, with an open parapet above, and is surmounted by four pinnacles. The total height to the top of the pinnacles is 135 feet. This square stone tower has a most graceful appearance as seen from Queen Victoria Street, and forms an agreeable relief to the monotonous and uninteresting buildings which predominate in that thoroughfare. Like all other buildings, the church of St. Mary Aldermary has no doubt its faults, but, taking it as a whole, one cannot fail to concur in the opinion of Newcourt, that it was " very nobly rebuilt."

In 1835, on the demolition of some houses in Watling Street, a crypt was discovered, 50 feet long by 10 feet wide, having five pointed arches on each side. In all probability this crypt belonged to the church built by Keble.

In 1874 the church of St. Antholin, which was situated at the south-west corner of Size Lane, at the junction of Watling Street and Budge Row, was pulled down, and the benefice, a rectory in the gift of the Dean and Chapter of St. Paul's, was united with that of St. Mary Aldermary. After the Fire, the church of St. John the Baptist upon Walbrook, so called from its position on the bank of that stream, was not rebuilt, and the rectory was united with that of St. Antholin. The patronage of St. John the Baptist was originally in the hands of the Dean and Chapter of St. Paul's, who about the year 1273 bestowed it upon the prioress and convent of St. Helen's, Bishopsgate. Since the dissolution of monasteries it has been retained by the Crown. Thus the church of St. Mary Aldermary now serves for four parishes, *i.e.*, its original parish, that of St. Thomas the Apostle, that of St. Antholin, and that of St. John the Baptist.

St. Antholin, or St. Antling, as the name was commonly pronounced, is a corruption of St. Anthony, the church being dedicated to that famous saint. Stow describes St. Antholin's as being in his time a "fair parish church," and tells us that it was "re-edified" by Thomas Knowles, grocer, twice Lord Mayor, in 1399 and 1410, and Thomas Knowles, his son, both of whom were there buried. Henry Colet, mercer, twice Lord Mayor, in 1486 and 1495, the father of the illustrious Dean Colet, was a great benefactor to St. Antholin's. He was not buried there; but, says Stow, "the pictures of him, his wife, ten sons, and ten daughters, remain in the glass window on the north side of the church." A later benefactor was Sir William Craven, Lord Mayor in 1610, the father of the Earl of Craven, who, though he afterwards resided in the parish of St. Andrew Undershaft, had his shop in that of St. Antholin. Besides gifts for the poor, Sir William contributed towards the endowment of the St. Antholin Lectures, which had been first instituted in 1559, were widely celebrated and numerously attended during the religious struggles of the seventeenth century, and are now delivered daily at St. Mary Aldermary, the service lasting from 1.15 p.m. to 2 p.m. Sir William Craven also subscribed liberally towards the reparation of the church in 1616.

St. Antholin's perished in the Great Fire, and was rebuilt by Wren in 1682-3. The beautiful stone spire was considered to rank amongst the greatest of Sir Christopher's achievements, and its destruction has deprived the City of one of its most striking ornaments. The site of the church is marked by a memorial, on which is a representation in fresco of the demolished edifice.

The church of St. John the Baptist appears to have been by no means rich in associations. It was rebuilt about 1412, and re-

St. Mary Aldermary.

paired in 1621. A memorial, surmounted by a small cross, which stands on the north side of Cloak Lane, near the east corner, still serves to remind us of the former existence of this church. The inscription is as follows :

> "Sacred
> To the memory of the
> dead
> Interred in the ancient church and churchyard
> of St. John the Baptist
> upon Walbrook
> during four centuries.
> The formation of the District Railway
> having necessitated the destruction of
> the greater part of the
> churchyard,
> All the human remains contained therein
> were carefully collected and reinterred in a
> vault
> Beneath this monument
> A.D. 1884."

THE church of St. Mary-at-Hill stands between the street or lane of that name and Love Lane; having its east front in the former, and its west front in the latter thoroughfare. It is so called from its position on the sloping ground which ascends from Billingsgate to Eastcheap.

The living is a rectory, the patronage of which appears to have been in private hands till the reign of Charles I., when the advowson was purchased by the parishioners, in whose possession it has ever since remained.

The sacred edifice was thoroughly renovated in 1616 at the cost of the parishioners, who afterwards, with highly commendable zeal, repaired it periodically every third or fourth year. The body of the church was destroyed in the Great Fire, and rebuilt by Wren but the old stone tower escaped the flames, and remained standing till 1780, when, being considered insecure, it was pulled down and replaced by the existing brick tower, an extremely commonplace appendage, quite unworthy of the church.

The church of St. Andrew Hubbard, which was probably so called in memory of a rebuilder or repairer named Hubert, stood in Love Lane near the west end of the church of St. Mary-at-Hill. It was not rebuilt after the Fire, and its parish was united with that of St. Mary. The rectory of St. Andrew Hubbard was in the gift of John, Earl of Pembroke, who was killed at a tourna-

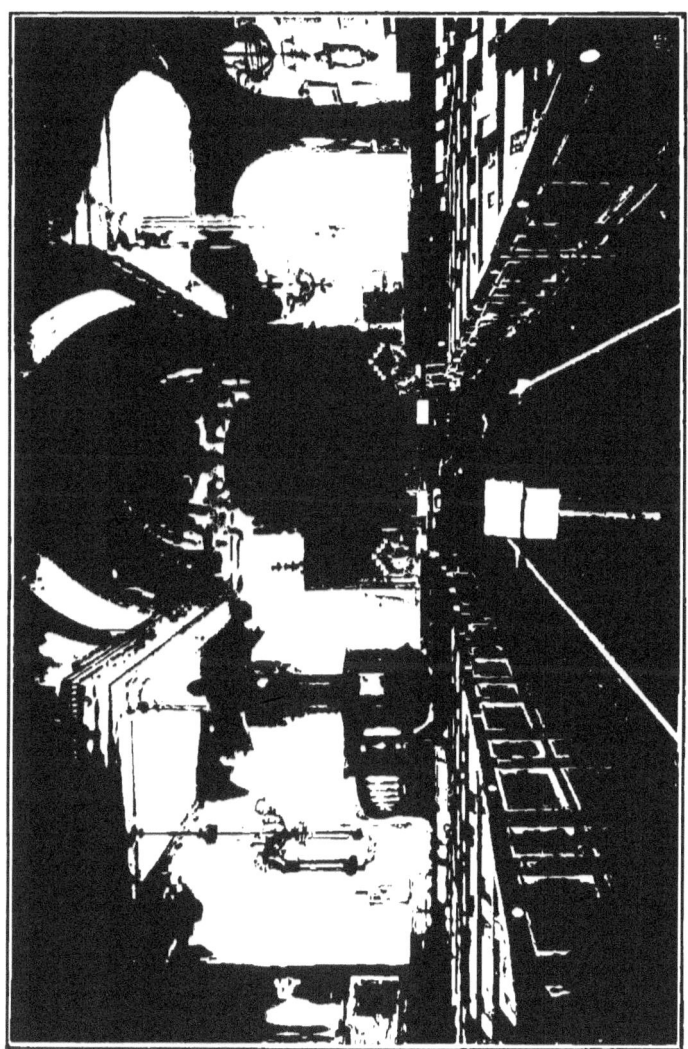

ST. MARY-AT-HILL.

St. Mary-at-Hill.

ment at Woodstock in 1389, and the advowson afterwards passed into the possession of the Talbots, Earls of Shrewsbury. In 1659 the Earl of Northumberland presented, and the patronage remained till recently in the Percy family. The present patron is Sir Henry Peck.

The body of the church of St. Mary-at-Hill was commenced by Wren in 1672, and completed in 1677. It measures 96 feet in length and 60 feet in breadth, and is crowned by a cupola, which attains the height of 38 feet. The cupola is divided into panels, which are ornamented with fretwork, and is lighted from the centre by a circular lantern. It is supported by four Doric columns, which form two side-aisles. The central ceiling is arched both to the east and west of the cupola, and the ceiling of each aisle is elevated into an arch in the space between the columns, the appearance of the roof being thus rendered cruciform. To the side walls are attached pilasters, by means of which the entablatures are carried on to the columns. The light is admitted at the east by two windows, one on each side of the altar-piece, neither of which is stained, but the north and south walls each possess a large central stained glass window, with a smaller plain window to the west of it. In the west wall are two side windows, which correspond to those at the east, but are hidden by the organ-gallery.

The church is abundantly adorned with carving, but this is all of a much later date than the fabric, having been executed by Mr. W. Gibbs Rogers in 1848-9, when the church was remodelled. The western gallery, which contains a fine organ by Hill, is excellently carved, and the pulpit, which is placed on the north side, is surmounted by a large sounding-board, which is most lavishly bedecked with carved foliage. The rector's pew and reading-desk are conspicuous for their carved open tracery, and display the lion and unicorn, each bearing a shield carved with the legend, "V. R. 1849." The Corporation pews, situated towards the west, one to the north, and the other to the south, of the middle aisle, are dominated by four handsome sword-rests.

Affixed to the east wall, a little to the south of the communion table, is an extremely simple tablet thus inscribed :

"Within the Communion Rails lies interred the body of the Rev. John Brand, 22 years and 6 months the faithful Rector of this and the united parish of St. Andrew Hubbard. He was also Perpetual Curate of Cramlington in the County of Northumberland; and he was Fellow and Secretary of the Society of Antiquaries of London. He died 11th September, 1806, in the 63rd year of his age. His affectionate Aunt, Mrs. Ann Wheatley, of Newcastle-upon-Tyne, has erected this monument to his memory."

Brand, whose name will ever be held in veneration by all lovers of the folk-lore and ancient customs of our country, was born in the county of Durham on August 19th, 1744. He first published his "Observations on Popular Antiquities" in 1777; he was elected Secretary of the Society of Antiquaries in 1784, the year in which he became rector of St. Mary-at-Hill, and he continued to hold that office till his death, being regularly re-elected every year.

Edward Young, the poet, was married on May 27th, 1731, at St. Mary-at-Hill, to Lady Elizabeth Lee, daughter of the Earl of Lichfield, and widow of Colonel Lee.

The church of St. Mary-at-Hill, after having remained closed for two years, during which period 3,000 bodies had been removed from beneath the church and re-interred at Norwood Cemetery, and

St. Mary-at-Hill.

the structure had been repaired and fitted with the electric light, was reopened on Friday, February 23rd, 1894. The opening service was attended by the Lord Mayor and Sheriffs in state, by Sir Reginald Hanson, Bart., M.P. for the City of London, Alderman of Billingsgate Ward, in which the church is situated, and by the representatives of the ward in the Common Council. The present rector is the Rev. W. Carlile, who is widely known on account of his work in connection with the Church Army, of which he is the founder and chief director. He has established at the rectory adjoining the church a "City Samaritan Office," which constitutes, in his own words, "A free club conducted by evangelists of the Church Army, to aid destitute but deserving clerks, warehousemen, and hopeless, starving outcasts."

Some fifteen years ago a scheme was mooted to demolish St. Mary-at-Hill for the purposes of a railway extension, and the church was only saved from destruction by the strenuous and laudable efforts of "The City Church and Churchyard Protection Society." But now that it has been launched upon a new and active career of usefulness, we may reasonably hope that many years will elapse before we hear of any fresh proposition threatening the existence of this beautiful sacred building.

St Mary-le-Bow.

THE music of Bow Bells rang in the ear of Whittington prophetic of his future greatness, and the fact of having been born within the sound of their melody constitutes a person a Cockney.

There is no church in London whose name is more familiar than that of St. Mary-le-Bow, commonly called Bow Church, which stands, as almost everybody knows, on the south side of Cheapside. It was anciently designated "New Marie" church, in distinction to the older foundation of St. Mary Aldermary, the earliest church in the city dedicated to the Virgin, out of the parish of which that of St. Mary-le-Bow was taken. It acquired the name of "Bow," or, in a Latin form, "De Arcubus," from its stone "bows" or arches, as Stow tells us, though he gives two different versions of their position and purpose. In the first edition of his "Survey" he explains that the church was "called De Arcubus of the stone arches or bowes on the top of the steeple or bell-tower thereof, which arching was as well on the old steeple as on the new, for no other part of the church seemeth to have been arched at any time." In his second edition, however, he states that it received its appellation, "in the reign of William Conqueror, being the first in this city built on arches of stone."

From the Latin title, "De Arcubus," is derived the name of the Court of Arches, which before the Great Fire held its sittings at

St. Mary-le-Bow.

St. Mary-le-Bow. This church was selected for the location of the Archbishop of Canterbury's court, as being one of the thirteen "peculiars" of the archbishop in the City of London.

Although the connection of St. Mary-le-Bow with the ecclesiastical courts has long ceased, it still enjoys the distinction of being used for the confirmation of the election of bishops.

"This church," observes Stow, "for divers accidents happening there, hath been made more famous than any other parish church of the whole city or suburbs." He then proceeds to give us details of these calamities. In the year 1090, it seems, "by tempest of wind," the roof was "overturned, wherewith some persons were slain." In 1196 "William Fitzosbert, a seditious tailor, took the steeple of Bow, and fortified it with munitions and victuals;" and the authorities, unable apparently to devise any other method of dislodging him, resorted to the very drastic expedient of setting fire to it. In 1271 "a great part of the steeple of Bow fell down, and slew many people, men and women." Not long afterwards, in 1284, one citizen having wounded another fled for refuge into the church, but "certain evil persons," friends of the injured party, got in during the night and killed him; in consequence of which sixteen men were hanged, and "a certain woman, named Alice, that was the chief causer of the said mischief, was burnt," and the church itself was interdicted, the door and windows being "stopped up with thorns."

The steeple, after its collapse, "was by little and little re-edified, and new built up, at the least so much as was fallen down, many men giving sums of money to the furtherance thereof." Among the contributors was Robert Harding, goldsmith, sheriff in 1478, who gave £40, and at length in the year 1512 the work of rebuilding the steeple, which had been so long in hand, was accomplished. A few years later, "the arches or bowes thereupon, with the lanthorns, five in number, to wit, one at each corner, and one on the top in the middle upon the arches, were also finished of stone brought from Caen in Normandy." These "lanthorns" were not merely ornamental, but were placed on the steeple with a very practical object, as Stow has not omitted to remind us:

"It appeareth that the lanthorns on the top of this steeple were meant to have been glazed, and lights in them placed nightly in the winter, whereby travellers to the city might have the better sight thereof, and not to miss of their ways."

In 1469 the Common Council ordained "that the Bow Bell should be nightly rung at nine of the clock," but the practice of ringing the curfew at this church had existed long before, and is referred to more than a century earlier. In 1472 John Donne, mercer, left by his will to the rector and churchwardens two tenements towards the bell's maintenance. By the time the steeple was completed, the number of bells amounted to five, the largest of which is said to have been presented by William Copland, tailor, the king's merchant, one of the churchwardens 1515-16, and to have been first rung as a knell at his funeral.

Among the civic dignitaries buried at St. Mary-le-Bow was Nicholas Alwine, Lord Mayor in 1499, whose name is familiar to readers of "The Last of the Barons."

The church was thoroughly repaired in 1620, but was totally destroyed by the Great Fire of 1666, which also consumed the neighbouring churches of St. Pancras, Soper Lane, and All Hallows, Honey Lane, which were neither of them rebuilt, their parishes being united to that of St. Mary-le-Bow.

St. Pancras, Soper Lane, which was one of the thirteen "peculiars" of the Archbishop of Canterbury, was dedicated to a

Phrygian saint, said to have been of noble family, who was put to death by the Emperor Diocletian. The site of Soper Lane was after the Fire occupied by Queen Street, so called in honour of Queen Catherine of Braganza, but the name of Needlers' Lane, in which St. Pancras actually stood, was altered into Pancras Lane in memory of the vanished church, and on its north side may yet be observed a portion of the old burial ground, situated a little to the west of that of St. Benet Sherehog.

All Hallows, Honey Lane, was slightly north of Cheapside. Its site after the Fire formed part of the Honey Lane Market, which existed till 1835, when the ground was utilized for the City of London School, now transferred to more spacious buildings on the Thames Embankment. Honey Lane, says Stow quaintly, was "so called, not of sweetness thereof, being very narrow, and somewhat dark, but rather of often washing and sweeping to keep it clean." John Norman, Lord Mayor in 1453, the first chief magistrate who went to Westminster by water, instead of riding, as had been hitherto the custom, was buried at All Hallows.

The advowson of the rectory of All Hallows, Honey Lane, belonged to Thomas Knoles, who was Lord Mayor both in 1399 and in 1410. He was a grocer, and from him or his descendants it passed some time in the fifteenth century into the hands of the Grocers' Company, who have ever since been the patrons. Amongst the rectors was one martyr, Thomas Garrard, or Garret, who was presented to the living in 1537, and suffered at the stake in Smithfield for his religious opinions towards the close of 1540.

The rebuilding of St. Mary-le-Bow was commenced by Wren in 1671, but the work was not finally completed till 1680. The cost was £15,400, a larger amount by over £3,000 than was expended on any other of Wren's parish churches. Towards this sum £2,000 was contributed by Lady Williamson, whose benefactions to St. Dunstan's in the East and St. Paul's Cathedral have already been noticed. Her liberality to Bow Church is commemorated by a tablet affixed to the north wall over the vestry-room door, with the following inscription :

" Dame Dyonis Williamson of Hale's Hall in the county of Norfolk gave to the inhabitants of this Parish £2,000 towards the rebuilding and splendid finishing this church and steeple, and furnishing the same with bells, etc.—which was demolished by the late dreadful Fire, Anno 1666."

Appended are the names of George Smallwood, rector, and the trustees.

In constructing this church Wren devoted more particular attention to the steeple than to the interior. The steeple of St. Mary-le-Bow, which is built of Portland stone, is the most elaborate of all those erected by Sir Christopher, and involved an expenditure of £7,388, almost one half of the total cost of the edifice. It stands at the north-west angle of the church, with which it is connected by a lobby, and measures at the base 32 feet square. The tower contains three storeys, of which the highest, or belfry, stage is ornamented with Ionic pilasters. The belfry is surmounted by a cornice and balustrade, from the angles of which rise tall finials, each supporting a vase. Upon the tower is placed a circular dome, on which rests a stone cylinder, which supports the lantern and spire. The cylinder is surrounded by a beautiful circular peristyle, consisting of twelve Corinthian columns, which constitutes the most charming feature of the steeple ; it terminates in a dome beneath the lantern, above which rises the spire, culminating in a weather-vane in the form of a dragon, the City emblem. The height of the tower at the top of the belfry is about 122 feet, and the total altitude of the steeple to the top of the dragon is 221 feet 9 inches—a height only exceeded amongst Wren's church steeples by that of St. Bride, which stands, however, on much lower ground, and therefore does not appear so lofty as that of St. Mary-le-Bow.

The steeple was repaired in the eighteenth century by Sir William Staines, and again in 1820 by Mr. George Gwilt, who found it necessary to rebuild 42 feet of the spire. At the same time the original Portland stone columns and entablatures of the lantern stage, having become decayed, were replaced by new ones of red granite. The dragon was also taken down and regilded. It measures 8 feet 10 inches in length, and carries on each wing an ornate cross of gilt copper.

The belfry was constructed to hold twelve bells, but not more than eight were at first hung there. In 1758 seven of the bells were recast, and two trebles added, and the ten thus formed were first rung on June 4th, 1762, in honour of King George III.'s birthday. During the late restoration a further addition of two bells was made, so that the full number of twelve has now been attained.

Visitors to Bow Church can hardly fail to notice affixed to the north face of the tower at its second storey, beneath the projecting clock, a balcony commanding a view of Cheapside. This balcony carries back our thoughts to the days when tournaments were held in "Cheape," for it was erected by Wren in memory of the "sild or shed" on the north side of the old church, which Edward III., after the collapse of a temporary wooden structure in 1331, "caused to be made, and to be strongly built of stone," as Stow tells us, "for himself, the queen, and other estates to stand in, there to behold the joustings and other shows at their pleasures." Long after the street below had ceased to be the scene of the contests of chivalry, "the kings of England and other great estates, as well of foreign countries repairing to this realm, as inhabitants of the same," still "repaired to this place, therein to behold the shows of this city passing through West Cheape."

Although the especial merit and attraction of St. Mary-le-Bow are to be found in its steeple, the interior of the church is nevertheless striking and handsome. It measures 65 feet in length and 63 feet in breadth, so that it is almost square, and the height from the pavement to the ceiling is 38 feet. The two side-aisles are separated from the main body of the church by Corinthian columns, which, with their entablature, support an arched ceiling, divided into panels and adorned with foliage and rosettes. The church possesses three windows at the east, with three circular lights above them, three windows at the west, and two large windows in the south wall, besides smaller and clerestory windows. The altar-piece, which was set up in 1706, is richly gilded, and is enclosed by Corinthian pilasters with entablature surmounted by a pediment. The pulpit, which stands on the north side, is of carved oak, and the marble font at the west end was presented by Francis Dashwood in 1675. The oak door-case at the north-west, opening into the vestibule, is very handsomely carved, and on the wall above are placed the royal arms.

The royal arms were formerly affixed to the front of the north gallery, but, as the galleries were taken away when the church was restored, they were transferred to their present position. A new organ was at the same time procured, and erected at the north of the chancel, and the windows were filled with stained glass representing scriptural subjects, which is well executed, and allows free admittance to the light.

A brass tablet on the north wall gives the particulars of the restoration, and states that a total sum of £7,572 was expended on the church between the years 1878 and 1882.

Against the west wall are three large memorials of the dead; namely, a monument with bust in memory of James Cart, who died in 1706, and six of his children; a monument to Colonel Charles Bainton, who died in 1712, and Elizabeth, his wife, who died in 1719, displaying both their busts in relief; and a sarcophagus, which is supported by a cherub, and an allegorical figure representing Faith, in memory of Bishop Newton. In a medallion on the sarcophagus is a bust of the bishop, beside which a female, apparently his widow, is seated in an attitude of sorrow.

Thomas Newton, who was born at Lichfield in 1704, obtained the rectory of St. Mary-le-Bow in 1744, through the influence of William Pulteney, Earl of Bath, the famous politician, who interested himself warmly on his behalf. In 1757 he was created Dean of Salisbury, in 1761 Bishop of Bristol, and in 1768 Dean of St. Paul's. He acquired considerable celebrity in the literary world as the editor of Milton, whose "Paradise Lost," with annotations, he first published in 1749. Encouraged by the favourable reception accorded to his work, he brought out several subsequent editions of the great poet. He was also the author of three volumes of "Dissertations on the Prophecies," the first of which appeared in 1754, and the last in 1758.

The memorials to Cart and Bainton appear to have been always at the west end of the church, but Newton's monument, which is from the chisel of Thomas Banks, was originally placed on the south side of the communion table.

To the south wall of the chancel is affixed a brass tablet, commemorating a much more recent rector, the Rev. Marshall Hall

Vine, who died at the age of seventy-five, on June 15th, 1887, after holding the living for thirty-five years.

Beneath the church, and supporting it, still remains an old Norman crypt, which in all probability formed a part of the building erected in the time of William the Conqueror. It consists of three aisles formed by massive columns, and extends under almost the whole of the church.

In 1876 the parish of All Hallows, Bread Street, was united with that of St. Mary-le-Bow, and the church itself was pulled down towards the close of the following year. The old church had been destroyed in the Great Fire, and the edifice lately demolished was built by Wren between the years 1680-1684. It was, to use Strype's words, "without any pillars, but very decent," and its tower, crowned by four tall pinnacles, rose to a height of about 104 feet.

The neighbouring church of St. John the Evangelist was not rebuilt after the Fire, its parish being united to that of All Hallows, Bread Street. A portion of its old burying-ground, which still remains at the corner of Friday Street and Watling Street, is beautifully planted with shrubs, and forms quite an oasis in the midst of the sombre warehouses.

All Hallows, Bread Street, was one of the "peculiars" of the Archbishop of Canterbury. Laurence Saunders, the martyr, was appointed rector by Archbishop Cranmer in March, 1553. He was also incumbent of Church Langton, in Leicestershire. The zeal with which, after the accession of Queen Mary, he preached against Popery in both his churches, caused him to be arrested, and, after an imprisonment of fifteen months, he was burnt at Coventry on February 8th, 1555.

With All Hallows is indissolubly linked the immortal name of

John Milton, who was born in Bread Street, and baptized in the old church on December 20th, 1608.

On the east side of Bread Street, just south of Watling Street, marking the spot formerly occupied by the church, there has been let into the wall a bust of Milton, beneath which is this inscription:

> "Milton
> Born in Bread Street
> 1608
> Baptized in Church of
> All Hallows
> Which stood here ante
> 1878."

On the west wall of St. Mary-le-Bow, facing Bow Churchyard is a tablet thus inscribed:

> "Three Poets in three distant Ages born,
> Greece, Italy, and England did adorn;
> The First in Loftiness of Thought surpasst,
> The Next in Majesty—in both the Last;
> The force of Nature could no further go:
> To make a Third she joined the former Two.
>
> John Milton
> was Born in Bread Street on Friday the 9th day of December 1608, and was Baptised in the Parish Church of All Hallows Bread Street on Tuesday the 20th day of December 1608.
> This Tablet was placed on the Church of All Hallows Bread Street Early in the 19th century, as a Memorial of the Event Therein recorded, and was removed in the year 1876—when that Church was pulled down and the Parish united for Ecclesiastica Purposes with the Parish of St. Mary-Le-Bow."

ST. MICHAEL BASSISHAW.

THE church of St. Michael Bassishaw stands on the west side of Basinghall Street, a little to the north of the Guildhall Library. Its parish is identical with the ward of Bassishaw or Basinghall; and the church, ward, and street still perpetuate the name of the ancient family of the Basings, once one of the most important in the City of London.

St. Michael's, which had been rebuilt in the fifteenth century, was destroyed in the Great Fire. It was again rebuilt by Wren, with brick walls and a stone tower, between the years 1676 and 1679.

The present church measures internally 70 feet in length, 50 feet in breadth, and 42 feet in height; it includes two side-aisles, which are separated from the nave by Corinthian columns. The ceiling is divided into panels, and is pierced with openings to admit the light. In the centre of the east wall there is a very large niche for a window; but this is blocked up, with the exception of a small portion at the top. On each side of it is a small circular window. The north and south walls each contain three spacious windows, and to the west of these a small circular window. The walls are panelled to the height of about eight feet. The pulpit and door-cases are handsome, and the altar-piece displays four Corinthian pilasters, with entablature and pediment.

The only noticeable monument is an elegant tablet, with Latin

St. Michael Bassishaw.

inscription, to Dr. Thomas Wharton, a physician, who covered himself with glory by his devoted labours during the Plague of 1665. He died in 1673 at the age of fifty-nine.

The tower is placed at the west. It contains four storeys, and is concluded by a cornice and a parapet, the angles of which are ornamented with pineapples. Above it is a lead-covered, octagonal lantern in two stages, surmounted by a short spire culminating in a ball, finial, and vane. The total altitude of the steeple is 140 feet.

The church, which is much out of repair, is now closed, and as a commission, bearing date December 23rd, 1893, has been issued by the Bishop of London, " to inquire into and report upon the expediency of" a proposition for uniting the rectory of St. Michael Bassishaw with that of St. Lawrence Jewry and St. Mary Magdalene, Milk Street, it will probably ere long be a thing of the past.

The rectory of St. Michael Bassishaw is in the gift of the Dean and Chapter of St. Paul's.

ST. MICHAEL CORNHILL

The rectory of St. Michael's, Cornhill, is in the gift of the Company of Drapers, who obtained it early in the sixteenth century from the abbot and convent of Evesham, its former patrons. Stow tells us that the old church was "fair and beautiful," and that a new steeple was added to it in 1421. In the early part of the seventeenth century it was several times repaired, and the parishioners seem to have spared no expense to render the sacred edifice as magnificent as possible. The body of the church was destroyed in the Great Fire of 1666, and was rebuilt by Wren in 1672. The tower also was much injured, and having been pulled down in 1722, was replaced by the present tower, which was likewise erected from the designs of Wren.

St. Michael's, Cornhill, measures 87 feet in length, by 60 feet in breadth, and the height from the pavement to the ceiling is 35 feet. It contains two aisles divided from the nave by Doric columns. The ceiling is groined. The appearance of the church, which was originally in the Italian style, was totally transformed by the alterations of 1858-60, executed by the late Sir Gilbert Scott, and at present it conveys the impression of a nineteenth century imitation of mediævalism; which is yet further heightened by the pretentious, but feeble, Gothic porch appended at the north-west, facing Cornhill, in 1857. The east window is circular, and that at the west oblong; these, and the windows of the side walls and clerestory are filled with very brightly stained glass, which somewhat obstructs the light. The organ is placed on the north of the chancel, and the pulpit is near the south wall. The old pews were removed during the alterations, and lower seats substituted. These are ornamented with excellent carvings of foliage and scriptural emblems, by the late Mr. Thomas Rogers, who executed his work with great skill and the most painstaking accuracy, even in the minutest details. On the ends of the seats in the middle aisle are displayed on small shields various coats of arms, including the royal arms, the arms of the City of London, the arms of the Drapers', Merchant Taylors', and Clothworkers' Companies, and those of various individuals connected with the church and parish.

To the west of the ordinary seats, and separated from them, are placed the high-backed pews of the churchwardens, which are also finely carved by Rogers. The font, which bears the inscription, "Donum Jacobi Paul, Arm^{ri} 1672," is located in a baptistery at the west beneath the tower, and behind it, close to the wall, standing on a pedestal, is a carved representation of a pelican, gilded over, which is attributed to Grinling Gibbons. To the sides of the tower arch are affixed brass tablets, recording the dates and particulars of various repairs to the church. Amongst them is one which gives the following list of benefactors to the rebuilding after the Great Fire:

"Sir John Langham £500
Sir John Mounson 20
Sir John Cutler 20
Sir Andrew Riccard 100
James Clitherow 50
Mary Scottow 20."

The tower is an imitation of that of Magdalen College, Oxford, and it was probably the desire to rebuild it in a similar style to the old one, that induced Wren to impose a Gothic steeple on his semi-classical church. It contains three storeys, and is crowned with a parapet from the angles of which rise four stately pinnacles. Its total altitude to the tops of the pinnacles is 130 feet, and the elevation of the ground on which it stands renders this beautiful tower an extremely prominent object, and gives it an appearance of far greater height than it actually possesses.

St. Michael's, Cornhill, has always been famous for its bells. Stow tells us that when the steeple was rebuilt, "a fair ring of five bells" was "therein placed," and that a sixth bell, which was named "Rus" after its part-donor, and was rung "nightly at eight of the clock," was given about 1430 "by John Whitwell, Isabel his wife, and William Rus, alderman and goldsmith." This William Rus, who was sheriff in 1429, was "a special benefactor" to the church, and his arms in Stow's time still remained in the windows. The present tower contains the large number of twelve bells.

Alderman Robert Fabian, sheriff in 1493, was buried here in 1513. He compiled an elaborate chronicle, dealing with France as well as England, which he called, "The Concordance of Histories," and which Stow characterizes as "a painful labour to the honour of the city and the whole realm."

St. Michael's, Cornhill, is particularly connected with John Stow. That indefatigable antiquary was a native of the parish, and both his father and grandfather, each of whom was named Thomas, were buried here, the former in 1559, and the latter in 1527. Thomas Stow the elder, citizen and tallow-chandler, bequeathed by his will, "my body to be buried in the litell Grene Churchyard of the Parysshe Church of Seynt Myghel in Cornehyll, betwene the Crosse and the Church Wall, nigh the wall as may

St. Michael, Cornhill.

be, by my Father and Mother, Systers and Brothers, and also my own Childerne." Stow also notes that his godfathers, Edmond Trindle and Robert Smith, and his godmother, Margaret, the wife of William Dickson, were interred at St. Michael's.

A monument in the present church, erected in place of one consumed in the Fire, commemorates John Vernon, a Merchant Taylor, and master of that company in 1609. The inscription is as follows:

"To the pious memory of Mr. John Vernon, late a worthy member of the Worshipful Company of Merchant Taylors: who by his last will gave many large legacies towards the annual relief of several Poor of that and other Companies of this City, amounting yearly to £200. All which Charities are duly paid by the said Company, who in gratitude to that great benefactor erected this monument at their charge in the place where one was ruined by the Fire, Anno 1666."

This monument, which is placed against the north wall, includes a half-length figure of Vernon. It is carefully preserved by the Merchant Taylors' Company, who cause it to be annually cleaned.

In the vestibule at the south-west are noticeable three monumental tablets to members of the Cowper family.

John Cowper, sheriff in 1551, the founder of the fortunes of the family, was an inhabitant of Cornhill, and his son, John Cowper, who died in 1609, had "a fair tomb in the Cloyster south," and "a hatchment." He was the father of Sir William Cowper, of Ratling Court, the first baronet, a zealous Cavalier, who survived the troubles of the Civil Wars, and died full of years and honours four years after the Restoration. He was succeeded in the baronetcy by his grandson, William, whose son, also named William, the third baronet, held the high office of

Lord Chancellor in Queen Anne's reign, and was elevated to the peerage as the first Earl Cowper. Earl Cowper was the great-uncle of the poet, whose father, the Rev. John Cowper, rector of Great Berkhampstead, was the son of Spencer Cowper, younger brother of the Lord Chancellor.

Cowper's Court, Cornhill, commemorates the connection of the Cowpers with St. Michael's parish, and marks the site of their residence.

There is a monument on the north wall to the Rev. Thomas Robert Wrench, who was rector of St. Michael's, Cornhill, for forty-two years, and was succeeded by his son, the Rev. Thomas William Wrench, who died in 1875, after holding the living for thirty-nine years. The younger Mr. Wrench and his widow, Diana Maria, whose death occurred in the following year, are commemorated by a brass tablet on the south-east wall.

The remainder of the monumental tablets, of which a considerable number are affixed to the north wall, possess no general interest.

St. Michael Paternoster Royal:

The church of St. Michael Paternoster Royal is situated in the Vintry Ward on the east side of College Hill. It derives its double appellation from the ancient names of two lanes which were adjacent to the church, Paternoster Lane and La Riole—of which "Royal" is a corruption—probably so called from its being inhabited by the wine merchants who traded with the town of La Riole, near Bordeaux.

This church was rebuilt by Sir Richard Whittington, who founded there a college of St. Spirit and St. Mary, whence College Hill takes its name. That great citizen, who was four times Lord Mayor—in 1396, 1397, 1406, and 1419—died in 1423, before his college was entirely finished; but the work was completed by his executors, John Coventrie, Jenkin Carpenter, and William Grove. The college was dissolved by Henry VIII., but the Whittington Almshouses, which formed part of the establishment, still exist, and are administered by Whittington's company, the Mercers'. They were removed to Highgate in 1808, and their old site on College Hill was occupied by the Mercers' School till its removal in 1894 to more commodious quarters in Barnard's Inn, Holborn.

Whittington was buried in the chancel of the church which he had so munificently benefited, under a marble tomb. His remains were, however, disturbed in the reign of Edward VI. by Thomas Mountain, then rector, who broke open the monument in the hope of discovering great treasure concealed there, and, failing to find any, tore from off the corpse the leaden sheet in which it was wrapped. But when Queen Mary had succeeded to the throne, this sacrilegious parson was ejected from the living, and the body of Whittington was again covered in lead and honourably interred, and his monument replaced. But it was destined to be totally destroyed in the Great Fire.

At St. Michael's John Cleveland, the Cavalier poet, found his last resting-place. He was buried on May 1st, 1658, and his funeral sermon was preached by Dr. John Pearson, afterwards Bishop of Chester.

The present church of St. Michael Paternoster Royal was built by Edward Strong, Wren's master-mason, under the superintendence of Sir Christopher. The body of the church was completed in 1694, but the steeple was not added till 1713. The building is of an oblong shape, and its internal measurements are 67 feet in length, 47 feet in width, and 38 feet in height. The ceiling is plain and flat in the centre, but at the sides it is coved. There is a well-carved pulpit, surmounted by a sounding-board, which is placed near to the north wall, and a very fine oak altar-piece, the work of Grinling Gibbons, above which is suspended a picture representing Mary Magdalen anointing the feet of Christ, by William Hilton, R.A., presented in 1820 by the directors of the British Institution.

The church was formerly too dark for this excellent painting to be adequately appreciated, but a great improvement has been recently effected by the opening of two windows in the east wall previously blocked up. Four memorial windows—the two easternmost of the north and south walls—were inserted in 1866, when the church was restored. The more western of the pair in the south wall is in memory of Whittington, the other three are to relatives of a late rector.

At the same period the old font, presented by Abraham Jordan in 1700, was also replaced by a new one in memory of Alderman Edward Conder, a parishioner, who was sheriff in 1858, and died in January, 1865.

The only monument of any interest is one to Sir Samuel Pennant, who died on May 20th, 1750, during his mayoralty. The cause of his death was the gaol fever, which, extending its ravages from Newgate Prison to the Sessions House, proved fatal to over sixty persons having business at the court, including two of the judges.

The tower, which is square, contains three storeys, and is terminated by a cornice surmounted by a pierced parapet, at the angles of which vases are placed. The steeple commences with a shallow dome resting on four arches, and encircled by a colonnade composed of eight Ionic columns. Above this circular stage the steeple becomes octagonal in shape, and is crowned by a pedestal supporting a finial and vane. The height from the ground to the top of the pedestal is 128 feet 3 inches. This steeple is graceful and beautiful, and the effect which it produces is wholly pleasing.

The rectory of St. Michael's is in the gift of the Dean and Chapter of Canterbury.

The church of St. Martin in the Vintry was destroyed in the Great Fire and not re-erected, its parish being united with that of St. Michael Paternoster Royal; but a portion of the old churchyard may still be observed at the corner of Queen Street and Upper Thames Street.

The advowson of the rectory of St. Martin in the Vintry was given by Ralph Peverell in the reign of William the Conqueror to the Abbey of Gloucester, in whose possession it remained till it came to the crown under Henry VIII. It was granted by Edward VI. to the see of Worcester, but the rectory is now in the gift of the Bishop of London.

There have now been added to these united parishes those of All Hallows the Great and All Hallows the Less, Upper Thames Street, which were themselves united after the Great Fire.

The patronage of the rectory of All Hallows the Great passed from the Le Despencers to the Beauchamps, Earls of Warwick, and thence into the hands of Richard Nevil, Earl of Warwick, the "King-maker." After his death at Barnet it fell into the possession of George, Duke of Clarence, Edward IV.'s brother, who had married the earl's elder daughter, Isabel, and in Henry VII.'s reign it came to the crown. Henry VIII. towards the close of his reign granted it to the archiepiscopal see of Canterbury, in which it has since continued.

All Hallows the Less, which was served by a curate, is said to have been built by Sir John Poultney, four times Lord Mayor, in 1330, 1331, 1333, and 1336. It stood over an arched gate, which formed the entrance to a large mansion called Cold Harbour, belonging to Sir John. Both All Hallows the Great and All Hallows the Less were destroyed in the Fire, while Cold Harbour had been pulled down in Queen Elizabeth's reign by its then owner, the Earl of Shrewsbury, who erected a quantity of small tenements on the site.

All Hallows the Great, which stands on the south side of Upper

St. Michael Paternoster Royal.

Thames Street, at the corner of All Hallows Lane, just to the east of Cannon Street Station, was rebuilt by Wren in 1683. The tower was taken down in 1876 to make room for the widening of Upper Thames Street, and the church itself, the site of which was sold by auction July 31st, 1894, is now in process of demolition.

The architectural features of All Hallows were not very striking, but the edifice was remarkable for the exceptional beauty of the pulpit and sounding-board, and the woodwork generally. The greatest ornament, however, was the chancel-screen of carved oak, which, together with the pulpit and sounding-board, has been transferred to St. Margaret, Lothbury.

The screen is composed of twisted columns excellently carved, which support an entablature; an eagle with open wings is placed over the doorway in the centre, through which admission is gained to the chancel; and the whole is crowned by the royal arms. The history of this noble specimen of workmanship is somewhat singular. It is said to have been made at Hamburg, and presented to the church by the 'Hanse merchants. The Hanse merchants, or "Easterlings," as they were called, had been long and closely connected with this neighbourhood. They were accorded a charter by Henry III., and remained in their "Steelyard" in Dowgate, the site of which is now occupied by the Cannon Street Railway Station, till early in the year 1598, when their exclusive privileges, which had been already curtailed by Edward VI., were finally abrogated by Elizabeth, and they were compelled to quit the country. They are stated, however, to have been mindful of their old association with the parish, and to have therefore bestowed the screen on the church of All Hallows; but the exact date of the gift is uncertain, as although tradition assigns it to the reign of Queen Anne, there is apparently no record of the year of its presentation. The eagle which adorns the screen was the emblem of the Hanseatic League.

The remainder of the woodwork has been utilized for the embellishment of St. Michael Paternoster Royal, the aspect of which has gained considerably both in dignity and grace from the skilful manner in which the materials have been adapted to their new surroundings. The old organ-case of All Hallows has also been re-erected on the south of the chancel, but it now encloses an entirely new organ. Two other interesting relics must not be forgotten—the stone figures of Moses and Aaron, which adorned the reredos of the demolished church, and may at present be seen standing on pedestals in the vestibule of St. Michael's.

The most illustrious of the rectors of All Hallows was Dr. Thomas White, who held the living from 1666 to 1679, and was created Bishop of Peterborough in 1685. He was one of the famous Seven Bishops, and, subsequently to the Revolution, a Nonjuror. White's successor, Dr. William Cave, remained at All Hallows till 1689. He was a man of great learning, and his "Lives of the Apostles," "Lives of the Fathers," and "Primitive Christianity," were regarded as extremely valuable works. He died at Windsor, where he had a canonry, in 1713.

S·Michael·Wood·Street·

THE church of St. Michael, Wood Street, stands at the south corner of Gresham Street and the west corner of Wood Street, and extends on the south into Huggin Lane. Stow calls it "a proper thing," and states that when he wrote it had been "lately well repaired." The body of the church perished in the Great Fire, and was rebuilt by Wren, who completed it in 1675.

Amongst those buried in the old church was Alderman John Lambarde, who served the office of sheriff in 1551, and died in 1554, and was, says Stow, "father to my loving friend, William Lambarde, esquire, well known by sundry learned books that he hath published."

William Lambarde, who was born in 1536, occupied himself with the study of jurisprudence and with antiquarian research. He published in 1568 "Archaionomia," and in 1570 a "Perambulation of Kent." He died in 1601.

In reference to this church Stow also tells us a strange tale, as to the truth of which we have no means of judging, with regard to the head of King James IV. of Scotland :

"There is also (but without any outward monument) the head of James, the fourth King of Scots of that name, slain at Flodden field, and buried here by this occasion : After the battle the body of the said king, being found, was enclosed in lead, and conveyed from thence to London, and so to the monastery of Shene in Surrey, where it remained for a time, in what order I am not certain; but since the dissolution of that house, in the reign of Edward VI., Henry Grey, Duke of Suffolk, being lodged and keeping house there, I have been shown the same body so lapped in lead, close to the head and body, thrown into a waste room amongst the old timber, lead, and other rubble. Since the which time workmen there, for their foolish pleasure, hewed off his head; and Launcelot Young, master glazier to Her Majesty, feeling a sweet savour to come from thence, and seeing the same dried from all moisture, and yet the form remaining, with the hair of the head and beard red, brought it to London to his house in Wood Street, where for a time he kept it for the sweetness, but in the end caused the sexton of that church to bury it amongst other bones taken out of their charnel."

The rectory of St. Michael's, Wood Street, was, prior to the dissolution of monasteries, in the gift of the abbot of St. Alban's, but in Queen Elizabeth's reign the advowson passed into the hands of trustees on behalf of the parish, and it has since then been always thus held in trust.

The church of St. Mary Staining, which was situated at the north end of Staining Lane, was not rebuilt after the Great Fire, and the rectory—an ancient appurtenance of the priory of St. Mary of Clerkenwell, now in the gift of the Lord Chancellor—was united with that of St. Michael, Wood Street.

The churchyard of St. Mary Staining still remains. It is situated at the top of Staining Lane, on the north side of Oat Lane, and, being tastefully laid out and carefully kept, forms a bright and agreeable contrast to the gloominess of the narrow streets by which it is encircled.

St. Michael, Wood Street.

The present church of St. Michael, Wood Street, is a very plain building without aisles, and was erected at a cost of less than £2,600. It measures 63 feet in length, 42 feet in breadth, and 31 feet in height from the pavement to the ceiling. The central part of the ceiling is flat, and is encircled by an ornamented cornice, beyond which the sides are coved. The church is lighted by three large windows at the east, and by four large windows in the south wall, but the north wall contains no apertures. The walls are panelled to the height of eight feet, and the oak altar-piece, which is surmounted by the royal arms well carved, and fixed at the centre of a broken pediment, is decidedly handsome. The pulpit, which is likewise of carved oak, stands at the extreme south-east. St. Michael's was repaired in 1888, and the high pews were then taken away and replaced by open benches and chancel-stalls. Although the western gallery was retained, the organ was brought downstairs, and now occupies a somewhat curious position at the north-west, between the gallery and the north wall. The font, which possesses a carved wooden cover, is located at the south-west. There are several monumental tablets fastened to the north and south walls, but none of them are of any interest.

The east front of St. Michael's, facing Wood Street, displays four Ionic pilasters supporting a pediment, and has a rather picturesque effect, which is heightened by the three circular-headed windows which appear in the spaces between the columns. The tower, which is connected with the church by a porch, through which admission is gained to the interior of the sacred edifice, stands at the south-west in Huggin Lane. It seems not to have been entirely destroyed by the Fire, but was considerably repaired by Wren. It contains three storeys, the middle one of which is lighted by a circular window, and is terminated by a parapet, from which rises a narrow lead-covered spire, culminating in a vane, and attaining a total height of 130 feet.

ST. MILDRED, BREAD STREET.

THE church of St. Mildred, Bread Street, is situated a little to the south of Cannon Street, having its west front on the eastern side of Bread Street.

With regard to its early history, we learn from Stow that "the Lord Trenchaunt of St. Alban's, Knight," who was buried here about 1300, "was supposed to be either the new builder of this church or best benefactor to the works thereof." Another benefactor was Sir John Shadworth, Lord Mayor 1401, "who gave the parsonage-house, a revestry, and churchyard to that parish." He was buried in the chancel, where a monument was erected to his memory.

The most distinguished rector of St. Mildred's was Hugh Oldham, who held the living from 1485 till 1488. Through the influence of the Lady Margaret, Henry VII.'s mother, whose chaplain he was, he obtained in 1504 the bishopric of Exeter, which he retained till his death in 1519. He was a benefactor to Corpus Christi College, Oxford, and founded a free school at Manchester, his native town.

The rectory was anciently in the gift of the prior and convent of St. Mary Overy, but since the reign of Henry VIII. the patronage has been in private hands. In the seventeenth century the advowson was in the possession of the Crispe family. Alderman Ellis Crispe was elected sheriff in 1625, a year in which there was

St. Mildred, Bread Street.

an outbreak of the Plague second only in virulence to the appalling visitation of 1665, and died almost immediately after entering on his office. He was buried in the family vault of the Crispes, on the south of the chancel, in which his wife's parents, John Ireland, master of the Salters' Company, and alderman's deputy of Bread Street Ward, and Elizabeth Ireland, had already been interred.

One of the sons of Ellis Crispe was Sir Nicholas Crispe, a captain of the city trained bands, and a devoted adherent of Charles I.; "a man of loyalty," says Dr. Johnson, "that deserves perpetual remembrance: when he was a merchant in the city, he gave and procured the king in his exigencies a hundred thousand pounds; and when he was driven from the Exchange, raised a regiment and commanded it."

At the Restoration, Crispe, who had shared the exile of the royal family, returned to England, and was created a baronet by Charles II. Before the commencement of the civil troubles he had built himself a palatial mansion at Hammersmith, and of this he now recovered possession. He set up in Hammersmith Church a bronze bust of Charles I. thus inscribed:

"This Effigies was Erected by the Special Appointment of Sir Nicholas Crispe, Knight and Baronet, As a grateful Commemoration of the Glorious Martyr King Charles the First of blessed Memory."

He died on February 26th, 1666, at the age of sixty-seven, and his heart was enclosed in an urn beneath the image of the sovereign whom he had served so faithfully.

"Within this urn," runs the simple inscription, "is entombed the Heart of Sir Nicholas Crispe, Knt. and Baronet, a loyal sharer in the sufferings of his late and present Majesty."

Crispe's house at Hammersmith was afterwards known as Brandenburg House; it was occupied by Queen Caroline during her trial, and in it she died, on August 7th, 1821. In the following year it was pulled down.

Crispe was a munificent benefactor towards his parish church. When St. Mildred's was extensively repaired in 1628, he erected at his sole cost a noble east window, containing five lights. The subjects represented on the glass were: The Spanish Armada, Queen Elizabeth, the Gunpowder Plot, the Plague of 1625, and figures of the donor himself, with his wife and children. He also presented a new font and two large sacramental vessels, which are still preserved in the church.

Sir Nicholas Crispe's great window was flanked by two smaller windows, the gifts respectively of his mother and his brother Samuel.

The Great Fire consumed St. Mildred's, Bread Street, and St. Margaret Moses, or Moyses, which was situated on the east side of Friday Street, toward the south end. Only the former was rebuilt, the parish of St. Margaret being united with that of St. Mildred.

St. Margaret Moses took its name from a certain Moses, or Moyses, a priest, who rebuilt it in the twelfth century. The advowson of the rectory was given by Robert Fitzwalter to the priory of St. Faith, at Horsham, in Norfolk, founded by him in the reign of Henry I., but since the time of Richard II. the benefice has been in the gift of the crown. John Rogers, the martyr, was instituted as rector in May, 1550, but resigned the living in the following year. The patronage is now alternately exercised by the Lord Chancellor for St. Margaret Moses, and the Storketh family for St. Mildred, Bread Street.

St. Mildred, Bread Street.

The present church of St. Mildred, Bread Street, was built by Wren, and first opened on March 23rd, 1683. It is constructed of brick, with the exception of the west front, which is of Portland stone. It measures 62 feet in length by 36 feet in breadth, and is crowned by a cupola, the height to the base of which is 40 feet, and to the summit about 52 feet. There is a niche for a window in each of the four walls, but only three windows now exist, that on the north side having been blocked up. Over each of these niches is an arch which meets the base of the dome. The cupola and the arches are richly decorated.

Fortunately St. Mildred's has not been afflicted with any of those "restorations" and "re-arrangements" which have obliterated the salient features and eradicated the indigenous charm of so many once interesting buildings. We now see it practically in its original state. The woodwork is exceedingly handsome. The spacious oak altar-piece is divided into compartments by Corinthian columns and pilasters, and is surmounted by a circular pediment. It contains paintings of Moses and Aaron. The pulpit, also of oak, which is placed on the north side of the church, is overshadowed by a magnificent sounding-board. The carvings about the altar-piece and those of the pulpit and sounding-board are of great merit. They are attributed, though not with absolute certainty, to Grinling Gibbons. The walls are panelled, and the substantial pews have not been disturbed. The capacious Corporation pew, the easternmost of the main block, is adorned at the ends with figures of the lion and unicorn, and at the centre with an elegant sword-rest. The font stands at the south-west. There is a western gallery, which contains the organ. The royal arms are affixed to the north wall beneath the window-niche.

A marble tablet against the north wall commemorates Lord

Trenchaunt, Sir John Shadworth, and other ancient benefactors. On the south wall is a tablet to Sir Thomas Crispe, son of Sir Nicholas Crispe, whose epitaph makes mention of his father's fidelity to Charles I. and Charles II.

The vestry room is situated to the south-east of the church. In it may be observed a large antique chest, wherein are kept the parish register-books, which are perfect from 1559. Among the entries is that of the marriage of Shelley and Mary Wolstonecraft Godwin, on December 30th, 1816.

The west front is adorned with a cornice and pediment, and is surmounted at the centre and extremities by pineapples. The steeple rises at the south-east, but only the upper portion of it is visible, owing to the close pressure of the surrounding buildings. It consists of a plain brick tower, lead-covered lantern, and slender spire, culminating in a ball and vane, and attains an altitude of 140 feet

St. Nicholas Cole Abbey

THE church of St. Nicholas Cole Abbey is situated between Queen Victoria Street and Knightrider Street, having its south front in the former, and its north front in the latter thoroughfare.

The name of this church has afforded a wide field for conjecture, but has not received a satisfactory explanation. Mr. Loftie surmises that St. Nicholas Cole Abbey "is probably a corruption of St. Nicholas Colby, and refers to a founder or restorer."

St. Nicholas was extensively repaired both externally and internally during the early part of the reign of Charles I., but was totally consumed in the Great Fire.

After the Fire the parish of St. Nicholas Olave was united with that of St. Nicholas Cole Abbey. The church which was not rebuilt had stood on the west side of Bread Street Hill. The name "Olave," which is another form of Olaf, may very possibly be derived from some benefactor of Danish family.

The present church of St. Nicholas Cole Abbey was completed by Wren in 1677. The cost of its construction, as is recorded on a tablet on the south wall, was £5,500. It is built chiefly of stone. The interior, which contains no aisles, measures 63 feet in length, 43 feet in breadth, and 36 feet in height. The ceiling is divided into compartments, which are delicately tinted a greyish blue. The walls are panelled to the height of seven feet, and the Corinthian pilasters which are affixed to the walls are encased in wood to the same level. The church is lighted at the east by three circular-headed windows filled with brightly stained glass, and by five similarly shaped windows in the north wall. Towards the west part of the south wall is a window, which, like those at the east, is brightly stained; and, still further west on this side, are two small windows, which are, however, concealed by the organ-gallery. The altar-piece is enclosed between two Corinthian pilasters, with entablature and broken pediment. The royal arms, which are of considerable size and very handsomely gilded, have been removed from their original position above the altar-piece, and are now placed in front of the easternmost window of the north wall.

The pulpit, which is well carved, stands on the north, and over the easternmost pew on the north side is elevated an excellently wrought sword-rest. At the west are high-backed seats for the churchwardens, and at this end of the church also stands the font, which has a carved wooden cover, culminating in the form of a crown. There are several monumental tablets, but none of any general interest. The parish register-books, however, contain a list of persons, with their ages, touched for the "king's evil" by James II. at his coronation.

A brass tablet on the south wall informs us that in the year 1873, "this edifice was restored, decorated, and repaired, and a new entrance from Queen Victoria Street formed."

Externally, the rows of windows displayed by the east and north fronts present a good appearance, each window being dominated by a horizontal cap. The roof is surmounted by a

St. Nicholas Cole Abbey.

pierced parapet. The steeple is at the north-west. The tower contains four storeys, and is concluded by a cornice ornamented at each angle by flaming urns, typifying the Great Fire. Above the tower is placed an octagonal lead-covered spire, which is pierced by two sets of elliptical openings, and is completed by a projecting balcony. A square pedestal, rising above the balcony, serves to support a moulded finial, and the whole is terminated by a large gilded ball and vane. The total altitude of the steeple is about 135 feet.

In 1871 the body of the church of St. Mary Somerset, in Upper Thames Street, was pulled down, and its parish was united with that of St. Nicholas Cole Abbey. St. Mary Somerset, or "Summerset," as he spells it, is described by Stow as "a proper church, but the monuments are all defaced." "I think the same," he adds, "to be of old time called Summer's hithe, of some man's name that was owner of the ground near adjoining, as Edred's hithe was so called of Edred owner thereof, and thence called Queene hithe, as pertaining to the Queen"—a conjecture which is very probably correct. St. Mary Somerset was "repaired and beautified" in 1624, and having been destroyed in the Great Fire, was rebuilt of stone by Wren, who completed the work in February, 1695.

Although the body of the church was taken down, the tower was spared, and still stands on the north side of Upper Thames Street, at the south-east corner of Lambeth Hill, formerly Old Fish Street Hill. It consists of five storeys, of which the lowest displays a doorway capped by an elliptical cornice; the second and fourth, round windows; and the third and highest, circular-headed openings with louvres. The tower is completed by a cornice and parapet, and is surmounted by eight pedestals, the central ones of which support obelisks crowned by balls, while those at the angles carry tall vases. The height to the top of the obelisks is 120 feet.

The church of St. Mary Mounthaw was not rebuilt after the Fire, and its parish was united with that of St. Mary Somerset.

Stow tells us that this church was originally a chapel attached to a mansion belonging to the Mounthauntes, a Norfolk family, and that, about the year 1234, Radulphus de Maydenstone, Bishop of Hereford, purchased the house and the patronage of the church, and bestowed them on his see.

But although the Bishops of Hereford were certainly patrons of the living, "the Mounthaunts," from whom Stow asserts they derived the advowson and their "inn," appear somewhat vague and shadowy people, and the name of the church, "Mounthaw," like that of St. Mary Bothaw, seems rather to point to a hatch or lock.

In 1701, after St. Mary Somerset had become the church of the united parishes, Gibert Ironside, Bishop of Hereford, was buried in its chancel. He was Warden of Wadham College, Oxford, for twenty-five years, and was vice-chancellor of the university when the president and fellows of Magdalene College were ejected by James II. Subsequently he was raised to the see of Bristol, and thence translated to Hereford. On the demolition of St. Mary Somerset, his remains were removed to Hereford Cathedral, and there deposited in the Lady Chapel.

The advowson of the rectory of St. Nicholas Cole Abbey was anciently in the gift of the collegiate church of St. Martin le Grand. This establishment was given by Henry VII. to the Abbey of Westminster, and the patronage of St. Nicholas was thereafter exercised by the abbot and convent of Westminster till the dissolution of monasteries, when it came into the hands of the

St. Nicholas Cole Abbey.

Crown. Queen Elizabeth granted it to two persons, named Thomas Reve and George Evelyn, and afterwards it was acquired by the Hackers, the last of whom to possess it was Colonel Francis Hacker, who commanded the guard at the trial and execution of Charles I. After the Restoration Hacker was hanged, and his estate being forfeited, the advowson returned to the Crown.

The rectory of St. Nicholas Olave, which was in the gift of Gilbert Foliot, Bishop of London from 1163 to 1187, was by him bestowed on the Dean and Chapter of St. Paul's, who ever afterwards retained it.

The earliest recorded patron of the rectory of St. Mary Somerset is Sir John de Peyton, who presented in 1335 and 1336; and the advowson subsequently passed through the hands of a long succession of private patrons.

With these four parishes have been also united those of St. Benet, Paul's Wharf, and St. Peter, Paul's Wharf. The church of St. Benet, Paul's Wharf, still stands, but it has ceased to be parochial, and is utilized for Welsh services. The united benefice of St. Nicholas Cole Abbey, St. Nicholas Olave, St. Mary Somerset, St. Mary Mounthaw, St. Benet, Paul's Wharf, and St. Peter, Paul's Wharf, is now in the gift of the Dean and Chapter of St. Paul's.

St. Peter Cornhill:

The church of St. Peter upon Cornhill is, like St. Michael's, situated to the south of that busy thoroughfare; but it stands further east than the church of the Archangel, its eastern front being in Gracechurch Street. St. Peter's claims an origin of great antiquity, the particulars of which are set forth on a brass tablet, which is mentioned by Stow:

"There remaineth in this church a table whereon it is written, I know not by what authority, but of a late hand, that King Lucius founded the same church to be an archbishop's see metropolitan and chief church of his kingdom, and that it so endured the space of four hundred years, until the coming of Augustin the monk."

This tablet was preserved from the Great Fire, and is now hung over the chimney-piece of the vestry room. The inscription is as follows:

"Bee it knowne to all men that the yeare of our Lord God 179 Lucius, the first Christian king of this land, then called Britaine, founded the first church in London, that is to say, the Church of St. Peter upon Cornehill. And hee founded there an Archbishop's See, and made the church the metropolitane and chief church of this kingdome; and so indured the space of

ST. PETER, CORNHILL.

400 yeares unto the coming of St. Austin, the Apostle of England, the which was sent into this land by St. Gregorie, the Doctor of the Church, in the time of King Ethelbert. And then was the Archbishop's See and Pall removed from the foresaid Church of St. Peter upon Cornehill unto Dorobernia, that now is called Canterburie, and there it remaineth to this day. And Millet, a monke, which came into this land with St. Austin, hee was made the first Bishop of London, and his See was made in Paul's Church. And this Lucius, king, was the first founder of St. Peter's Church upon Cornehill. And hee reigned in this land after Brute 1245 yeares. And in the yeare of our Lord God 124 Lucius was crowned king, and the yeares of his reigne were 77 yeares. And hee was buried after some Chronicles at London; and after some Chronicles hee was buried at Glocester where the order of St. Francis standeth now."

King Lucius seems hardly less mythical a personage than "Brute" himself, and in spite of the fact that the authorities of St. Peter's, Cornhill, thought fit to celebrate the 1700th anniversary of their foundation, one cannot do otherwise than dismiss this legend, which Stow himself appears not to have believed, as one of the many idle tales which have been told about the early history of London. At the same time, St. Peter's may very possibly be one of the most ancient churches of the city.

In the fourteenth century the advowson of the rectory of St. Peter upon Cornhill belonged, like that of St. Margaret Pattens, to the Nevils. In 1408 they were both confirmed by the then owners, Robert Rykedon, of Essex, and Margaret, his wife, to Richard Whittington and other citizens, who in their turn confirmed them in 1411 to the mayor and commonalty of London, who have ever since continued to be the patrons both of St. Margaret's and St. Peter's.

The church was so extensively repaired as to be practically rebuilt in the reign of Edward IV., but the old steeple remained. In 1628-29 this steeple was repaired, and in 1632-33 the church itself was thoroughly renovated and "richly and very worthily beautified" at the cost of the parishioners, who expended about £1,000 on the restoration of the sacred building. But when little more than thirty years had elapsed, it was reduced to ashes by the devouring flames.

The present church of St. Peter's, Cornhill, was built by Wren in 1680-81. It is entered by a door at the north-west from Cornhill, and from the churchyard by a door at the south-west, exactly opposite. It contains two aisles, which are divided from the nave by Corinthian columns elevated on high panelled bases, and measures in length 80 feet and in breadth 47 feet, while the height from the pavement to the ceiling is 40 feet. The roof is arched and divided into panels. The chancel, on the north and south of which are side chapels, is separated from the nave by a carved wooden screen—St. Peter's, Cornhill, and All Hallows, Thames Street, the latter of which has been demolished, being the only ones amongst all Wren's churches which were thus ornamented. The screen of St. Peter's is not so handsome as that of All Hallows,[1] but is nevertheless finely carved. It is surmounted at the centre by the royal arms, between the lion and the unicorn. The pulpit, which is covered by a large sounding-board, and stands at the north side of the church, also displays some good carving. The walls are panelled to a height of ten feet, the same level as is attained by the bases of the pillars.

The church is lighted by a row of five windows at the east, and

---

[1] Transferred to St. Margaret Lothbury.

above these is another window, flanked by two smaller circular windows. There are three large windows in the south wall, and the north wall possesses two large windows and a circular window, the last of which is over the north-west door. The organ, which occupies the western gallery, was the work of Father Smith, dating from 1681, and has since been much enlarged. It is considered one of the finest instruments constructed by that illustrious builder, and is enclosed in a very handsome case.

In front of the organ gallery is placed the marble font, presented by Samuel Purchas in 1681, and surmounted by an excellently carved cover, which belonged to the old church and was fortunately saved from the Fire.

The vestry room, which is situated to the west of the church, and is entered through an elegantly carved doorway, contains, in addition to the tablet about King Lucius, a curious old Bible, bearing the date 1290, magnificently illuminated by a monk attached to St. Peter's, and the old key-board and stops of the organ, which have now been replaced by new ones. They have a peculiar interest, as having been used by Mendelssohn, whose autograph, with the date—September 30th, 1840—on which he played at St. Peter's, Cornhill, hangs in a frame above them. Both the mediæval Bible and the key-board and stops are carefully enclosed in glass cases. The stops are very handsomely inlaid with pearl, and the different actions are engraved on small silver plates.

Over the fireplace, on each side of the Lucius tablet, hang the portraits of Bishop Beveridge and Bishop Waugh, both of whom were rectors of St. Peter's, Cornhill.

Dr. William Beveridge was born in 1638. He was rector of St. Peter's from 1672 to 1704, and thus it was during his incumbency that the church was rebuilt. It was he who caused the chancel screen to be erected, and he made mention of it in the sermon delivered by him on the occasion of the opening of the church, November 27th, 1681. He resigned the living on being elevated to the see of St. Asaph, and died on March 5th, 1708, and was buried in St. Paul's Cathedral. He was a great scholar, and the author of a large work on the Apostolical Canons; but the special objects of his study were the Semitic languages, on the use of which he composed a very learned treatise, to which he prefixed a Syriac grammar. He is described as a most exemplary man, and was conspicuous for the zeal and devotion with which he performed his clerical duties.

Dr. John Waugh was made Bishop of Carlisle in 1723, but he continued to hold the rectory of St. Peter's till his death in 1734, and was buried here.

The view of the exterior of St. Peter's is blocked on the north side by the intervening houses, but on the south the church is open to the churchyard, which extends as far as St. Peter's Alley. The east front, abutting on Gracechurch Street, displays at the lower stage a row of six Ionic pilasters, between which are the five windows, and in the upper storey appear the three higher windows within the gable. When the church is lighted up for a service on a dark winter's evening, the glow of the light through all these windows, as seen from the opposite side of Gracechurch Street, produces a beautiful effect. The steeple, which rises at the south-west, attains a total height of 140 feet. The tower, which is of brick, is ornamented at the belfry stage by triple openings, and is concluded by a cornice; above the tower are a lead-covered cupola, a pierced octagonal lantern, and a spire; the whole terminating in a large vane in the shape of St. Peter's emblem, the key.

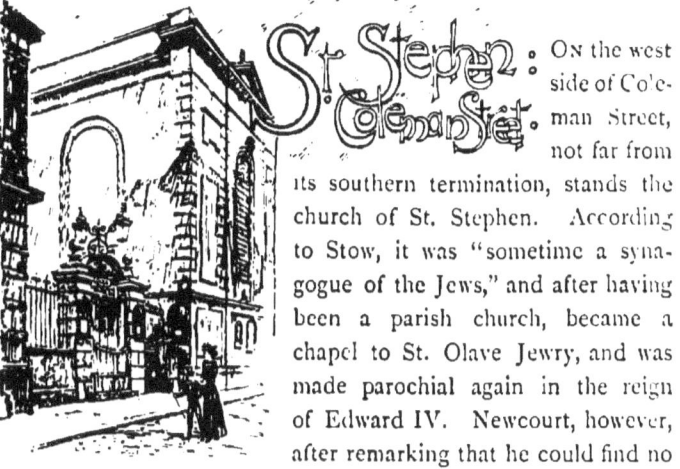

St. Stephen Coleman Street

On the west side of Coleman Street, not far from its southern termination, stands the church of St. Stephen. According to Stow, it was "sometime a synagogue of the Jews," and after having been a parish church, became a chapel to St. Olave Jewry, and was made parochial again in the reign of Edward IV. Newcourt, however, after remarking that he could find no authority for Stow's statement about the Jewish synagogue, explains that the church anciently belonged to the canons of St. Paul's, and was in the year 1182 held of them by the prior and convent of Butley in Suffolk, to whom they had also granted St. Olave Jewry. It was in 1456, he tells us, and thus before the close of the reign of Henry VI., that St. Stephen's was made parochial, and a vicarage ordained and endowed there by Thomas Kemp, then Bishop of London, who arranged matters with the prior and convent of Butley, the parishioners, and the vicar of St. Olave's, to whose church St. Stephen's had been a chapel. The patronage remained with the prior and convent till the dissolution of monasteries, but since the reign of Queen Elizabeth the vicarage has been in the gift of the parishioners.

Anthony Munday, the dramatist, the arranger of the city pageants, and the continuator of Stow's survey, who died in his eightieth year on August 10th, 1633, was buried at St. Stephen's, but his monument perished in the destruction of the old church by the Great Fire.

St. Stephen's, having been consumed by the Fire, was rebuilt by Wren. The gateway, leading into the churchyard from Coleman Street, is adorned with some curious carving in high relief, measuring about five feet by two and a half feet, representing the Day of Judgment. The Judge is enthroned above; Satan is falling; and the dead are rising from their coffins; while angel forms are hovering about, to marshal them to the tribunal of the Creator.

The east front, abutting on Coleman Street, is embellished with a cornice and pediment, and displays a large central window; the south wall, facing the churchyard, is pierced with five tall and handsome windows. The steeple, which rises at the north-west, consists of a stone tower, lead-covered lantern, and small spire; the whole terminating in a gilded vane in the form of a cock. The tower, which is 65 feet high, contains eight bells; the height of the lantern is about twenty feet.

Internally St. Stephen's is a plain building without aisles. It is long and narrow, measuring 75 feet in length by 35 feet in breadth, and is extremely low, the altitude of the ceiling, which is flat in the central part, but coved at the sides, hardly exceeding 24 feet. The oak pulpit is finely carved, and the altar-piece, of the same material, is enriched with Corinthian pilasters. The lower parts of the walls are panelled, and there are two inner door-cases on the north, and two on the south side, all handsomely wrought.

Against the south wall is a large and ornate monument of white marble to Henry Vernon, an Oriental merchant, who died at Aleppo in 1694 in his thirty-first year. He was the son of Sir Thomas Vernon, a parishioner.

St. Stephen·Walbrook·

THE church of St. Stephen Walbrook, stands behind the Mansion House at the northeastern corner of Walbrook, a street which still preserves the name of the ancient stream, now concealed beneath the ground, which, rising among the swamps beyond Moorgate, flowed down into the Thames at Dowgate. The period of the original foundation of this church is unknown, but it dates at least as far back as the time of Henry I., for we read that St. Stephen's, Walbrook, was one of the churches presented by Eudo, sewer to that monarch, to the monastery of St. John of Colchester, in whose possession the advowson continued as late as the year 1422. It then passed, but by what means is not recorded, into the hands of John, Duke of Bedford, uncle of Henry VI., who sold it to Sir Robert Whittingham, a draper. Whittingham bestowed it, "Edward IV., in the 2nd of his reign," on Sir Richard Lee, who had been Lord Mayor in 1460. Lee was a grocer, and either he or his son not many years afterwards gave the patronage of St. Stephen's to the Grocers' Company, who still present to the rectory.

St. Stephen's was rebuilt early in the reign of Henry VI., chiefly through the instrumentality of Robert Chicheley, who had been twice Lord Mayor—in 1411 and 1421. It was repaired in the reign of Charles I. at a cost of over £500, but was totally consumed by the Great Fire. Amongst its monuments was that of Sir Thomas Pope, the founder of Trinity College, Oxford. He was Master of the Mint and Treasurer of the Court of Augmentations, and died in 1559.

After the Great Fire the neighbouring church of St. Benet Sherehog, which was situated opposite to Sise Lane in Pancras Lane, was not rebuilt, and the benefice—a rectory—was united with that of St. Stephen Walbrook. The advowson of St. Benet belonged, previously to the dissolution of monasteries, to the prior and convent of St. Mary Overy in Southwark, but has ever since that event been retained by the Crown.

The history of this appellation, "St. Benet Sherehog," is somewhat singular. The church was originally dedicated to St. Osyth, a Saxon saint, described as "queen and martyr," whose name in a corrupted form still survives in "Sise" Lane. But after it had been repaired or rebuilt—Stow says, "in the reign of Edward II.," but very probably at an earlier period—by Benedict Sherehog, "sometime a citizen and stock-fishmonger of London," the benefactor drove out the patron saint from connection with the church, and St. Osyth's became St. Benedict's, or Benet's, from the Christian name, with the distinctive title of Sherehog from the surname, of the "stock-fishmonger."

According to Dean Peckard, in his "Life of Nicholas Ferrar," Nicholas Ferrar the elder, the father of that religious enthusiast, "repaired and decently seated at his own expense" the church and chancel of St. Benet Sherehog; "and as there was not any morning preacher there, he brought from the country Mr. Francis White." Ferrar was a merchant adventurer, trading extensively

with the East and West Indies, of high repute in the city, and personally acquainted with the great seamen, Drake, Hawkins, and Raleigh, in whose ventures he frequently had an interest. Francis White, whom he thus introduced to London, was made Bishop of Carlisle in 1626, translated to Norwich in 1629, and again to Ely in 1631. He died in 1638.

At St. Benet Sherehog were buried Sir Ralph Warren, twice Lord Mayor, in 1435 and 1444, and Dame Joan White, daughter of John Lake, of London, gentleman, who was married, firstly to Sir Ralph Warren, and secondly to Sir Thomas White, Lord Mayor in 1553, the founder of St. John's College, Oxford. She died in 1573, at Hinchinbrook, in Huntingdonshire, at the house of Sir Henry Cromwell, who had married Joan, her daughter by her first husband. A younger son of this Sir Henry Cromwell and his wife Joan was Robert Cromwell, the father of the Protector Oliver.

Here also was interred Edward Hall, the chronicler, whose narrative extends from the end of the reign of Richard II. to the death of Henry VIII. in 1547, in which year Hall himself died; and, not long before the final destruction of the church, St. Benet Sherehog received the remains of Mrs. Katharine Philips of Cardigan, the poetess, the "matchless Orinda," whose untimely death, on June 22nd, 1664, was bewailed by Cowley in an elaborate elegy.

A portion of the old burying-ground of St. Benet Sherehog is still to be seen on the north side of Pancras Lane, exactly opposite the northern termination of Sise Lane.

The first stone of the present church of St. Stephen Walbrook, was laid on October 16th, 1672, and the edifice was completed in 1679 at a cost of £7,652. The church is, next to

St. Paul's Cathedral, considered Wren's masterpiece. It is of an oblong shape, and is traversed by four rows of Corinthian columns elevated on bases; so that it is divided into five aisles, of which the central aisle is the broadest, while those nearest the walls are the least wide. An open space having been formed by the omission of two columns from each of the two central rows, the church is crowned by a circular dome supported on eight arches. This dome contains compartments decorated with palm-branches and roses, and the light is admitted by a circular lantern at the apex. The spandrels of the arches which support the dome are ornamented with shields.

The effect of the circle thus springing from an octagonal base is singularly beautiful. The architect evidently took extraordinary pains with the proportions of this building, and his mathematical genius stood him in good stead in enabling him to produce so magnificent a work in such a limited space; for the extent of St. Stephen's, Walbrook, is by no means large, though it possesses the property of appearing much greater than it really is. Its interior length is 82 feet 6 inches, its breadth 59 feet 6 inches; the height to the summit of the dome is 63 feet, and the diameter of the dome at the base is 45 feet; the height to the ceiling of the side aisles is 36 feet.

The walls and columns are of stone, but the dome consists of timber and lead. The ceiling of the centre aisle is groined; those of the side aisles are flat, and are divided into compartments by mouldings. The wainscoting and pews were presented, at the rebuilding of the church, by the patrons of the living, the Grocers' Company, but at the last restoration, in 1888, the pews were removed—a step as to the expediency of which different opinions have been expressed. The present mosaic pavement

St. Stephen, Walbrook.

was also laid down at this restoration. The organ is placed at the west, and on the organ-gallery and case are displayed the arms of the Grocers' Company. Two old prints of the interior of the church are hung on the north part of the west wall. The oak pulpit, which stands south of the central aisle, is well carved, and is overshadowed by a handsome sounding-board. The marble font at the north-west is capped with a carved wooden cover ornamented with figures.

A picture of the "Martyrdom of St. Stephen," by Benjamin West—one of the finest works of that artist—was presented to the church by Dr. Wilson, rector, in 1779, and was at first placed over the altar, thus blocking the east window. During the repairs of 1847-48, however, it was removed to the north wall, where it is still suspended, and the east window was filled with stained glass representing the life and death of the patron saint, executed by Willement at the expense of the Grocers' Company. There are two smaller windows at the east end, one on each side of the large central window, which correspond to two similar windows in the west wall. On the former are represented the Crucifixion and Ascension, and on the latter the Nativity and Baptism—the work of Gibbs, by whom also are the windows in the north and south walls, depicting respectively the Parables and Miracles of our Lord. All these constitute a memorial to the poetical rector, Dr. George Croly, who died in 1860. The glass of the windows of the clerestory is plain.

Admission is gained to the interior of the church by ascending a flight of steps in an enclosed porch opening out of Walbrook.

St. Stephen's, Walbrook, must be seen to be appreciated. All description of it, however exact, falls flat, it being totally impossible to convey by words any adequate impression of the loveliness of this delightful church.

The tower of St. Stephen's, which is very plain, contains four storeys. Upon it is placed the steeple, consisting of two open square storeys, tapering into a spirelet which culminates in a finial and vane. The total height is about 130 feet. The spire is extremely elegant, but the tower is commonplace. Wren probably considered that, owing to the smallness of the space at his command, and the obstruction to the view caused by the surrounding houses, it would be waste of labour to construct an elaborate tower where it could not be seen to advantage, and therefore wisely concentrated his energies on the interior and the spire.

The great Italian sculptor, Canova, when in London, inspected this church, and was charmed with its beauty. He is said to have remarked that he would gladly pay another visit to England, in order to again have the pleasure of beholding St. Paul's Cathedral, Somerset House, and St. Stephen's, Walbrook.

The oldest monument in the church is one of white marble, affixed to a pillar at the south-east, in memory of John Lilbourn, citizen and grocer of London, who died in 1678. On the north wall is a tablet to Nathaniel Hodges, a physician who wrote a treatise on the Plague. He died in 1688.

On the same wall, further east, is a white marble monument, with bust, which perpetuates the name of another medical practitioner, Percival Gilbourne, an apothecary, who died in 1694. On a pillar at the north-east, opposite Lilbourne's monument, is a memorial to Robert Marriott, a rector, described in his epitaph as "Vir in prædicando vere Divinus." He died, or, as the epitaph puts it, "in celestem Patriam emigravit," May 14th, 1689.

Two later rectors, the Rev. Thomas Wilson, D.D., and the Rev. G. S. Townley, are also commemorated by tablets. Between them they held the living for nearly a century. Dr. Wilson died in 1784, after having been rector for forty-six years; but this lengthy period of incumbency was exceeded by that of Mr. Townley, who had ministered here for over fifty years when he passed away in 1835. Dr. Croly, in addition to the memorial windows, has a monument on the north wall, near that of Gilbourne, with his bust by Behnes.

In his family vault at St. Stephen's, Walbrook, was interred Sir John Vanbrugh, who departed this life on March 26th, 1726, the playwright and architect, author of "The Relapse," "The Provoked Wife," and "The Confederacy," and designer of Blenheim and Castle Howard, whom Benjamin Disraeli calls "an imaginative artist, whose critics I wish no bitterer fate, than not to live in his splendid creations."

St. Swithin, with the parish of London Stone.

THE church of St. Swithin, dedicated to the Saxon Bishop of Winchester of that name, is situated on the north side of Cannon Street, opposite the railway station, and is bounded on the east by St. Swithin's Lane, and on the west by Salters' Hall Court.

After the dissolution of monasteries the advowson of the rectory of St. Swithin, which had previously belonged to the prior and convent of Tortington, in Sussex, was granted, together with the "inn" or town-house of the prior of Tortington, by Henry VIII., to John, Earl of Oxford; and thence is derived the name of Oxford Court, in which the "inn" was situated. Edward, Earl of Oxford, a nobleman described by Scott in "Kenilworth" as "a young unthrift," sold both the advowson and the house to Sir John Hart, who was Lord Mayor in 1589, and from him they passed to his son-in-law, Sir George Bolles, Lord Mayor in 1617. From the Bolles family they were purchased by the Company of Salters, whose hall, to the west of St. Swithin's Lane, in Oxford Court, still occupies the site of the old mansion. They disposed, however, of the advowson of St. Swithin's, about the beginning of this century, to a gentleman named Watkins, whose descendants are now the patrons.

Sir John Hart and Sir George Bolles were both buried in the

church, but their monuments were destroyed in the Great Fire, when the whole building was consumed. Less than three years before that catastrophe, on December 1st, 1663, Dryden was married at St. Swithin's to Lady Elizabeth Howard.

The church of St. Mary Bothaw, the name of which has been explained as meaning Boat-hatch, or Board-hatch, was situated to the south of Cannon Street, or Candlewick Street, as it was formerly called. It was not rebuilt after its destruction by the Fire, and the rectory, which is in the gift of the Dean and Chapter of Canterbury, was united with that of St. Swithin.

St. Swithin's was rebuilt by Wren in 1678. It measures internally 61 feet in length, 42 feet in breadth, and 41 feet in height. It is surmounted by an octagonal cupola, divided by bands into compartments, and powdered with stars on a blue ground. This cupola is illumined by four circular lights, and adorned in the spaces between the lights by four paintings; it rests on pillars fixed against the walls, and on one separate column on the north side. There is a small north gallery, against the face of which, at its upper part, is fastened a curious old gilded clock. The royal arms occupy a prominent position on the west wall, and below them stands the font.

The church has been very much modernized; it was "rearranged" in 1869, and in 1879 the chancel was renewed, and at the same time a new vestry was constructed beneath the north gallery. The large east window, which is flanked by two smaller windows, is filled with stained glass representing the Crucifixion, and the central window of the south wall is also richly stained. There is a handsome oak communion table, and also an oak pulpit, which is placed at the south of the chancel. The organ is located on the north side of the chancel, just east of the column.

The lower portions of the walls are panelled, and the higher parts are delicately tinted.

Affixed to the column on the north side of the church is a large monumental tablet to Michael Godfrey, nephew to Sir Edmundsbury Godfrey, whose mysterious death created such a ferment in London at the time of the "Popish Plot." Michael Godfrey, who was born in 1658, was a man of great financial capacity, and his practical knowledge was of the utmost value in formulating the scheme for the establishment of the Bank of England. On the incorporation of the Bank in 1694, he was chosen to be its first deputy-governor. In the following year he was despatched on some important business to the camp of King William, who was then besieging Namur, and having ventured within range of the enemy's fire, he was on July 17th, 1695, slain by a cannon ball from the town, while the king, who was close at his side, and had just been remonstrating with him on his rashness in thus needlessly exposing himself, escaped without the slightest injury. His body was brought over to England, and interred in this church, close to his father's grave. The monument to him was erected by his mother, Mrs. Ann Mary Godfrey, whose remains, nearly thirteen years afterwards, were laid by those of her beloved son.

The tower of St. Swithin's rises at the north-west, which accounts for the somewhat peculiar form of the north side of the church. It is square, but is contracted at the top into an octagonal shape, and surrounded with a cornice and balustrade; thence rises a lead-covered spire, of a perfectly simple character, which is terminated by a ball and vane. The total height of the steeple is 150 feet.

Built into the south wall of St. Swithin's church, facing Cannon Street, and protected by a grating, are the remains of the ancient London Stone, about the origin and purpose of which varying theories have been advanced, but which the best authorities consider with Camden to have been the central Roman milestone, from which, as from the Milliarium in the Forum at Rome, the Roman roads started, and the distances on them were measured.

This is the stone which Cade, when he led the men of Kent through London, struck with his sword, in token of the subjugation of the city—a scene pictured for us by Shakespeare in "King Henry VI., Part II."

Stow describes the stone as it appeared more than a century later: "On the south side of this high street, near unto the channel, is pitched upright a great stone called London Stone, fixed in the ground very deep, fastened with bars of iron, and otherwise so strongly set, that if carts do run against it through negligence, the wheels be broken, and the stone itself unshaken."

Subsequently it became considerably worn, and was encased with a new stone to keep it from further injury. In 1742 it was removed from the south to the north side of Cannon Street, and in 1798 it was placed in its present position in the church wall, through the exertions of Mr. Thomas Maiden, a printer of Sherborne Lane, who, justly indignant at a proposal which had been made to destroy it as an obstruction, prevailed upon the parochial authorities to give shelter to this venerable relic of antiquity.

Above the stone are two parallel inscriptions, Latin and English. The English inscription runs thus:

"London Stone
Commonly believed to be a Roman Work
Long placed about 35 Feet hence
Towards the South West
And afterwards built into the Wall of this Church
Was for more careful Protection
And transmission to Future Ages

Better secured by the Churchwardens
In the Year of Our Lord 1869.

Edward Allfree M.A. Rector

Henry Edward Murrell	John Land
Charles Cann	Charles Curtoys
Churchwardens	Churchwardens
St. Swithin.	St. Mary Bothaw.[10]

ST. VEDAST, FOSTER LANE.

On the east side of Foster Lane, a little above its junction with Cheapside, stands a church dedicated to St. Vedast, a bishop of Arras, who flourished in the sixth century, and about whom many miraculous legends are narrated. This church was formerly commonly known as St. Fauster's, or Foster's, and is described by Stow as "a fair church lately new built." It was repaired and enlarged in 1614, but, though not entirely destroyed, was severely damaged by the Great Fire.

St. Vedast's was rebuilt of stone by Wren, mostly upon the old walls; the ancient steeple remained standing till 1694, but owing to the injuries which it had sustained from the flames, it was then found necessary to take it down, and Wren erected a new steeple, which was completed in 1697.

The steeple of St. Vedast's, which is placed at the south-west, is remarkably graceful. It shows to the best advantage from the western end of Newgate Street, whence it can be discerned rising beyond that of Christ Church. The two steeples harmonize well together, and both attain a height of about 160 feet. The tower of St. Vedast's measures 20 feet square at the base, and its altitude is about 90 feet. Above this are three stages, the lowest of which is concave, and the second convex, both displaying piers at the angles, while the third consists of an obelisk-shaped spire, and the whole is surmounted by a ball, finial, and vane. There are six bells.

St. Vedast's measures internally 69 feet in length by 51 in breadth, and the height to the ceiling of the nave is about 36 feet. It includes a south aisle, which is separated from the main body of the building by arches supported on four Tuscan columns. The church is lighted by three windows at the east, three at the west, four in the north wall, and one in the western portion of the south wall, and also by four windows in the clerestory. The windows at the west are plain, but all the others were filled with stained glass at the restoration of 1885, as is recorded on a tablet on the north wall. The ceiling of the nave is formed by ornamental bands into one large outer panel, and within this are smaller compartments, which are likewise decorated. The sides of the ceiling are slightly coved. The oak altar-piece, which is attributed to Grinling Gibbons, is very handsome. It contains four Corinthian columns with entablature and pediment, and displays the figure of a pelican, cherubim, urns, palm branches, and other embellishments. The pulpit and sounding-board, which are placed on the south side, are also of oak, and finely carved. The font stands at the south-west. During the restoration of 1885 the organ was re-constructed, and transferred from the west gallery to the south of the chancel. The royal arms are affixed to the centre of the north wall.

Robert Herrick, the poet, who was the son of Nicholas Herrick, a goldsmith of Cheapside, was baptized at St. Vedast's on August 24th, 1591.

The parish of St. Vedast was one of the Archbishop of Canterbury's thirteen "peculiars." The patronage of the rectory, originally in the hands of the prior and chapter of Canterbury,

By permission of the London Stereoscopic Co., Cheapside.

ST. VEDAST.

passed to the archbishop somewhere about the beginning of the fifteenth century.

Thomas Rotherham was rector of St. Vedast from 1465 to 1467, when he resigned the living on being promoted to the see of Rochester. He was translated to Lincoln in 1471, and in 1474 Edward IV. made him Lord Chancellor. In 1480 he was further advanced to the archbishopric of York, which he held till his death in 1500. He was deprived of his chancellorship, and for a short time imprisoned by Richard III. He was a lover of learning, and a liberal benefactor to both Oxford and Cambridge, at the latter of which universities he had received his education, but he does not appear to have shown any particular ability as a statesman.

The church of St. Michael-le-Querne, *i.e.*, at the Corn, so called "because in place thereof was sometime a corn market, stretching by west to the shambles," stood at the east end of Paternoster Row; it was burnt down by the Great Fire, and its parish was united with that of St. Vedast. The rectory had from ancient times been in the patronage of the Dean and Chapter of St. Paul's.

St. Michael-le-Querne was the burial-place of John Leland. That great antiquary was born in London about the year 1506. He became chaplain and librarian to Henry VIII., and was in 1533 commissioned by that sovereign to search for records of antiquity in all the cathedrals, abbeys, colleges, etc., of England. For six years he was perambulating the country in the diligent performance of this task, and afterwards he applied himself to the arrangement of the immense mass of information which he had gathered in his journeys. But the intense ardour with which he prosecuted his studies proved fatal to his reason, and he passed the last years of his life in a state of insanity, from which he was delivered by death on April 18th, 1552. His monument perished in the destruction of the church, but his great work, "The Itinerary," replete with priceless stores of knowledge, remains *monumentum ære perennius.*

Sir Thomas Browne, the author of the "Religio Medici," who was born on October 19th, 1605, was baptized at St. Michael-le-Querne.

The church of St. Matthew, Friday Street, which stood on the west side of Friday Street at the north end, close to Cheapside, was taken down in 1881, and its parish united with that of St. Vedast. It was a plain brick building without aisles, measuring 64 feet by 33 feet, and having a tower 74 feet high, and was built by Wren in 1685 in place of the old church, which was destroyed by the Fire.

The rectory was in the gift of the abbot and convent of Westminster, and when Henry VIII. made a bishopric there, it was transferred to the bishop; but the new see being dissolved by Edward VI., the advowson was bestowed by him on the Bishop of London.

That ardent Puritan, Henry Burton, was rector of St. Matthew, Friday Street. Having published a sermon in which he vehemently attacked the bishops, he was, in June, 1637, placed in the pillory, together with Prynne and Bastwick, and subsequently imprisoned, first in Lancaster Castle, and afterwards in Guernsey. He was released by the Long Parliament, and re-entered London in triumph. After his return he was one of the first to avow himself an Independent, in contradistinction to the Presbyterians.

Sir Hugh Myddelton, the designer and constructor of the New River, was a parishioner of St. Matthew's, and served the office of churchwarden in 1598, 1599, and 1600. Several of his children were baptized here. He was the son of Richard Myddelton, who had been governor of Denbigh Castle, and followed the occupation of a goldsmith. In connection with his business he worked a silver mine in Cardiganshire, and thus acquired knowledge and experience in engineering, which enabled him to accomplish his great enterprise. The works were first opened on Michaelmas day, 1613, when Sir John Swinnerton was Lord Mayor, and Sir Thomas Myddelton, Hugh's brother, Lord Mayor elect. He was created a baronet by James I. in 1622, but although the New River was of the utmost value as affording London a pure water supply, it proved of little profit commercially to its contriver. Sir Hugh died on December 10th, 1631, and was buried in St. Matthew's churchyard.

The church of St. Peter, West Cheap, which was called St. Peter at the Cross in Cheape, from its proximity to one of the crosses erected by Edward I. in memory of his queen, Eleanor of Castile, stood at the south-west corner of Wood Street.

It was not rebuilt after the Great Fire, its parish being united with that of St. Matthew, Friday Street. A portion of the old burying-ground, however, still remains, and in it stands the graceful plane-tree which affords so pleasing a relief to the eye as one turns into Wood Street from the turmoil of Cheapside.

The patronage of St. Peter's was, until the dissolution of monasteries, in the hands of the abbots of St. Alban's; King Henry VIII. granted the advowson to Thomas Wriothesley, the first Earl of Southampton, and after the extinction of that family in the male line, it passed, like that of St. Andrew's, Holborn, to the Dukes of Buccleugh.

CHURCHES SUBSEQUENT TO WREN.

X

All Hallows London Wall

THE church of All Hallows on the Wall is situated on the north side of London Wall, just before its junction with Old Broad Street, and takes its name from its proximity to the old wall of the city. The benefice is a rectory, the patronage of which appertained, before the dissolution of monasteries, to the Priory of the Holy Trinity, Aldgate; it is now in the gift of the Lord Chancellor.

There is but little noteworthy in the history of All Hallows, though the parish books contain some interesting entries with reference to a fifteenth century "anker," *i.e.*, anchorite, who dwelt hard by the church—perhaps in a bastion of the wall—and was on several occasions a benefactor to it; and the marriage is recorded on December 26th, 1588, of Sir Francis Knollys, the Elizabethan statesman, to his second wife, Lettice Barratt. The old church escaped the Fire, but as it had fallen into a ruinous state, the parishioners in 1764 obtained an Act of Parliament for its demolition, and in its stead the present edifice was erected at a cost of a little under £3,000. The first stone was laid on July 10th, 1765, and the church was consecrated on September 8th, 1767. The architect was George Dance the younger.

The body of the church, which is broadest at the east end, is built of brick, but the steeple, which stands at the west, and includes a sort of Corinthian temple above the tower, is composed of stone. Access is gained to the interior through a vestibule beneath the tower. To the north and south walls respectively are attached four Ionic columns which support a frieze. The ceiling is arched, and divided into small panels. At each side of it are three semicircular windows, and there is also a small window in the west part of the north wall, just behind the font. Above the altar is placed a picture representing Saul restored to sight by Ananias at Damascus. This is a copy of a painting in the church of the Conception at Rome, by the Florentine artist, Pietro Berretini di Cortona (1596-1669), and was executed and presented to the church by Sir Nathaniel Dance Holland, a brother of the architect. At the sides of the altar are painted figures of Moses and Aaron. The pulpit, which stands against the north wall, is remarkable from the fact that it is entered by means of a flight of steps from the vestry-room. The organ, which is very small, stands in a gallery at the west. The south-easternmost bench is surmounted by an elegant sword-rest.

The interior of All Hallows was renovated and greatly improved in 1891.

Towards the west end, affixed one to the north and the other to the south wall, are two marble monuments preserved from the old church, commemorating Edmond Hammond, a benefactor to the parish, who died in 1642, and Mrs. Joan Bencè, who died in 1684. On the south of the chancel is a large monument, with bust, to Joseph Patience, an architect, who died in 1797; and on the north side is a tablet in memory of the Rev. William Beloe, the translator of Herodotus and Aulus Gellius, who died on April 11th, 1817, after having been rector of the parish for twenty years.

Beloe was succeeded by the Rev. Robert Nares, the Shakespearean glossary writer, who died in 1829.

In the churchyard wall, to the north of the church, a fragment of the old London wall may be discerned, and the vestry is said to be built with the material and on the foundation of one of the bastions.

ST. ALPHAGE, LONDON WALL

ST. ALPHAGE, London Wall, was anciently in the patronage of the collegiate church of St. Martin-le-Grand, being among the churches confirmed to the dean of that establishment by a charter of William the Conqueror in 1068. When St. Martin's-le-Grand was annexed by Henry VII. to the Abbey of Westminster, the abbot and convent became patrons, and, finally, Queen Mary bestowed the advowson on the see of London, in whose gift the rectory has ever since remained.

The parish church of St. Alphage originally stood on the north side of London Wall, where the churchyard may still be noticed. Within this churchyard is preserved a fragment of the old wall of the city, to which attention is attracted by an inscription.

The present church is situated on the south side of London Wall, extending on the east into Aldermanbury, and occupies a portion of the site of the church of the Elsing Hospital and Priory, founded by William Elsing, a mercer, who in 1329 commenced a hospital "for sustentation of one hundred blind men," and in 1332 established a priory, of which he himself became the first prior.

The Elsing Hospital and Priory having been surrendered to Henry VIII., "the principal aisle of this church towards the north," says Stow, "was pulled down, and a frame of four houses set up in place: the other part, from the steeple upward, was converted into a parish church of St. Alphage; and the parish church which stood near unto the wall of the city by Cripplegate was pulled down, the plot thereof made a carpenter's yard with saw-pits."

The hospital itself was at first utilized as a private dwelling-house, but the ground was afterwards occupied by the buildings of Sion College, which were completed in 1630, and the college remained on the site of Elsing's old foundation till its removal to its present premises on the Victoria Embankment in 1886.

The remnant of the priory church which had thus become parochial was extensively repaired by the parishioners between the years 1624 and 1628, and in 1649 they were compelled to rebuild the whole of the upper portion of the steeple. The church escaped the Fire, and was again repaired in 1701, but in 1774, having become hopelessly dilapidated, it was taken down, and the present edifice was erected by Sir William Staines, and first opened on July 24th, 1777.

The church of St. Alphage presents an eastern front in Aldermanbury and one at the north-west in London Wall, the rest of the building being concealed by the adjacent houses. Both these fronts are of brick, with stone columns and dressings to the doorways, and are extremely commonplace. The north-west door leads into a porch, the pointed arches of which proclaim it to have once formed a portion of the old priory church. It is, in fact, the only existing relic of the ancient building, having constituted the basement of the tower, which was spared when the upper part was demolished in 1649. The eastern arch, which is ornamented with two sculptured heads, gives admission to a vestibule, on the wall of which hangs a table of benefactors, and thence one passes through a door into the church.

St. Alphage, London Wall.

The interior is plain and uninteresting. Light is obtained by windows at the south and east; the ceiling is flat, and there are no aisles. The pulpit is placed on the south side, and the font at the north-west, and over the north-west door are affixed the royal arms. The organ is located at the west, and as there is no gallery, it stands upon the floor.

St. Alphage is, however, redeemed from utter dreariness by a very handsome monument on the north wall to Sir Rowland Hayward, twice Lord Mayor, in 1570 and 1591. Sir Rowland inhabited the hospital, and was a benefactor to the parish. The monument displays his figure kneeling in the centre between two pillars, and facing the church, and at the sides the kneeling figures of his two wives and sixteen children. Above the figure is a canopy, and the monument is adorned with Sir Rowland's coat-of-arms and the arms of his wives' families.

Sir Rowland Hayward's monument was placed on the south wall of the chancel of the old church. At the rebuilding it was repaired at the expense of the parishioners, in memory of his liberality, and re-erected in its present position.

On the same wall, a little farther to the east, a marble monument, bearing on its upper portion an allegorical representation of Charity tending children, commemorates Samuel Wright, who at his death in 1736 left charitable bequests to the amount of £20,950.

One of the parish books of St. Alphage contains a register of about forty persons who certified that they had been touched for the king's evil by Charles II.

St. Bartholomew the Less

The church of St. Bartholomew the Less, which in monastic times served as the chapel to the hospital, has since the dissolution of the priory been used as a parish church for the dwellers within the hospital precincts. The benefice is a vicarage in the gift of the governors of St. Bartholomew's Hospital.

The old tower, which stands at the west, and is surmounted by a small turret, still remains, but the interior, which had become much dilapidated, was entirely remodelled on an octagonal plan by the younger Dance in 1789. Dance's work, which was of timber, soon fell into decay, and the church was practically rebuilt in 1823 by Thomas Hardwick, who adhered to Dance's plan, but substituted for the timber stone and iron. The church has since then been again restored, so that it now presents an extremely modern appearance, with the exception of the vestibule beneath the tower, which still displays traces of the old work.

The area enclosed by the walls is almost square, but the octagonal shape is obtained by means of clustered columns and arches, above which is a clerestory, pierced with windows. The ceiling is groined. The organ is placed at the south of the chancel, and on the north is a handsome marble pulpit.

St. Bartholomew the Less.

The old church contained a large number of monuments, and a few of them have been preserved. The most ancient is a brass with male and female figures to William Markeby, who died in 1439, and Alice, his wife; and there may also be observed a tablet erected by Sir Thomas Bodley, the founder of the Bodleian Library at Oxford, in memory of his wife, Anne, and a monument, displaying a kneeling figure, to Robert Balthrope, "Sergeant of the Chirurgeons" to Queen Elizabeth, who died in 1591. But we now look in vain for the memorial of John and Margaret Shirley, who are described by Stow as "having their pictures of brass, in the habit of pilgrims, on a fair flat stone."

"This gentleman," continues Stow, "a great traveller in divers countries, amongst other his labours, painfully collected the works of Geffrey Chaucer, John Lidgate, and other learned writers, which works he wrote in sundry volumes to remain for posterity; I have seen them, and partly do possess them."

Sir Ralph Winwood, James I.'s ambassador to Holland, and Secretary of State, was buried at St. Bartholomew the Less, as was also James Heath, author of the "Flagellum, or the Life and Death of Oliver Cromwell, the late Usurper," characterized by Carlyle as a "mournful brown little book," and the "Chronicle of the Civil Wars," which the same historian considers as "little other than a tenebrific book." Inigo Jones was baptized here on July 19th, 1573.

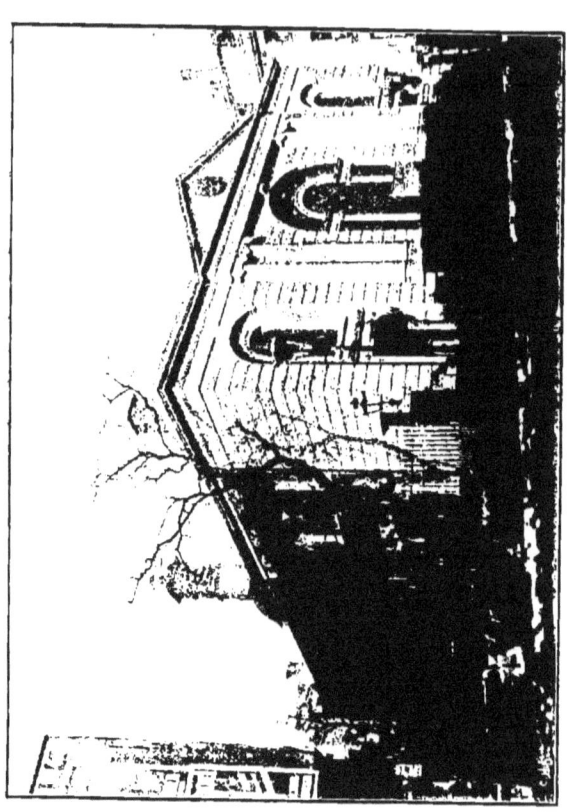

ST. BOTOLPH, ALDERSGATE.

To St. Botolph, an East Anglian saint of the seventh century, who gave his name to Boston, *i.e.*, Botolph's Town, in Lincolnshire, where he founded a celebrated monastery, were dedicated four churches in London, each of which stood by a gate of the city. One of these, St. Botolph's, Billingsgate, was not rebuilt after the Great Fire, but the other three, St. Botolph's, Aldersgate, St. Botolph's, Aldgate, and St. Botolph's, Bishopsgate, are still in existence.

St. Botolph's, Aldersgate, is situated opposite the General Post Office, at the corner of Little Britain. The benefice was anciently a rectory in the gift of the dean of St. Martin's-le-Grand, but Richard II. in the last year of his reign appropriated the rectory to that collegiate church, and St. Botolph's was afterwards served by a curate. The patronage passed to the abbot and convent of Westminster in the reign of Henry VII., and their successors, the dean and chapter, now appoint the vicar.

The church was repaired at a cost exceeding £400 by the parishioners in 1627, at which time a large portion of the steeple was rebuilt. It was but slightly damaged by the Great Fire, but in 1790, having become very dilapidated, it was pulled down, and a new church erected at an expenditure of about £10,000.

The present church of St. Botolph, Aldersgate, is divided into a nave and side-aisles by Corinthian columns. There are galleries on the north, south, and west; the last of which contains the organ. The ceiling, which is arched, has four central compartments, and is pierced on each side by four semicircular windows. The north and south walls each possess two rows of stained glass windows. The recess at the east, in which the altar is placed, is lighted by a spacious window, flanked by two smaller ones. The glass of the central window represents angels ministering to our Lord in the wilderness, and the side windows display figures of St. Peter and St. John. The pulpit, which stands on the south side of the church, is imposing from its height, but not otherwise interesting; on the opposite side a sword-rest is conspicuous.

The oldest remaining monument is that of Dame Anne Packington, a benefactress to the parish, who died on August 22nd 1563. She was the widow of Sir John Packington, described as "late Chirographer in the Court of the Common Pleas."

There is a monument with bust to Elizabeth, daughter of Sir William Hewitt, of St. Martin's-in-the-Fields, and wife of Sir Thomas Richardson, of Honingham, in Norfolk, who died in 1639 at the age of thirty-two; and two seventeenth century medical practitioners, Sir John Micklethwait and Dr. Francis Bernard, have here memorials. Micklethwait was physician to Charles II., and President of the College of Physicians, and died in 1683; Bernard, who died in 1698, was held up to ridicule by Garth, in the "Dispensary," under the name of Horoscope. An ornamental tablet commemorates Richard Chiswell, one of the principal booksellers of his time, who was a benefactor to St. Botolph's parish, in which he was born. He died on May 3rd, 1711, in his seventy-second year. The name of Elizabeth Smith, daughter of Philip and Elizabeth Smith, of this parish, who died, aged fifteen, in 1750, is perpetuated by a white marble bust, the work of Roubiliac; and a tablet is inscribed to Daniel Wray, F.R.S., F.S.A., who died on December 29th, 1783, aged eighty-two. Wray was for thirty-seven years Deputy-Teller of the Exchequer, one of the original Trustees of the British Museum, and part-author of the "Athenian Letters;" but he is especially noteworthy as the esteemed friend of the poets Dyer and Akenside. His widow, who long survived him, is commemorated by a smaller separate tablet.

St. Botolph's is built of brick. The tower rises at the west, and is crowned by a very insignificant turret. The east front displays a façade, consisting of four Ionic columns, placed two on each side of the central window, and supporting a pediment, within which is a clock-face. This façade did not form part of the original building, but was constructed in Roman cement in the year 1831, when the eastern limit of the church was curtailed, in order to widen the pavement. The rest of the exterior does not call for comment.

The churchyard, which is of considerable size, extends to the south and west of the church. It is beautifully laid out, and is open to the public during the summer months.

ST. BOTOLPH, ALDGATE.

THE church of St. Botolph, Aldgate, is placed at the junction of Aldgate High Street and Houndsditch. It is said to have been originally founded about the reign of William the Conqueror, and belonged to the burgesses of the Knighten Guild, descendants of thirteen knights who had land on the east part of the city conferred upon them by King Edgar, and were formed into a guild, whose privileges were confirmed by Edward the Confessor, and subsequently by William Rufus. These burgesses in 1115 gave the church of St. Botolph to the Priory of the Holy Trinity, Aldgate, then newly founded by Queen Matilda, and the cure continued to be served by one of the canons till the priory was surrendered to Henry VIII. in 1531.

Stow describes St. Botolph's as having been "lately new built at the special charges of the Priors of the Holy Trinity; patrons thereof, as it appeareth by the arms of that house, engraven on the stone work." But he goes on to complain that "the parishioners of this parish being of late years mightily increased, the church is pestered with lofts and seats for them." The old church remained standing till 1741, when, having become extremely dilapidated, it was pulled down, and replaced by the present church, which was designed by the elder Dance, the architect of the Mansion House, and completed in 1744 at an expenditure of over £5,500.

St. Botolph's is built of brick, with stone dressings. The tower, which is surmounted by a small spire, stands at the south, facing Aldgate High Street. The altar is placed at the north. The interior includes two side-aisles, separated from the central portion by Tuscan columns, which support a flat ceiling. There are galleries at the east, west, and south, the last of which contains the organ. The church is well furnished with windows, there being two rows in each of the side walls, one above and one below the gallery. The window over the altar is divided into three compartments, and the eastern and western aisles are each terminated by a window at the northern extremity. All these windows are filled with stained glass. The altar-piece displays Corinthian columns brightly gilded, with entablature and circular pediment. The pulpit stands on the east, and on the same side of the church appears a handsome sword-rest; the font is located at the south-east. The royal arms are placed in the vestibule at the south, over the doorway which leads into the church, and on the vestibule walls are some old paintings, which were originally placed above the altar, but were transferred to their present situation in 1875, when St. Botolph's was repaired, and the heaviness of its former aspect considerably modified.

The most interesting monument in St. Botolph's is a tomb of alabaster, overshadowed by a canopy, and bearing a well-sculptured recumbent figure in white marble, the lower parts of which are wrapped in a winding-sheet. It is inscribed to the memory of Thomas, Lord Darcy of the North, Sir Nicholas Carew, and various members of their families.

Lord Darcy and Sir Nicholas Carew were concerned in the Catholic plots against Henry VIII., and were both beheaded on Tower Hill, the former in 1537, and the latter in 1538. Their monument stood in the chancel of the old church over the family vault; when the new church was built, the monument was placed in the vestibule, but at the restoration it was removed to the west gallery. There is also a tablet against the south-west wall to Sir Edward Darcy, a grandson of Lord Darcy of the North, who died in 1612.

Robert Dowe, the charitable Merchant Taylor, who gave money for the ringing of the bell at St. Sepulchre's at the time of executions, died, at the age of eighty-nine, in 1612, and was buried at St. Botolph's. Besides various other acts of munificence, he was a benefactor to St. Botolph's parish, and to his own company of the Merchant Taylors, who erected to his memory a monument with half-length effigy, in which he is represented in his gown and cap, with peaked beard, and resting his hand on a skull. Dowe's monument was affixed to a pillar in the chancel of the old church, and after the rebuilding was again set up in the chancel; it has now, however, been removed to the east gallery.

To the north of the church, and at the east and west sides, is a churchyard, which is well planted and laid out, and is daily open to the public.

The right of presentation to St. Botolph's, which remained in the crown from the dissolution of the priory at Aldgate till the reign of Queen Elizabeth, passed afterwards through the hands of a number of private persons. The vicarage is now in the gift of the Bishop of London.

White Kennett, the historian and anti-Jacobite preacher, was incumbent of St. Botolph's from 1700 till 1707, when, after obtaining the deanery of Peterborough, he removed to St. Mary Aldermary, where, his parochial duties being less exacting, he was enabled to devote more time to study. He was raised to the bishopric of Peterborough in 1718, and dying on December 19th, 1728, was buried in his cathedral, "a practical sermon," as his biographer informs us, " being preached at his funeral, as he himself had also desired."

Saint Botolph's Bishopsgate

The church of St. Botolph, Bishopsgate, is situated in Bishopsgate Street Without, opposite Houndsditch. It is described by Stow as standing "in a fair churchyard, adjoining to the town ditch, upon the very bank thereof, but of old time inclosed with a comely wall of brick, lately repaired by Sir William Allen, mayor in the year 1571, because he was born in that parish, where also he was buried."

Of the early history of the church scarcely any facts of interest are recorded; but in later times its annals become more interesting. Edward Alleyn, the actor and founder of Dulwich College, who was the son of an innkeeper in the parish, was baptized here in 1566; an infant son of Ben Jonson was buried here in 1600; and Archibald Campbell, the seventh Earl of Argyll, and father of the celebrated first marquis, was married here in 1609 to his second wife, Anne, daughter of Sir William Cornwallis.

In 1615 the city gave to the parishioners additional ground on the west for their burying-ground, which had become too small for their needs. At the west end of the burying-ground, occupying the site of the present New Broad Street, was "a quadrant called Petty France of Frenchmen dwelling there."

The story of a curious interment not many years after the enlargement of the burying-ground is thus related by Anthony Munday:

"August 10. 1626. In Petty France out of Christian buriall was buried Hodges Shaughsware a Persian Merchant, who with his sonne came over with the Persian Ambassadour, and was buried by his owne Son, who read certaine prayers, and used other ceremonies, according to the custome of their owne Country, morning and evening, for a whole month after the buriall; for whom is set up at the charge of his sonne a Tombe of stone with certain Persian characters thereon; the exposition thus, 'This grave is made for Hodges Shaughsware, the chiefest Servant to the King of Persia, who came from the King of Persia and dyed in his service. If any Persian commeth out of that Country, let him read this and a prayer for him, the Lord receive his soule, for here lyeth Maghmote Shaughsware, who was borne in the Towne of Novoy in Persia."

In the burying-ground in Petty France the remains of the intrepid Puritan, John Lilburne, were interred in 1657.

A great benefactor to the church and parish was Sir Paul Pindar, a portion of whose mansion in Bishopsgate Street Without, afterwards the "Sir Paul Pindar's Head" public-house, remained standing till recently, but has now been entirely swept away in the extensions of the Liverpool Street Station. Sir Paul was one of the richest merchants of his time, and was sent ambassador to Turkey by James I. He was a munificent contributor towards the restoration of Old St. Paul's. Charles I. found in him a most faithful adherent, and enormous were the sums which he advanced to the king; but, like many another loyal subject,

> "Whose fate has been through good and ill
> To love his Royal Master still,"

his devotion to the cause of his prince plunged him into poverty, and he died in very embarrassed circumstances.

St. Botolph, Bishopsgate.

He was buried at St. Botolph's, where a monument was erected to his memory, with the following inscription :

> " Sir Paul Pindar, Kt.
> His Majesty's Ambassador to the Turkish Emperor
> Anno Dom. 1611, and Nine Years Resident.
> Faithful in Negotiations, Foreign and Domestick ;
> Eminent for Piety, Charity, Loyalty, and Prudence.
> An Inhabitant Twenty-six Years, and bountifull Benefactor
> to this Parish
> He died the 22d of August, 1650,
> Aged 84 years."

The old church, having become ruinous early in the eighteenth century, was taken down, and the first stone of the present structure was laid on April 10th, 1725, by Edmund Gibson, the learned Bishop of London. The new church was completed in 1729 at an expense of over £10,400. The architect is stated to have been James Gold.

St. Botolph's is a spacious and imposing, though not lofty, building, and includes two aisles, which are separated from the main body by Composite columns. The steeple is placed at the east end, so as to dominate Bishopsgate Street, and in consequence the chancel is formed beneath the tower. The ceiling is arched, and embellished with ornamental panels. It is pierced in the centre with a lantern, which was introduced in 1820, to remedy the deficiency of light in the church. There are galleries at the north, south, and west. The east and west windows are richly stained, and the organ is divided, so as to allow the west window to be seen. In the north and south walls are two rows of windows, one above and one below the gallery. The lower rows, together with windows on the same level at the north-west and south-west, are filled with stained glass representations of

scriptural subjects in memory of benefactors to the poor of the parish, and in front of each window is a marble tablet with names inscribed. The pulpit, which is of oak, and has a substantial appearance, is placed on the south side, and the font stands at the north-west.

On the north side of the chancel is Sir Paul Pindar's monument, and opposite to it is one to Andrew Willow, a benefactor to the parish, who died in 1700. There is also in the chancel a brass plate in memory of Sir William Blizard, President of the Royal College of Surgeons, who resided many years in the parish, and died in 1835 at the age of ninety-two.

The steeple is built of stone. The lowest storey has a large arched window in the centre, flanked by Doric pilasters and surmounted by their entablature and pediment. At each side is a doorway, and over each doorway are two small windows, the higher ones being circular. The second storey is adorned at the angles with pilasters supporting a cornice, above which a clock-dial is inserted on each face, while the sides are ornamented with carved scrolls. The third stage displays Ionic pilasters and entablature, and is finished at each corner with a flaming urn; and a small Composite temple, encircled at the base by a balustrade, and surmounted by a flaming urn, completes the whole. The tower contains eight bells. The remainder of the exterior is of red brick with stone dressings.

John Keats was baptized at St. Botolph's, Bishopsgate, on October 31st, 1795.

The infant school stands in the churchyard, and harmonizes well with the church. On its south front, on each side of the door, are placed figures of a boy and girl in quaint old costume. Close by it is the large tomb of Sir William Rawlins, sheriff in

1801. He was an upholsterer, and Thomas Dibdin was at one time his apprentice. He died in his eighty-sixth year on March 26th, 1838, and bequeathed £1,000 to the parish school.

Opposite the churchyard, but divided from it by the passage leading from Bishopsgate Street to New Broad Street, is an additional piece of ground which was bestowed on the parish by the Common Council in 1760. It has been prettily laid out, and is furnished with seats.

The rectory of St. Botolph, Bishopsgate, has been from ancient times in the gift of the Bishop of London. Stephen Gosson, rector from 1600 till his death in 1623, was the author, amongst other works, of "The Schoole of Abuse, conteining a Plesaunt Invective against Poets, Pipers, Plaiers, Jesters, and such like Catterpillers of a Commonwelth," published in 1579. Bishop Blomfield was appointed rector in 1819, and remained here till he was elevated to the see of Chester in 1824. The living, which is worth £1,200 a year, is the richest in the city of London.

St Dunstan in the West

THE church of St. Dunstan in the West, one of the most prominent landmarks on the north side of Fleet Street, is so called from its position almost at the extreme western boundary of the city, and in contradistinction to the fellow church of St. Dunstan in the East.

This church seems to have originally belonged to the monastery of Westminster, but in the year 1237 Richard de Barking, then abbot, granted it to King Henry III., who applied the profits to the maintenance of the asylum for converted Jews, an establishment subsequently transformed by Edward III. into the Rolls Court and Chapel. After the year 1361 the rectory of St. Dunstan's was bestowed on the abbot and convent of Alnwick in Northumberland, and the cure was served by one of their canons or by a priest of their nomination. About 1437 a vicarage was ordained and endowed, the patronage of which remained in the hands of the abbot and convent till they were dissolved by Henry VIII. Edward VI. gave the advowson of the vicarage to Lord Dudley, but it soon afterwards passed, together with the rectory, into the possession of the Sackvilles, Earls of Dorset, who retained the patronage for many years. The benefice is now a rectory, the advowson of which is held by the Simeon trustees.

William Tyndale, the translator of the New Testament, was a frequent preacher at St. Dunstan's in the West, where he attracted great attention by his unflinching advocacy of the reformed doctrines. Dr. Thomas White, the founder of Sion College, was presented to the vicarage in 1575. He became a prebendary of St. Paul's in 1588, treasurer of the church of Salisbury in 1590, Canon of Christ Church in 1591, and Canon of Windsor in 1593. He died on March 1st, 1623, and was buried in St. Dunstan's near the altar. He endowed a lecture at St. Dunstan's, and also a moral philosophy lecture at Oxford, of which university he was a graduate. His successor was Donne, the illustrious Dean of St. Paul's, who held the living till his death, March 31st, 1631. Coming down to a more recent epoch, William Romaine was appointed Lecturer at St. Dunstan's in 1749, and for some years drew large crowds to listen to his fervent and eloquent discourses.

Ralph Bane, Bishop of Lichfield and Coventry, and Oglethorpe, Bishop of Carlisle, the prelate who officiated at the coronation of Queen Elizabeth, both of whom died in 1559, were buried at St. Dunstan's. And here were baptized the great Earl of Strafford, born 1593, and Bulstrode Whitelocke, born 1605, the ambassador and author of the "Memorials of English Affairs."

St. Dunstan's escaped the Great Fire of 1666, but only very narrowly, as the flames extended to within three doors of the sacred building. In 1671 a new clock was supplied by Thomas Harrys, of Water Lane, to whom the parish accorded in payment the old clock and the sum of £35. To Harrys's clock were attached the two figures of giants with clubs to strike the hours and quarters, which became famous throughout London, and are noticed by many writers, as for example Cowper:

St. Dunstan in the West.

"When labour and when dullness, club in hand,
Like the two figures at St. Dunstan's stand,
Beating alternately in measured time
The clockwork tintinnabulum of rhyme,
Exact and regular the sounds will be,
But such mere quarter-strokes are not for me."

In 1701 the church was extensively repaired, and the old arched roof was removed, and a square roof, at a higher elevation, substituted. In 1730 the edifice a second time was threatened by an adjacent fire, but fortunately again escaped injury.

When Lud-gate was rebuilt in 1580, its west side was adorned by a statue of Queen Elizabeth. In 1760 Lud-gate was finally demolished, as an obstruction to the traffic; and the statue was presented by the City to Sir Francis Gosling. Sir Francis, who was alderman of the Ward of Farringdon Without, in which St. Dunstan's is situated, bestowed the statue on the church, and it was set up outside the east end, with a suitable inscription beneath.

The old church, which displayed a picturesque medley of different styles of architecture added at various times, was taken down towards the close of 1829. The giants were purchased by the Marquis of Hertford, who re-erected them outside his villa in Regent's Park.

The present church is set further back than its predecessor, which, projecting forward into the street, unduly narrowed the thoroughfare, and stands in what was formerly the churchyard. The first stone was laid on July 27th, 1831, and the building was consecrated on July 31st, 1833. The architect was John Shaw, who a few years previously had designed the new hall of Christ's Hospital. He died, before the church was quite completed, on July 30th, 1832, and the work was finished by his son.

The body of St. Dunstan's is principally composed of brick, but the tower, which rises at the south, facing Fleet Street, is of yellow freestone. The lowest storey contains the entrance doorway, which is ornamented with heads of Tyndale and Donne. In the panels at the sides are carved the royal arms and the arms of the City of London. The second storey is relieved merely by narrow loop-holes; the third, however, displays on each front a clock-face and large pointed opening. At each angle of the tower is placed a large pinnacle. Above the tower is a pierced octagonal lantern, having at the angles buttresses concluded by pinnacles, and the whole is terminated by a high, open parapet. The height of the tower is 90 feet, and the total height of the steeple 130 feet. The form, not a common one, is said to have been suggested to the architect by the steeples of St. Botolph's, Boston, and St. Helen's, York. The tower contains eight bells, which belonged to the old church.

The statue of Queen Elizabeth now stands in a niche at the east end of the south front, over the door leading to the vestry-room and parochial schools.

To the west of the main entrance, between the church rails, is placed a fountain, "The Gift of Sir James Duke, Bart., M.P., and Ald. of this Ward, 1860."

Access is gained to the church by means of a porch beneath the tower and a vestibule. The interior is octagonal in shape, and contains seven recesses, one on every side, except the entrance, which are separated from each other by clustered columns and pointed arches, supporting a clerestory pierced with eight windows. The roof is groined, and is formed by eight beams of iron, which are united at the centre. The altar occupies the northern recess. The altar-piece is of oak, and elaborately carved. It is crowned by three carved canopies of Flemish workmanship. The organ is located in a gallery at the south, above the entrance door. The font, which is of stone, is adorned on its upper portion with angel figures.

To the walls are affixed a large number of monuments belonging to the old church. The earliest consists of two brass kneeling figures, male and female, with labels protruding from their mouths. Beneath them is the following inscription:

"Here lyeth buryed the body of Henry Dacres, Cetezen and Marchant Taylor and sumtyme Alderman of London, and Elizabeth his Wyffe, the whych Henry decessed the — day of — the yere of our Lord God — and the said Elizabeth decessed the xxiii day of Apryll the yere of our Lord God MD^e and xxx."

A monument with male and female figures commemorates Gerard Legh, a member of the Inner Temple, who died in 1563, and his wife. The inscription is in Latin, but the greater part of it has become obliterated. Another monument of the Elizabethan period is a square tablet with a long Latin inscription to Sir Matthew Carew, Doctor of Law.

An ornate monument, which displays a female figure kneeling at a desk, and three children kneeling below, is that of Elizabeth North, who died in 1612. A kneeling male figure, the inscription beneath which is utterly illegible, appears to represent her husband, Roger North.

Cuthbert Fetherstone, the king's doorkeeper, who died in 1615, has a tablet with bust in frame, and there are several other seventeenth-century monuments, including an oval tablet to Alexander Layton, "ye famed Swordman," who died in 1679.

> "His Thrusts like Light'ing flew, more Skilful Death
> Parr'd 'em all, and beat him out of breath."

Among the later monuments are those of two Sir Richard Hoares, both Lord Mayors. The elder, who was elected to the chief magistracy of the city in 1712, died at the age of seventy in 1718; the younger Sir Richard's term of office commenced in 1745, "in which alarming crisis he discharged the great trust reposed in him with honour and integrity, to the approbation of his sovereign and the universal satisfaction of his fellow-citizens." He died in October, 1754. Their descendants, the Brothers Hoare, were liberal benefactors to the new church, to which they presented the window over the altar and the carved canopies of the altar-piece.

There is also a plain round tablet to an estimable professional man, thus inscribed:

"To the Memory
of Hobson Judkin Esq.
late of Clifford's Inn
The Honest Solicitor
who departed this Life June the 30 1812

This Tablet was erected by his Clients
as a Token of Gratitude and Respect for his
honest, faithful and friendly Conduct to them
thro' Life.
Go Reader and imitate
Hobson Judkin."

A tablet over the door of the vestibule records the dates of the foundation and consecration of the church, and the death of the architect, John Shaw. There are several memorial windows in the walls of the recesses, amongst them being one inserted in 1881 in memory of the Rev. E. Auriol, who was rector of the parish for many years.

On April 5th of the present year was unveiled a stained glass

St. Dunstan in the West.

window at the north-west in memory of Izaak Walton, the author of " The Compleat Angler," who was a parishioner of St. Dunstan's. The centre of the window is occupied by a figure of Walton, and at the sides are half-length figures of his brother-in-law, Bishop Ken, and the subjects of his " Lives," Sir Henry Wotton, George Herbert, Donne, Hooker, and Dr. Robert Sanderson.

To draw public attention to Walton's connection with the parish, and the insertion of this window in his honour, a tablet has been affixed to the south wall of the church, west of the doorway.

Holy Trinity Minories

The Minories derives its name from the Minoresses, or Nuns of the Order of St. Clare, for whom an abbey, situated on the east side of this street, was founded in 1293 by Edmund, Earl of Lancaster, the brother of Edward I. The abbey was surrendered to Henry VIII. in 1539, and Holy Trinity has since remained a parish church for the inhabitants of the old monastic precincts. It stands at the end of Church Street, the first turning out of the Minories on the left hand as one comes from Aldgate. The vicarage is in the gift of the Lord Chancellor.

The church and steeple were repaired in 1618-20, and the interior " well and very commendably beautified" in 1628. But, though it escaped the Great Fire, Holy Trinity had become very ruinous at the beginning of the eighteenth century, and was therefore entirely rebuilt, as we now see it, in 1706. The cost of the erection of the new church was about £700, towards which a Mr. Daniel King subscribed £200, and Lady Pritchard, widow of Sir William Pritchard, who had been Lord Mayor in 1682, £100, while the remainder was paid by the parishioners.

The present church is a very unpretending little structure, but contains at the west end some handsome carving from the old church, bearing the date 1620. There are monuments on the north side of the chancel to Colonel William Legge, Groom of the Bedchamber and Lieutenant-General of the Ordnance to Charles I., and subsequently to Charles II., who died on October 13th, 1672, and his son, George, the first Lord Dartmouth, Admiral of the Fleet, who died on October 25th, 1691. The Dartmouth family continued to be buried in the vaults beneath the church until their closure in 1849.

During the examination of the vaults in that year a very curious relic was brought to light, namely, a head, which is said to be that of Henry Grey, Duke of Suffolk, the father of Lady Jane Grey, who was beheaded on February 23rd, 1554, and to whom the abbey of the Minoresses had been granted by Edward VI. The head, having been cast into sawdust after being severed from the trunk, has been preserved from decay; the skin has very much the appearance of leather, and the features are perfectly clear and distinct. At its first discovery the teeth were entire, but since then several have dropped or been pulled out. The hair on the top of the head has fallen off, but some of a reddish colour remains about the chin. The head is kept in the vestry-room, and is enclosed in a small glass case to protect it from damage.

The exterior of Holy Trinity, Minories, is extremely plain. It has no proper tower, only a turret at the west end. A small square stone in front of the church is inscribed "1745;" beneath it was deposited a box filled with bones brought from the field of Culloden.

This was the church attended by Sir Isaac Newton when Master of the Mint.

St· Katherine· Coleman·

The church of St. Katherine Coleman is situated a little to the south of Fenchurch Street, and east of Mark Lane. Its name, says Stow, "was taken of a great haw-yard or garden, of old time called Coleman haw."

Anthony Munday considers that the south aisle of this church was rebuilt by William White, Lord Mayor 1489, giving his reasons as follows:

"Mr. Wright, the learned Parson here, gave me his gentle furtherance, shewing mee a glasse window in the south ile of the church, where is figured the shape of an Alderman in Scarlet, kneeling on his knees, and the words set downe by him doe expresse his name to be William White, Maior of this honourable Citie: Whereby he is perswaded, and I am likewise of his opinion (by divers opinions thereto inducing) that all that ile was either of his building or (at least) repairing, it appeareth so novell to the rest."

The church was repaired in 1620, and in 1624 a vestry was built, and "a gallery new made for the Poor of the Parish to sit in." In 1703 more repairs and adornments took place, but in 1734 the old structure was pulled down, and the present church erected from the designs of an architect named Horne. It is built of brick with stone dressings, having a tower at the west, but presents no features of interest.

The benefice of St. Katherine Coleman is a rectory, and was anciently in the gift of the Dean of St. Martin's-le-Grand, and afterwards in that of the abbot and convent of Westminster. The patronage now appertains to the see of London, to which the advowson was given by Queen Mary.

ST. MARY WOOLNOTH.

THE church of St. Mary Woolnoth is situated at the junction of Lombard Street and King William Street. The date of its original foundation is unknown, and but little is recorded of its early history.

It was rebuilt, as Newcourt tells us, "from the very foundations, as it seems," about 1438, and consecrated in that year by an Irish bishop, acting under a commission from the Bishop of London. But the work was apparently not completed till considerably later, for we are informed by Stow that "Sir Hugh Brice, Goldsmith, Mayor in the first year of Henry VII., Keeper of the King's Exchange at London, and one of the Governors of the King's Mint in the Tower of London," who died in 1496, and was buried here, "built in this church a chapel called the Charnell, as also part of the body of the church and of the steeple, and gave money toward the finishing thereof, besides the stone which he had prepared."

The advowson of the rectory of St. Mary Woolnoth, which had been among the possessions of the priory of St. Helen's, Bishopsgate, was, after the suppression of that establishment, granted by Henry VIII. to Sir Martin Bowes. Sir Martin, who was a goldsmith, and Lord Mayor in 1545, resided in Lombard Street, the site of his house being now occupied by the bank of Messrs. Glyn, Mills and Co. He died on August 4th, 1566, and was buried in the chancel together with his three wives. He left some charitable bequests to the parish, for the distribution of which he appointed his company trustees. The advowson, after remaining for several generations in the Bowes family, passed into the hands of the Goldsmiths' Company.

Sir Thomas Ramsey, Lord Mayor in 1577, was buried here in 1590, and "a very goodly monument" in the chancel was erected over him and his first wife. His second wife, who survived him, was Dame Mary Ramsey, the benefactress of Christ's Hospital.

The church of St. Mary Woolchurch Haw stood close to the Stocks Market, which was held on the site now occupied by the Mansion House. It was "so called," says Stow, "of a beam placed in the churchyard, which was thereof called Woolchurch Haw, of the tronage, or weighing of wool there used." If this explanation be correct, the name of St. Mary Woolnoth, which has proved very difficult to account for, may also very probably contain an allusion to the wool trade.

St. Mary Woolchurch was built, as we learn from Newcourt, subsequently to the Conquest, by Hubert de Ria, the father of Eudo, steward to Henry I. Eudo founded the abbey of St. John at Colchester, and bestowed upon it the patronage of this church of St. Mary, described as "Ecclesiam S. Mariæ de Westcheping, London, quæ vocatur Niewechirche," and that of the neighbouring church of St. Stephen, Walbrook. The abbot and convent of Colchester continued patrons of St. Mary Woolchurch till the dissolution of monasteries, since which time the advowson of the rectory has been retained by the Crown.

St. Mary Woolchurch, which Stow considered "reasonable fair and large," was "new built by license granted in the 20th of

St. Mary Woolnoth.

Henry VI.;" but having been consumed by the Great Fire, it was not again erected, its parish being united with that of St. Mary Woolnoth.

St. Mary Woolnoth, though damaged by the Fire, was not destroyed. The steeple remained standing, as did also part of the walls. Wren repaired it in 1677, entirely rebuilding the north side, facing Lombard Street, but constructing almost all the remainder upon the old walls. Sir Robert Vyner, Lord Mayor in 1674, contributed munificently towards the expenses of this restoration. He was a goldsmith, and had a mansion in Lombard Street, on the spot where the Branch Post Office and the Guardian Assurance Office now stand, and in compliment to him vines were spread about the church on the side fronting his house, "insomuch," says Strype, "that the church was used to be called Sir Robert Vyner's church."

The injuries which St. Mary Woolnoth had received from the Fire were, however, so severe that Wren's repairs proved of no avail to secure a prolonged existence for the shattered structure. During the reign of Queen Anne the building fell into an extremely dangerous state, and the parishioners having obtained an Act of Parliament enabling the commissioners who had charge of the erection of fifty new churches under Queen Anne's Act to advance money for the rebuilding, the old church and steeple were pulled down in 1716, and the present church commenced. It was first opened for divine worship on Easter Day, 1727. The architect was Nicholas Hawksmoor, Wren's pupil, and St. Mary Woolnoth is undoubtedly one of the finest of his works.

The interior of St. Mary Woolnoth is almost square. It contains twelve handsome Corinthian columns, which are placed at the angles in groups of three, and support an entablature, which is prolonged to the walls by means of pilasters. Above the entablature is a clerestory, which is pierced on each of its four sides with a large semicircular window. There are also four small windows in the south wall, but none at the north. The clerestory windows are filled with stained glass, but those in the south wall are plain. The ceiling is flat, and is divided into panels and richly ornamented. The altar-piece, which occupies an arched recess at the east, is of oak, and displays two prominent twisted columns. The pulpit, likewise of oak, and a fine piece of work, stands on the north side, and is surmounted by a very large sounding-board.

There were formerly highly-ornamented oak galleries at the north, south, and west, but in 1876, when the high pews were taken away, these were also removed, though there is still a diminutive gallery over the entrance doorway at the west, from which project the banners of the Goldsmiths' Company. The supports of the galleries, and the gallery fronts, however, which are very handsome, remain against the walls. The organ, which was built by Father Smith, and is enclosed in an imposing case, was transferred at the same time to the north of the chancel.[1]

To the north wall is affixed a white marble tablet in memory of Cowper's friend, John Newton, who was rector of the united parishes for twenty-eight years. It bears the epitaph which he had written for himself:

"John Newton, Clerk, once an infidel and libertine, a servant of slaves in Africa, was, by the rich mercy of Our Lord and Saviour, Jesus Christ, preserved, restored, pardoned, and appointed to preach the faith he had long laboured to destroy."

[1] The organ has been thoroughly renovated, and was reopened on Sunday, November 11th, 1894.

St. Mary Woolnoth.

Some curious old documents are appended to the south wall; the most ancient, by which a small sum of money was bequeathed to the church, dates from about 1290, but the name of the donor does not appear to be known.

St. Mary Woolnoth occupies one of the most conspicuous positions in the city, and its exterior is certainly striking, although too heavy to be entirely pleasing. The tower is placed at the west; its basement storey contains the doorway, and over it a semicircular window; above the cornice is a pedestal, which supports Composite columns, and the summit is divided into two turrets surmounted by balustrades, which present a very original appearance. The north front is varied by three niches, each of which encloses two Ionic columns on pedestals; but the south front is unadorned, for the reason that it was hidden from view by the adjacent buildings previously to the formation of King William Street. A projecting clock is attached by a bracket to the north wall towards the west end.

St. Mary Woolnoth was threatened with destruction in 1863, but it was preserved by the exertions of some of the parishioners, including the then Lord Mayor, Alderman Rose, a parishioner in respect of his occupancy of the Mansion House. Again during the last year something has been heard of a scheme for pulling it down; it has, however, found able defenders, and no effort will be spared to frustrate this barbarous design, and to guard from the wanton hand of the destroyer the beautiful and unique church of St. Mary Woolnoth.

ST. PETER-LE-POER.

THE church of St. Peter-le-Poer is situated on the north side of Old Broad Street. The reason of its distinguishing title is not certainly known. Stow conjectured that it was "sometime peradventure a poor parish," "but at this present," he adds, "there be many fair houses, possessed by rich merchants and other." As, however, the church is styled in ancient documents "Parvus," "Poer" may perhaps more probably be a corruption of that designation.

The church was enlarged and very extensively repaired, both internally and externally, between the years 1615 and 1630. In the former year, additional space having been gained on the north side, Sir William Garaway, a wealthy merchant, built a new north aisle at his own expense. He died in 1625 at the advanced age of eighty-eight, and was buried in a vault at the east end of this aisle, and "a fair and comely monument" marked the site of his grave. The whole cost of the repairs and alterations is stated to have amounted to almost £1,600, £400 of which was paid by Garaway, and the rest by the parishioners.

The rectory of St. Peter-le-Poer has been from time immemorial in the gift of the Dean and Chapter of St. Paul's. Dr. Richard Holdsworth, who was rector at the commencement of the Civil War, was sequestered, and for a time imprisoned, by the Long

Parliament. "This most eminent and loyal person," as Newcourt calls him, was born at Newcastle-upon-Tyne, and was educated at St. John's College, Cambridge. He was Master of Emmanuel College, and several times Vice-Chancellor of the University, and he was also professor of divinity at Gresham College. Before the outbreak of the war he had declined the bishopric of Bristol, but in 1645 he accepted the deanery of Worcester. He attended on Charles I. during his confinement at Hampton Court and Carisbrooke, and did not long survive his sovereign, dying on August 22nd, 1649. He was buried in St. Peter-le-Poer, where a monument was set up to his memory, which, after the demolition of the old church, lay for nearly a century hidden in the vaults and totally forgotten, but, having been accidentally discovered, has been brought above ground again, and erected against the wall above the stairway leading to the organ-gallery.

Dr. Benjamin Hoadly, the famous Whig theologian and controversialist, became rector of St. Peter-le-Poer in 1704. In 1715 he was raised to the see of Bangor, but continued to hold the rectory till 1720. In 1721 he was translated to Hereford, in 1723 to Salisbury, and finally in 1734 to Winchester. He died, when considerably over eighty, on April 17th, 1761.

The old church, having become much decayed, was taken down in 1788, and the present church, which stands farther back than the old one, which was an obstruction to the thoroughfare, was erected in its stead from the designs of Jesse Gibson, and consecrated, as is recorded by an inscription below the organ, by Bishop Porteous on November 19th, 1792. It is by no means a beautiful edifice, is circular in shape, having a recess at the north for the altar, and is lighted by a large lantern with glass sides in the centre of the ceiling. There was originally a gallery running round the church to the sides of the recess in which the altar is placed, but at the restoration in 1888 this was taken away, with the exception of a small portion at the south, which contains the organ. On the east side of the church may be observed a sword-rest, and at the south is a handsome marble font, with an inscription notifying that it was given by the present rector, the Rev. J. H. Coward, in memory of his wife. On the walls of the vestry-room, which is situated at the south-east, are hung engravings of the two churches, the old and the new, and also engravings of the old Navy and Excise Offices, besides plans of the church and parish.

The steeple rises at the south, the only side on which the exterior is visible, the rest of it being concealed by the surrounding buildings. The square tower supports a stone cupola dominated by a vane. The basement storey contains the entrance doorway, which is flanked on each side by two attached columns, and surmounted by an entablature and pediment. There are two windows, one on each side of the doorway. The church is rather a prominent object in Old Broad Street, but the outside is quite as commonplace as the interior.

The church of St. Benet Fink in Threadneedle Street derived its title from its re-builder, Robert Finke, whose name is likewise perpetuated in Finch Lane, in which his mansion stood.

The benefice was originally a rectory, and the advowson was in the possession of the Neville family. From them it appears to have passed to the adjacent Hospital of St. Anthony of Vienna, to which the church was appropriated in 1440. From this time it became a curacy, the curate being appointed by the master and brethren of the hospital. In 1474 Edward IV. annexed the hospital to St. George's, Windsor, and St. Benet Fink was thence-

St. Peter-le-Poer.

forth served by one of the canons of Windsor or by a curate of their nomination.

The church was repaired and beautified in 1633, but perished in the Great Fire. It was rebuilt by Wren between the years 1673-76 at a cost of over £4,000, towards which £1,000 was contributed by a Mr. George Holman. The parishioners, as a mark of their gratitude, presented him with two pews and a vault, which were to be for him and his heirs for ever, and his arms were emblazoned on the east window. Wren's church was elliptical in shape, and measured 63 feet by 48. It was traversed by six Composite columns, which, with the arches connecting them, supported the roof. The steeple, which attained a total altitude of about 110 feet, consisted of a tower, lead-covered cupola, and lantern.

Richard Baxter, the great Nonconformist divine, was married at St. Benet Fink to Margaret Charlton on September 10th, 1662; and the parish register records the burial, on August 12th, 1679, of Magdalen, the first wife of Alexander Pope the elder, and mother of Mrs. Racket, the poet's half-sister.

St. Benet Fink was demolished between 1842 and 1844 on the erection of the present Royal Exchange, and its parish was united with that of St. Peter-le-Poer.

St. Sepulchre.

At the eastern end of Holborn Viaduct, on the north side of the way, and just to the west of Giltspur Street, stands the church of St. Sepulchre, the name of which carries us back to Crusading times. This church with its appurtenances was bestowed in the twelfth century by Roger, Bishop of Salisbury, on the prior and canons of St. Bartholomew, West Smithfield; to whom it was confirmed by a charter of Henry III. in 1253, and in whose possession it continued till the dissolution of monasteries.

Stow, who calls it St. Sepulchre's "in the Bayly, or by Chamberlain gate" (an old name for Newgate), states that it was rebuilt about the reign of Henry VI. or Edward IV. "One of the Pophames," he adds, "was a great builder there, namely of one fair chapel on the south side of the choir, as appeareth by his arms and other monuments in the glass windows thereof, and also the fair porch of the same church towards the south; his image, fair graven in stone, was fixed over the said porch, but defaced and beaten down; his title by offices was this, Chancellor of Normandy, Captain of Vernoyle, Pearch, Susan, and Bayon, and treasurer of the King's household: he died rich, leaving great treasure of strange coins, and was buried in the Charterhouse church by West Smithfield."

The south porch and the tower—considerably altered—are all that now remain of Pophame's building, as the main part of the church was destroyed by the Great Fire of 1666. It was rebuilt about 1670, some say under the direction of Sir Christopher Wren; but others maintain that the parishioners were in too great a hurry to wait till he had leisure to undertake the work, and completed their church without his assistance. It is, in fact, quite uncertain whether Wren did, or did not, participate in the rebuilding; neither is it a matter of much interest, for St. Sepulchre's has been so frequently restored that it now presents an extremely modern appearance. It was extensively repaired in 1738, and again in 1837, when a new roof was put on. More alterations took place in 1863; and in 1875 the pinnacles of the tower, which had received considerable repairs in Charles I.'s time, and again after the Fire, were rebuilt. The tower and porch, which latter contains three floors, were then refaced, and the tracery of their windows was renewed, while a new oriel was constructed on the front of the porch at the spot once ornamented by Pophame's statue. Between 1878 and 1880 the body of the church was completely transformed both inside and out; new windows were inserted, and fresh buttresses and battlements substituted.

St. Sepulchre's in its present condition is an imposing church, consisting of a nave, chancel, and two side-aisles, and an adjunct on the north side called the chapel of St. Stephen. The church is entered through a vestibule, and its total length is 150 feet, the width, inclusive of the side chapel, being 81 feet. The height of the tower, to the top of the pinnacles, was before its restoration 152 feet 9 inches, but its altitude has been slightly reduced, and it now measures 149 feet 11 inches. It contains ten bells. The font, which is surmounted by a well-carved wooden cover bearing the date 1670, stands in the vestibule, having been removed to its present position from St. Stephen's Chapel, which was also formerly used for a Sunday School, in order to make room for the organ, by which the chapel is now occupied. This organ was built by Renatus Harris, and was considered to be one of his finest productions. It has been many times repaired and altered since its first erection on the rebuilding of the church after the Fire. The case is very handsome, and is said to have been the work of Grinling Gibbons.

In St. Sepulchre's was buried Roger Ascham, the tutor of Queen Elizabeth, and author of "Toxophilus" and the "Scholemaster," who died December 30th, 1568; but he has no memorial. Here also was interred the adventurous soldier, Captain John Smith, author of the "General History of Virginia." His monument has perished, but its position, on the south wall just outside the chancel, is marked by a brass plate with a replica of the original inscription:

> "To the living memory of his deceased Friend
> Captain John Smith
> Sometime Governour of Virginia
> And Admiral of New England
> Who departed this life the 21st of June 1631.
> Accordiamus, Vincere est Vivere.
>
> Here lyes one conquered that hath conquered Kings,
> Subdu'd large Territories, and done Things,

St. Sepulchre.

> Which to the World impossible would seem,
> But that the Truth is held in more Esteem.
> Shall I report his former Service done
> In honour of his God and Christendom?
> How that he did divide from Pagans three
> Their Heads and Lives, Types of his Chivaldry;
> For which great Service in that Climate done,
> Brave Sigismundus, King of Hungarion,
> Did give him as a Coat of Arms to wear
> These Conquered Heads got by his Sword and Spear.
> Or shall I tell of his Adventures since,
> Done in Virginia, that large Continent?
> How that he subdu'd Kings unto his Yoke,
> And made those Heathen flee, as Wind doth Smoke;
> And made their Land, being of so large a Station
> An Habitation for our Christian Nation,
> Where God is glorify'd, their Wants supply'd;
> Which else for Necessaries must have dy'd.
> But what avails his Conquests, now he lyes
> Interred in Earth, a Prey to Worms and Flyes?
> O! May his Soul in sweet Elysium sleep,
> Until the Keeper, that all Souls doth keep,
> Return to Judgment: and that after thence,
> With Angels he may have his Recompence."

The remains of Sir Robert Peake, a gallant cavalier and distinguished engraver, who died in 1667, were entombed at St. Sepulchre's, but no one else of importance appears to have been buried here, though there are several small monuments and tablets affixed to the walls.

In 1605 Robert Dowe, citizen and merchant taylor, gave to the parish the sum of £50, on condition that the parochial authorities should on the night before every execution day send to the neighbouring prison of Newgate a person who would take his stand in front of the window of the condemned prisoners' dungeon, and "give there twelve solemn towles with double strokes" with a handbell presented by Dowe for this purpose; and having thus aroused their attention, would "deliver with a loud and audible voice" an exhortation intended to bring them to a proper sense of their condition. Dowe also stipulated that the largest bell of St. Sepulchre's should toll on the mornings of the executions "in manner as the passing-bell is used," "to the end and purpose that all good people hearing this passing-bell may be moved to pray for those poor sinners going to execution." His donation has now been transferred from the parish into the hands of the Charity Commissioners.

After the dissolution of the Priory of St. Bartholomew, the patronage of St. Sepulchre's was retained by the Crown till 1610, when James I. granted the advowson to Francis Philips; it subsequently came into the possession of the President and Fellows of St. John's College, Oxford, who still present to the vicarage. The greater part of the parish is situated within the city boundaries in the Ward of Farringdon Without, but as a small portion, about a fifth, of it lies beyond the civic jurisdiction, two sets of churchwardens, in accordance with the custom prevailing in such cases, are annually appointed.

John Rogers, one of the first who suffered martyrdom at the stake in the reign of Queen Mary, was vicar of St. Sepulchre's.

St. Sepulchre's churchyard was originally very extensive. In Stow's day it was "not so large as of old time, for the same is letten out for buildings and a garden plot;" but it continued long afterwards to stretch on the south side some distance into the road, from which it was separated by a high wall. In 1760 the wall was pulled down, and the churchyard curtailed; when the Holborn Viaduct was constructed, it was still further abridged,

St. Sepulchre.

and many bodies were exhumed in 1871 and re-interred in the City Cemetery at Ilford. The small remnant of it still left has been planted with trees and flowers, and fitted with seats for the accommodation of the public, to whom it is open during the summer months

INDEX OF CHURCHES.

St. Alban, Wood Street, 8, 113-115.
All Hallows Barking, 2, 5, 6, 8, 15-27.
All Hallows, Bread Street, 10, 250, 251.
All Hallows, Honey Lane, 3, 10, 244, 245.
All Hallows, Lombard Street, 8, 116-121, 176.
All Hallows on the Wall, 2, 9, 307-309.
All Hallows Staining, 6, 11, 101, 102, 109, 110.
All Hallows the Great, Upper Thames Street, 2, 5, 7, 10, 206, 262-264, 282.
All Hallows the Less, 2, 10, 262.
St. Alphage, London Wall, 6, 9, 311-313.
St. Andrew by the Wardrobe, 8, 122-125.
St. Andrew, Holborn, 3, 5, 8, 126-132, 303.
St. Andrew Hubbard, 2, 10, 238, 239.
St. Andrew Undershaft, 2, 5, 6, 8, 28-36, 236.
St. Anne and St. Agnes, Aldersgate, 8, 133, 134.
St. Anne, Blackfriars, 10, 123.
St. Antholin, Watling Street, 10, 235, 236.

St. Augustine, Watling Street, 8, 135-138, 222.

St. Bartholomew by the Exchange, 7, 10, 202, 207, 208, 211.
St. Bartholomew the Great, West Smithfield, 6, 8, 37-51, 209.
St. Bartholomew the Less, 6, 9, 314, 315.
St. Benet Fink, 7, 10, 350, 351.
St. Benet Gracechurch, 10, 102, 119, 120.
St. Benet, Paul's Wharf, 8, 9, 139-141, 279.
St. Benet Sherehog, 10, 245, 288, 289.
St. Botolph, Aldersgate, 9, 317-319.
St. Botolph, Aldgate, 9, 317, 321-324.
St. Botolph, Billingsgate, 10, 181, 317.
St. Botolph, Bishopsgate, 6, 9, 317, 325-330.
St. Bride, Fleet Street, 4, 8, 142-149, 157, 215, 247.

Christ Church, Newgate Street, 2, 4, 8, 136, 150-157, 199, 299.
St. Christopher-le-Stocks, 7, 10, 206, 207, 211.
St. Clement, Eastcheap, 8, 159-162.

St. Dionis Backchurch, 10, 120, 121.

St. Dunstan in the East, 4, 8, 9, 163-175, 246, 331.
St. Dunstan in the West, 6, 9, 163, 331-337.

St. Edmund the King and Martyr, 8, 176-179.
St. Ethelburga, Bishopsgate Street, 6, 8, 52-54.

St. Faith under St. Paul's, 10, 135, 136, 221, 222.

St. Gabriel Fenchurch, 10, 120, 213.
St. George, Botolph Lane, 8, 181, 182.
St. Giles, Cripplegate, 5, 6, 8, 55-72.
St. Gregory by St. Paul's, 10, 221, 222.

St. Helen, Bishopsgate, 5, 6, 8, 73-93.

St. James, Duke's Place, Aldgate, 6, 11, 99.
St. James, Garlickhithe, 8, 183-188.
St. John the Baptist upon Walbrook, 10, 133, 235, 236, 237.
St. John the Evangelist, 10, 250.
St. John Zachary, 10, 133, 134.

St. Katherine Coleman, 9, 340, 341.
St. Katherine Cree, 2, 6, 8, 94-99.

St. Lawrence Jewry, 8, 189-196, 229, 253.
St. Lawrence Poultney, 2, 10, 223, 225, 226.
St. Leonard, Eastcheap, 10, 120.
St. Leonard, Foster Lane, 10, 154, 155.

St. Magnus the Martyr, 4, 8, 197-204, 208.

St. Margaret, Lothbury, 8, 205-211, 263, 282.
St. Margaret Moses, 2, 10, 272.
St. Margaret, New Fish Street, 10, 197, 198, 203.
St. Margaret Pattens, 8, 212-215, 281, 282.
St. Martin, Ludgate, 8, 216-222.
St. Martin Orgar, 10, 159, 160, 161, 162.
St. Martin Outwich, 6, 11, 76, 77, 79, 89, 90, 93.
St. Martin Pomary, 10, 209, 211.
St. Martin Vintry, 10, 261, 262.
St. Mary Abchurch, 1, 4, 8, 223-227.
St. Mary, Aldermanbury, 1, 8, 228-231.
St. Mary Aldermary, 1, 8, 232-237, 242, 323.
St. Mary-at-Hill, 1, 8, 9, 238-241.
St. Mary Bothaw, 1, 10, 278, 295, 298.
St. Mary Colechurch, 1, 10, 211.
St. Mary-le-Bow, 1, 3, 4, 8, 143, 165, 215, 242-251.
St. Mary Mounthaw, 2, 10, 278, 279.
St. Mary Somerset, 1, 4, 7, 11, 277, 278, 279.
St. Mary Staining, 1, 10, 266.
St. Mary Woolchurch Haw, 1, 10, 344, 345.
St. Mary Woolnoth, 1, 3, 6, 9, 343-347.
St. Mary Magdalene, Milk Street, 10, 191, 253.
St. Mary Magdalene, Old Fish Street, 10, 220, 221, 222.
St. Matthew, Friday Street, 11, 302, 303.
St. Michael Bassishaw, 7, 8, 252, 253.

Index of Churches.

St. Michael, Cornhill, 8, 66, 254-258, 280.
St. Michael, Crooked Lane, 7, 11, 203, 204.
St. Michael-le-Querne, 10, 301, 302.
St. Michael Paternoster Royal, 4, 8, 259-264.
St. Michael, Queenhithe, 11, 187, 188.
St. Michael, Wood Street, 8, 265-268.
St. Mildred, Bread Street, 4, 8, 269-274.
St. Mildred, Poultry, 11, 209, 210, 211.

St. Nicholas Acon, 10, 177, 178.
St. Nicholas Cole Abbey, 9, 141, 275-279.
St. Nicholas Olave, 10, 275, 279.

St. Olave, Hart Street, 5, 6, 8, 100-110, 119.
St. Olave Jewry, 11, 100, 208, 209, 211, 265.

St. Olave, Silver Street, 10, 100, 114.

St. Pancras, Soper Lane, 3, 10, 244, 245.
St. Peter, Cornhill, 5, 9, 280-284.
St. Peter-le-Poer, 9, 348-351.
St. Peter, Paul's Wharf, 10, 140, 279.
St. Peter, Westcheap, 10, 303.

St. Sepulchre, 3, 9, 152, 323, 252-357.
St. Stephen, Coleman Street, 9, 285, 286.
St. Stephen, Walbrook, 4, 9, 287-293, 344.
St. Swithin by London Stone, 4, 9, 294-298.

St. Thomas the Apostle, 10, 233, 235.
Trinity, Holy, the Less, 10, 188.
Trinity, Holy, Minories, 9, 338, 339.

St. Vedast, Foster Lane, 4, 9, 299-303.

INDEX OF PROPER NAMES.

Abbis, Rev. John, rector of St. Bartholomew the Great, 41.

Addington, Henry, baptized at St. Andrew's, Holborn, 131.

Addison, Joseph, married at St. Edmund the King and Martyr, 179.

Aelmund, gave advowson of St. Giles, Cripplegate, to Dean and Chapter of St. Paul's, 55.

Akenside, Mark, a friend of Daniel Wray, 319.

Albany, Duchess of, at St. Bartholomew the Great, 49.

Albemarle, Duke of, his monument in Westminster Abbey, 25.

Alcock, John, afterwards Bishop of Ely, rector of St. Margaret, New Fish Street, 198.

Alfune, founder of St. Giles, Cripplegate, 55, 56.

Allen, Joseph, afterwards Bishop of Bristol, vicar of St. Bride, Fleet Street, 146.

Allen, Miss Mary, organist at St. Andrew Undershaft, 30.

Allen, Sir William, repaired St. Botolph, Bishopsgate, 325.

Alleyn, Edward, memorial window to, at St. Giles, Cripplegate, 59, 60; baptized at St. Botolph, Bishopsgate, 325.

Alwine, Nicholas, buried at St. Mary-le-Bow, 244.

Alwyne, Bishop of Helmeham, conveyed the remains of King Edmund to London, 73.

Andrewes, Lancelot, afterwards Bishop of Winchester, vicar of St. Giles, Cripplegate, 61, 70; Earl of Essex baptized by, 109.

Anne, Queen, 48, 258; screen said to have been presented by Hanse merchants to All Hallows the Great in her reign, 263; Act of, for building new churches, 345.

Anne of Bohemia, queen of Richard II., monument to, in Westminster Abbey, 197.

Annesley, Samuel, vicar of St. Giles, Cripplegate, 70.

Anthony, St., St. Antholin's dedicated to, 236.

Apsley, Lucy, married to John Hutchinson at St. Andrew's, Holborn, 131.

Argyll, Archibald, seventh Earl of, married at St. Botolph, Bishopsgate, 325.

Armer, William, monument to, in All Hallows Barking, 23.

Arundel, Thomas, Archbishop of Canterbury, obtained advowson of St. Mary Aldermary for his see, 233.

Index of Proper Names. 363

Arundel, Earl of, 85, 97.
Ascham, Roger, buried at St. Sepulchre's, 354.
Ashmole, Elias, married at St. Benet, Paul's Wharf, 141.
Asshfeld, Alice, prioress of the convent of St. Helen, 74.
Audley, Lord, priory of Holy Trinity, Aldgate, and advowson of St. Katherine Cree bestowed on, by Henry VIII., 93.
Augustine, first Archbishop of Canterbury, St. Augustine's Church dedicated to, 135.
Auriol, Rev. E., memorial window to, at St. Dunstan's in the West, 336.
Avenon, Dame Alice, benefactress to St. Lawrence Jewry, 190, 191; memorial window to, 193.
Avenon, William, porch given by, to St. Katherine Cree, 97.

Bacon, Francis, Viscount St. Albans, death of, 85; his attachment to Lady Elizabeth Hatton, 130; his marriage, 159; one of his uncles an alderman, 164; edition of his "Letters and Speeches," by Birch, 214.
Bacon, Alderman James, buried at St. Dunstan's in the East, 164.
Bacon, John, brass to, at All Hallows Barking, 22.
Bacon, John, sculptor, bust of Milton in St. Giles, Cripplegate, by, 65, 66; bas-relief in St. Katherine Cree by, 98; monument in St. Andrew by the Wardrobe by, 124, 125; monument in St. Edmund the King and Martyr by, 178.

Bacon, John, junior, sculptor, monument in St. Andrew by the Wardrobe by, 125.
Baillie, Messrs., stained glass in St. Dunstan's in the East by, 168.
Bainton, Colonel Charles, monument to, in St. Mary le-Bow, 249.
Baker, Sir Richard, buried at St. Bride's, Fleet Street, 146, 147.
Balthrope, Robert, monument to, at St. Bartholomew the Less, 315.
Bancroft, Francis, monument to, in St. Helen, Bishopsgate, 79, 80, 92.
Bane, Ralph, Bishop of Lichfield, buried at St. Dunstan's in the West, 332.
Banks, Thomas, monument in St. Giles, Cripplegate, by, 67, 68; monument in St. Mary-le-Bow by, 249.
Barber, Alderman, house of, on Lambeth Hill, 141.
Barclay, Alexander, rector of All Hallows, Lombard Street, 116; his poems, 117.
Barham, Rev. Richard Harris, rector of St. Augustine and St. Faith, 138; buried at St. Mary Magdalene, Old Fish Street, 222.
Barking, Richard de, abbot of Westminster, granted St. Dunstan's in the West to Henry III., 331.
Barnham, Alice, married Francis Bacon, 159.
Barnham, Benedict, buried at St. Clement, Eastcheap, 159.
Barnham, Francis, buried at St. Clement, Eastcheap, 159.
Barratt, Lettice, married to Sir Francis

Knollys at All Hallows on the Wall, 307.

Barton, Elizabeth, the "Holy Maid of Kent," buried in the Grey Friars' Church, 152; 233.

Basinge, William de, munificence of, to the priory of St. Helen, 74.

Bastwick, John, set in the pillory, 302.

Bateman, William, benefactor to St. Dunstan's in the East, 169.

Bath, Marquis of, brass at All Hallows Barking restored by, 21.

Battishill, Jonathan, organist at St. Clement, Eastcheap, 162.

Baxter, Richard, buried at Christ Church, Newgate Street, 156; married at St. Benet Fink, 351.

Baxter, Robert, first stone of St. Lawrence Jewry laid by, 196.

Bayning, Andrew, monument to, in St. Olave's, Hart Street, 104, 106.

Bayning, Paul, monument to, in St. Olave's, Hart Street, 104, 106.

Bayning, Sir Paul, first Viscount Bayning of Sudbury, buried in St. Olave's, Hart Street, 104.

Beauchamp, Sir John, builder of the Great Wardrobe, 122.

Becket, Thomas, Archbishop of Canterbury, Hospital of St. Thomas of Acon dedicated to, 211.

Beckford, Alderman William, sword-rest inscribed to, in St. George, Botolph Lane, 182.

Bedford, John, Duke of, patron of St. Stephen, Walbrook, 287.

Behnes, William, bust in St. Stephen, Walbrook, by, 293.

Beloe, Rev. William, tablet to, in All Hallows on the Wall, 308.

Bence, Joan, monument to, in All Hallows on the Wall, 308.

Bennett, Mirabelle, benefactress to St. Dunstan's in the East, 168, 169.

Benolte, Thomas, brass to, in St. Helen, Bishopsgate, now lost, 90.

Berkeley, Thomas, Lord, patron of St. Andrew by the Wardrobe, 122.

Bernard, Dr. Francis, monument to, in St. Botolph, Aldersgate, 318.

Berry, Thomas, benefactor to St. Mary Magdalene, Old Fish Street, 220.

Bertha, Queen, mother of St. Ethelburga, 52.

Bethell, Slingsby, buried at All Hallows Barking, 25; his sword-rest, 26.

Beveridge, William, afterwards Bishop of St. Asaph, rector of St. Peter, Cornhill, 283, 284.

Birch, Dr. Thomas, rector of St. Margaret Pattens, 214.

Blades, John, his munificence, 144.

Blizard, Sir William, brass plate to, in St. Botolph, Bishopsgate, 329.

Blomberg, Dr. Frederick William, tablet to, in St. Giles, Cripplegate, 68.

Blomfield, Sir A., monument to Pepys designed by, 107.

Blomfield, Charles James, Bishop of London, his arms in St. Dunstan's in the East, 168; rector of St. Botolph, Bishopsgate, 330.

Blow, John, played for Father Smith, 128.

Bodley, Dame Anne, tablet to, in St. Bartholomew the Less, 315.

Index of Proper Names.

Bolingbroke, Viscount, appealed to by Swift on behalf of Sacheverell, 129; his "Letters on the Study of History," 215.

Bolles, Sir George, patron of St. Swithin by London Stone, 294; buried there, 294, 295.

Bolton, Prior, his work at St. Bartholomew the Great, 40, 46, 49.

Bond, Martin, monument to, in St. Helen, Bishopsgate, 80, 81; first stone of St. Katherine Cree laid by, 94.

Bond, William, monument to, in St. Helen, Bishopsgate, 81.

Bosworth, Sir John, monument to, in Christ Church, Newgate Street, 156.

Botolph, St., 317.

Bourchier, Elizabeth, married to Oliver Cromwell at St. Giles, Cripplegate, 69.

Bowes, Sir Martin, monuments in the Grey Friars' Church sold by, 152; patronage of St. Mary Woolnoth granted to, 343; buried there, 344.

Boydell, John, buried at St. Olave Jewry, 209.

Boyer, Rev. James, buried at Christ Church, Newgate Street, 156.

Boyle, Robert, Life of, by Birch, 214.

Brand, Rev. John, tablet to, in St. Mary-at-Hill, 240.

Brandt, Sebastian, his "Narrenschiff," 117.

Brice, Sir Hugh, benefactor to St. Mary Woolnoth, 343.

Bridget, St., 142.

Bridgewater, Earl of, Milton's "Comus" presented to, 69.

Brieux, John, brass to, in St. Helen, Bishopsgate, 89.

Brihtmerus, patron of All Hallows, Lombard Street, 116.

Brittany, John, Duke of, body of the Grey Friars' Church built by, 150.

Brooke, John Charles, monument to, in St. Benet, Paul's Wharf, 141.

Browne, Sir Thomas, baptized at St. Michael-le-Querne, 302.

Buckeridge, John, afterwards Bishop of Ely, vicar of St. Giles, Cripplegate, 70.

Buckingham, Duke of, his monument in Westminster Abbey, 25.

Buckler, John, window in St. Dunstan's in the East by, 168.

Buggin, Sir George, tablet to, in St. Dunstan's in the East, 174.

Bullen, Anne, queen of Henry VIII., great-granddaughter of Sir Geffrey Bullen, 190.

Bullen, Sir Geffrey, buried at St. Lawrence Jewry, 190; memorial window to, 192.

Bullen, Richard, buried at St. Giles, Cripplegate, 62, 63.

Bullen, Thomas, buried at St. Lawrence Jewry, 190.

Bullen, William, buried at St. Giles, Cripplegate, 62, 63.

Burnet, Gilbert, Bishop of Salisbury, Tillotson's funeral sermon preached by, 195.

Burnet, Dr. Thomas, rector of St. James, Garlickhithe, 185.

Burney, Dr. Charles, organist of St. Dionis Backchurch, 121.

Burney, Admiral James, his daughter's wedding, 210.

Burton, Henry, rector of St. Matthew, Friday Street, 302.
Burton, Simon, tablet to, in St. Andrew Undershaft, 34.
Busby, Thomas, monument to, in St. Giles, Cripplegate, 60, 67.
Butler, Samuel, his "Hudibras," 123.
Byng, Alice, monument to, in St. Andrew Undershaft, 34, 35.

Cade, Jack, at London Stone, 297.
Cæsar, Sir Julius, monument to, in St. Helen, Bishopsgate, 85, 86.
Cage, Robert, monument to, in St. Giles, Cripplegate, 67.
Calamy, Benjamin, buried at St. Lawrence Jewry, 229.
Calamy, Edmund, minister of St. Mary, Aldermanbury, 228; buried there, 229.
Calamy, Edmund, grandson, buried at St. Mary, Aldermanbury, 229.
Caldwell, Dr. Richard, buried at St. Benet, Paul's Wharf, 139.
Camden, William, his opinion of the origin of London Stone, 297.
Canning, George, Addington ridiculed by, 131.
Canova, Antonio, his admiration of St. Stephen, Walbrook, 292.
Carden, Sir Thomas, pulled down the Black Friars' church, 123.
Carew, Sir Matthew, tablet to, in St. Dunstan in the West, 335.
Carew, Sir Nicholas, father-in-law of Sir Nicholas Throckmorton, 97; executed, 322; monument to, in St. Botolph, Aldgate, 322, 323.

Carlile, Rev. W., rector of St. Mary-at-Hill, 241.
Carlyle, Thomas, his opinion of Heath's works, 315.
Caroline, Queen, cause of, maintained by Sir Matthew Wood, 69; place o her death, 272.
Cart, James, monument to, in St. Mary-le-Bow, 249.
Catherine of Braganza, Queen, 128; Queen Street, Cheapside, named after, 245.
Cave, Dr. William, rector of All Hallows the Great, 264.
Caxton, William, patronized by the Earl of Worcester, 16.
Cecil, Robert, Earl of Salisbury, Bacon's request to him, 159.
Cecil, William, Lord Burleigh, his patronage of Fox, 62; grandfather of Lady Elizabeth Hatton, 130.
Cely, Richard and Robert, benefactors to St. Olave, Hart Street, 100, 105.
Challis, Alderman Thomas, his arms in St. Giles, Cripplegate, 69.
Chamberlayne, Sir Robert, monument to, in St. Bartholomew the Great, 45, 48.
Champion, Sir Richard, benefactor to St. Dunstan's in the East, 168.
Champneys, Basil, vicarage of St. Bride designed by, 149.
Chandler, John and Richard, monuments to, in St. Mary, Aldermanbury, 230.
Chapone, or Caponius, Peter, monument to, in St. Olave's, Hart Street, 103.
Charles I., King, conspiracy in favour

of, 20; portrait of, in stained glass, at St. Andrew Undershaft, 29; statue of, at Charing Cross, 46; 67, 86, 98, 101, 126, 131, 143, 238; bust of, set up in Hammersmith Church, 271; 274, 275, 279, 288; fidelity of Sir Paul Pindar to, 326; 339; attended during his confinement by Holdsworth, 349; 353.

Charles II., King, portrait of, in stained glass, at St. Andrew Undershaft, 29; 48, 67; arms of, in St. Helen, Bishopsgate, 88; Sir Andrew Riccard knighted by, 105; 148, 160; his obligations to Sir John Moore, 171; Restoration of, 229; Sir Nicholas Crispe created a baronet by, 271; 274; parishioners of St. Alphage touched for the king's evil by, 313; 318, 339.

Charlton, Margaret, married to Baxter at St. Benet Fink, 351.

Chatterton, Thomas, burial of, recorded in register of St. Andrew's, Holborn, 130; his Rowley poems, 178, 179.

Chaucer, Geoffrey, earliest complete edition of his poems, 21; uncertainty as to his parentage, 232; his works collected by Shirley, 315.

Chaucer, Richard, benefactor to St. Mary Aldermary, 232.

Cheke, Sir John, buried at St. Alban's, Wood Street, 113, 114.

Cheney, Sir William, buried at St. Benet, Paul's Wharf, 139.

Cherry, Sir Francis, buried at All Hallows Barking, 25.

Chichcley, Robert, rebuilder of St. Stephen, Walbrook, 287, 288.

Chiswell, Richard, tablet to, in St. Botolph, Aldersgate, 318.

Chitty, Sir Thomas, sword-rest of, 26.

Churchill, Charles, his friendship with Lloyd, 147.

Clarendon, Edward Hyde, Earl of, his account of the executions of Hewet and Slingsby, 222.

Cleveland, John, buried at St. Michael Paternoster Royal, 260.

Clitherow, Sir Christopher, monument to, in St. Andrew Undershaft, 34.

Clitherow, James, benefactor to St. Michael, Cornhill, 255.

Cobham, Lord, added to St. Dunstan's in the East, 163.

Cockerell, Charles Robert, R.A., St. Bartholomew, Moor Lane, built by, 208.

Coke, Sir Edward, married at St. Andrew's, Holborn, 130, 131.

Coke, Robert, buried at St. Andrew's, Holborn, 130.

Coleridge, Samuel Taylor, remark of, about Boyer, 156.

Colet, Henry, benefactor to St. Antholin's, 236.

Colleton, Sir Peter, monument erected by, in All Hallows Barking, 25.

Compton, William, Lord, married daughter of Sir John Spencer, 90; erected monument to him in St. Helen, Bishopsgate, 91.

Condell, Henry, buried at St. Mary, Aldermanbury, 228.

Conder, Alderman Edward, font in memory of, at St. Michael Paternoster Royal, 261.

Constantine, Emperor, said to have founded church of St. Helen, 73.
Conway, Viscountess, benefactress to St. Dunstan's in the East, 169.
Cooke, Edward, monument to, in St. Bartholomew the Great, 46, 47.
Copeland, Alderman William Taylor, memorial window to, in St. Helen, Bishopsgate, 92.
Copland, William, benefactor to St. Mary-le-Bow, 244.
Cornwallis, Anne, married to Earl of Argyll at St. Botolph, Bishopsgate, 325.
Cortona, Pietro Berretini di, copy of a painting of his, in All Hallows on the Wall, 308.
Coverdale, Miles, Bishop of Exeter, rector of St. Magnus the Martyr, 198; his remains transferred to St. Magnus, 202; his monument there, 202, 203; buried at St. Bartholomew by the Exchange, 207; his monument there destroyed by the Great Fire, 208.
Coward, Rev. J. H., font presented to St. Peter-le-Poer by, 350.
Cowley, Abraham, his lament for the "matchless Orinda," 289.
Cowper, John, memorial window to, at St. Lawrence Jewry, 193; an inhabitant of Cornhill, 257.
Cowper, Judith, first wife of first Earl Cowper, monument to, in St. Augustine's, 137.
Cowper, William, the poet, ancestry of, 257, 258; giants at St. Dunstan's in the West mentioned by, 332, 333; his friend John Newton, 346.

Cox, Dr. J. E., window at St. Helen, Bishopsgate, inserted by, 93; tablet to, 93.
Cranmer, Thomas, Archbishop of Canterbury, appointed Saunders to All Hallows, Bread Street, 250.
Craven, Earl of, baptized at St. Andrew Undershaft, 35; 236.
Craven, Sir William, buried at St. Andrew Undershaft, 35; benefactor to St. Antholin's, 236.
Crispe, Ellis, sheriff, 269; buried in St. Mildred, Bread Street, 271.
Crispe, Sir Nicholas, his loyalty, 271; his benefactions to St. Mildred, Bread Street, 272; 274.
Crispe, Samuel, window presented to St. Mildred, Bread Street, by, 272.
Crispe, Sir Thomas, tablet to, in St. Mildred, Bread Street, 274.
Croke, John, tomb at All Hallows Barking conjectured to be his, 24.
Croly, Dr. George, memorial windows to, at St. Stephen Walbrook, 291; monument to, 293.
Cromwell, Oliver, married at St. Giles, Cripplegate, 69; his ancestry, 74, 289; brother-in-law of Wilkins, 194; account of, by Heath, 315.
Crosby, Brass, churchwarden of All Hallows Barking, 27.
Crosby, Sir John, hired ground from the priory of St. Helen, 74; his bequest to St. Helen's, 75; monument to, in St. Helen's, 87, 88; figure of, in stained glass, 92.
Crowley, Robert, vicar of St. Giles, Cripplegate, 62.
Crowther, Rev. Samuel, monument to

in Christ Church, Newgate Street, 155, 156.
Cunningham, Peter, his "Life of Inigo Jones," 140.
Cutler, Sir John, benefactor to St. Michael, Cornhill, 255.

Dacres, Henry, monument to, in St. Dunstan in the West, 335.
Dale, Rev. Thomas, afterwards Dean of Rochester, vicar of St. Bride's, Fleet Street, 146.
Dance, George, architect of St. Botolph, Aldgate, 321.
Dance, George, the younger, architect of All Hallows on the Wall, 307; remodelled St. Bartholomew the Less, 314.
Danckers, Cornelius, lithograph after, at St. Dunstan's in the East, 170.
Darcy, Sir Edward, tablet to, in St. Botolph, Aldgate, 323.
Darcy, Thomas, Lord, of the North, monument to, in St. Botolph, Aldgate, 322, 323.
Dashwood, Francis, font of St. Mary-le-Bow presented by, 248.
Davenant, Dr. Charles, buried at St. Bride's, Fleet Street, 147.
Day, William, tablet to, in St. Giles, Cripplegate, 66.
Deane, Sir James, monument to, in St. Olave's, Hart Street, 103, 104.
Deane, Sir John, brass to, in St. Bartholomew the Great, 49.
Defoe, Daniel, born in St. Giles, Cripplegate, parish, 70.
Delmé, Sir Peter, monument to, in St. Margaret Pattens, 215.

Denham, Sir John, married at St. Bride's, Fleet Street, 147.
Dethike, Sir Gilbert, buried at St. Benet, Paul's Wharf, 139.
Deykes, –, altar-piece at St. Bride's, Fleet Street, designed by, 145.
Dibdin, Thomas, apprenticed to Sir William Rawlins, 330.
Dickson, Margaret, Stow's godmother, buried at St. Michael, Cornhill, 257.
Digby, Sir Kenelm, buried at Christ Church, Newgate Street, 153.
Digby, Venetia, buried at Christ Church, Newgate Street, 153.
Dionysius the Areopagite, St. Dionis Backchurch dedicated to, 120.
Disraeli, Benjamin, Earl of Beaconsfield, baptized at St. Andrew's, Holborn, 132; his praise of Vanbrugh, 293.
Disraeli, Isaac, his account of Stow, 32.
Dobbes, Sir Richard, interested himself in the establishment of Christ's Hospital, 152.
Donne, John, Dean of St. Paul's, vicar of St. Dunstan in the West, 332; carved head of, 334; figure of, in stained glass, 337.
Donne, John, benefactor to St. Mary-le-Bow, 244.
Doré, Peter, gravestone of, in Christ Church, Newgate Street, 156.
Dormer, Sir Michael, buried at St. Lawrence Jewry, 190; memorial window to, 193.
Douglas, Dr. John, afterwards Bishop of Salisbury, rector of St. Augustine and St. Faith, 138.

Dowe, Robert, monument to, in St. Botolph, Aldgate, 323; his bequest to St. Sepulchre's, 355, 356.

Downe, William, rector of St. Martin, Ludgate, 216.

Draghi, Baptiste, played for Renatus Harris, 128.

Drake, Sir Francis, Ferrar acquainted with, 289.

Dryden, John, his "Absalom and Achitophel," 21; his monument in Westminster Abbey, 25; criticised by Milbourn, 54; his praise of Sir John Moore, 171, 172; married at St. Swithin by London Stone, 295.

Duke, Sir James, fountain presented by, to St. Dunstan's in the West, 334.

Duncombe, Sir Charles, clock and organ of St. Magnus presented by, 201.

Dunstan, St., first ecclesiastical statesman, 163.

Dyer, John, a friend of Daniel Wray, 319.

Dyke, John, gifts by, to St. Katherine Cree, 96.

Edgar, King, charter of, 126; land granted to thirteen knights by, 321.

Edmund, King, the Martyr, remains of, deposited in St. Helen's, 73; his death, 176.

Edward the Confessor, privileges of the Knighten guild confirmed by, 321.

Edward I., King, benefactions of, to All Hallows Barking, 16; expulsion of the Jews by, 189; crosses erected by, in memory of his queen, Eleanor of Castile, 303.

Edward II., King, his heart buried in the Grey Friars' Church, 151; 288.

Edward III., King, 2; his Great Wardrobe, 122; Abbey of Graces founded by, 207; 216; shed built beside Bow Church by, 247; asylum for converted Jews transformed into Rolls Court and Chapel by, 331.

Edward IV., King, interested in All Hallows Barking, 16; his esteem for Sir John Crosby, 87; Morton preferred by, 165; 262, 282, 285, 287; Rotherham made Lord Chancellor by, 301; annexed Hospital of St. Anthony of Vienna to St. George's, Windsor, 350; 352.

Edward VI., King, 23, 28; portrait of, in stained glass, at St. Andrew Undershaft, 29; 62, 86; taught by Sir John Cheke, 114; bishopric of Westminster abolished by, 142; Bridewell given to the citizens of London by, 149; charter of Christ's Hospital signed by, 152; 184; Coverdale made a bishop by, 198; College of Corpus Christi surrendered to, 223; 260; advowson of St. Martin in the Vintry granted to see of Worcester by, 262; privileges of Hanse merchants curtailed by, 263; 266; advowson of St. Matthew, Friday Street, granted to see of London by, 302; advowson of St. Dunstan in the West granted to Lord Dudley by, 331; Abbey of the Minoresses granted to Duke of Suffolk by, 339.

Edward the Black Prince, labours of, against corruption, 183.

Elizabeth, Queen, 2, 23; envoy sent to Russia by, 25; portrait of, in stained glass at St. Andrew Undershaft, 29; Sir Walter Mildmay, one of her statesmen, 43; 62; military dress in her time, 81; Cæsar, Admiralty Judge under, 85; Pickering employed by, 86; and Throckmorton, 97; Turner's "Herbal" dedicated to, 103; 109; Westminster Abbey formed into a Collegiate Church by, 142; account of her progresses, etc., by Nichols, 147; great-great-granddaughter of Sir Geffrey Bullen, 190; attitude of, towards Coverdale, 198, 208; "Memoirs" of her reign by Birch, 214; advowson of St. Mary Abchurch granted to Corpus Christi College, Cambridge, by, 223; 262; privileges of Hanse merchants abrogated by, 263; 266; portrait of, in stained glass at St. Mildred, Bread Street, 272; advowson of St. Nicholas Cole Abbey granted to Reve and Evelyn by, 279; 285, 315, 323; coronation of, 332; statue of, at St. Dunstan's in the West, 333, 334; 354.

Elmore, Bartholomew, monument to, in St. Katherine Cree, 98.

Elsing, William, hospital founded by, 228, 311, 312.

Emery, John, tablet in St. Andrew's, Holborn, to, 131.

Erasmus, copy of his "Paraphrase of the Books of the New Testament" at St. Andrew Undershaft, 36.

Erkenwald, Bishop of London, reputed founder of the convent of Barking, 15.

Ernest, alias Metyngham, Matthew, benefactor to St. Dunstan's in the East, 168.

Essex, Robert Devereux, second Earl of, his house in Seething Lane, 109; his condemnation, 129.

Essex, Robert Devereux, third Earl of, baptism of, 109.

Ethelbert, King of Kent, father of St. Ethelburga, 52.

Ethelburga, St., 52.

Eudo, sewer to Henry I., gave to the monastery of Coichester advowson of St. Stephen, Walbrook, 287; and that of St. Mary Woolchurch Haw, 344.

Evyngar, Andrew, brass to, in All Hallows Barking, 21.

Ewin, John, co-operated with the Grey Friars, 150.

Eyles, Sir John, sword-rest of, 26.

Fabian, Robert, the chronicler, buried at St. Michael, Cornhill, 256.

Faithorne, William, buried at St. Anne, Blackfriars, 123.

Felton, George Matthew, tablet to, in St. Giles, Cripplegate, 68.

Ferrar, Nicholas, the elder, benefactions of, to St. Benet Sherehog, 288; position of, in the city, 288, 289.

Fetherstone, Cuthbert, tablet to, in St. Dunstan in the West, 335.

Fieldynge, Geffrey, buried at St. Lawrence Jewry, 190; memorial window to, 192.

Finke, Robert, St. Benet Fink named after, 350.

Finnis, Colonel John, monument to, in St. Dunstan's in the East, 174, 175.

Fisher, John, Bishop of Rochester, temporarily interred at All Hallows Barking, 20.

Fitzosbert, William, insurrection of, 243.

Fitztheobald, Agnes, sister of Thomas Becket, founded, with her husband, Thomas, Hospital of St. Thomas of Acon, 211.

Fitzwalter, Robert, patron of St. Margaret Moses, 272.

Fitzwilliam, Canon, praised by Macaulay, 25.

Fitzwilliams, William, his work at St. Andrew Undershaft, 29; ancestor of the Earls Fitzwilliam, 73, 74.

Foliot, Gilbert, Bishop of London, advowson of St. Nicholas Olave bestowed on Dean and Chapter of St. Paul's by, 279.

Fowke, John, benefactor to St. Dunstan's in the East, 169.

Fox, John, copies of his "Acts and Monuments" at St. Andrew Undershaft, 36; monument to, in St. Giles, Cripplegate, 61, 62; his connection with that church, 62; tutor in the family of Sir Thomas Lucy, 63.

French, Elizabeth, married Tillotson, 195.

Freshwater, Elizabeth, monument to, in St. Bartholomew the Great, 48.

Frobisher, Sir Martin, monument to, in St. Giles, Cripplegate, 63, 64.

Fuller, Thomas, memorial to, in St. Clement, Eastcheap, 161, 162; his description of Old St. Paul's, 221.

Fuller, William, vicar of St. Giles, Cripplegate, 70.

Garaway, Sir William, benefactor to St. Peter-le-Poer, 348.

Garrard, or Garret, Thomas, rector of All Hallows, Honey Lane, martyrdom of, 245.

Garth, Sir Samuel, his "Dispensary," 121, 318.

Gascoyne, Sir Crisp, ancestor of the Marquis of Salisbury, 193.

Gayer, Sir John, brass plate to, in St. Katherine Cree, 98; bequest of, 98.

Geddes, A., A.R.A., picture by, in St. James, Garlickhithe, 185.

Gentilis, Albericus, tablet to, in St. Helen, Bishopsgate, 81; account of, 81, 82.

Gentilis, Matthew, father of Albericus, accompanied him to England, 81; buried in St. Helen's churchyard, 82.

Gibbons, Grinling, carvings at All Hallows Barking ascribed to, 18; pulpit at St. Giles, Cripplegate, ascribed to, 58; pulpit at St. Olave's, Hart Street, ascribed to, 102; pulpit at St. Dionis Backchurch carved by, 120; carvings at St. Dunstan's in the East by, 169, 170; carvings at St. Michael, Queenhithe, attributed to, 188; font at St. Margaret, Lothbury, attributed to, 206; carvings at St. Mary Abchurch by, 225; carvings at St. Michael, Cornhill, ascribed to, 255; altar-piece at St. Michael Paternoster Royal by, 260; carvings at St.

Mildred, Bread Street, attributed to, 273; altar-piece at St. Vedast's attributed to, 300; organ-case at St. Sepulchre's attributed to, 354.
Gibbs, Rev. Michael, monument to, in Christ Church, Newgate Street, 155, 156.
Gibbs, —, windows in St. Stephen, Walbrook, by, 291.
Gibson, Edmund, Bishop of London, first stone of St. Botolph, Bishopsgate, laid by, 327.
Gibson, Jesse, architect of St. Peter-le-Poer, 349.
Gilbert, Rev. Philip Parker, tablet to, in St. Giles, Cripplegate, 68; portrait of, 71.
Gilbert, Thomas, brass to, in All Hallows Barking, 22.
Gilbourne, Percival, monument to, in St. Stephen, Walbrook, 292, 293.
Gladerinus, patron of St. Andrew's, Holborn, 126.
Glyn, Mills, and Co., Messrs., bank of, 343.
Godart, or Goddard, Simon, patron of St. Bartholomew by the Exchange, 207.
Godfrey, Michael, monument to, in St. Swithin by London Stone, 296.
Godwin, Mary Wolstonecraft, married to Shelley at St. Mildred, Bread Street, 274.
Godwinus, patron of St. Nicholas Acon, 177.
Gold, Henry, rector of St. Mary Aldermary, execution of, 233.
Gold, James, architect of St. Botolph, Bishopsgate, 327.

Goldsmith, Oliver, 147.
Goode, Rev. William, monument to, in St. Andrew by the Wardrobe, 124, 125.
Gore, Elizabeth, monument to, in St. Olave's, Hart Street, 108.
Gore, Sir Paul, ancestor of the Earls of Arran, 193.
Gosling, Sir Francis, statue of Queen Elizabeth presented to St. Dunstan's in the West by, 333.
Gosson, Stephen, rector of St. Botolph, Bishopsgate, 330.
Gower, John, the poet, 163.
Gravesend, Richard de, Bishop of London, St. Katherine Cree built during his episcopate, 2, 94; vicarage ordained at St. Lawrence Jewry by, 189.
Green, Rev. John Richard, his account of St. Dunstan, 163.
Gresham, Sir Richard, buried at St. Lawrence Jewry, 190; memorial window to, 193; purchase of the Hospital of St. Thomas of Acon by the Mercers' Company arranged by, 211.
Gresham, Sir Thomas, monument to, in St. Helen, Bishopsgate, 82, 85; memorial window to, 82, 92; promised to rebuild steeple of St. Helen's, 83; his parentage, 190; his house in Lombard Street, 201.
Grey, Lord Thomas, buried at All Hallows Barking, 20.
Grindal, Edmund, Bishop of London, afterwards Archbishop of Canterbury, presented Coverdale to rectory of St. Magnus, 198, 208.

Gwilt, George, steeple of St. Mary-le-Bow repaired by, 247.

Hacker, Colonel Francis, patron of St. Nicholas Cole Abbey, 279.

Hacket, John, afterwards Bishop of Lichfield, rector of St. Andrew's, Holborn, 129.

Haddon, Sir Richard, brass to, in St. Olave's, Hart Street, 102, 103.

Hale, Richard, buried at St. Dunstan's in the East, 165; his monument, 172, 173.

Hall, Edward, the chronicler, buried at St. Benet Sherehog, 289.

Halliday, Sir William, monument to, in St. Lawrence Jewry, 194.

Hammersley, Sir Hugh, monument to, in St. Andrew Undershaft, 33, 34.

Hammond, Edmond, monument to, in All Hallows on the Wall, 308.

Hand, Mrs., monument to, in St. Giles, Cripplegate, 67, 68.

Hanger, George, benefactor to St. Dunstan's in the East, 169.

Hanson, Alderman Sir Reginald, Bart., M.P., reopening of St. Mary-at-Hill attended by, 241.

Harding, Robert, benefactor to St. Mary-le-Bow, 243.

Hardwick, Thomas, St. Bartholomew the Less repaired by, 314.

Harris, Renatus, organ at All Hallows Barking by, 19; organ at St. Andrew Undershaft by, 30; organ at St. Giles, Cripplegate, by, 59; organ at St. Andrew's, Holborn, by, 128, 129; organ at St. Sepulchre's by, 354.

Harris, Roger, benefactor to the poor of Christ Church, Newgate Street, 154.

Harrison, Edmund, monument to, in St. Giles, Cripplegate, 67.

Harrys, Thomas, maker of the clock with giants at St. Dunstan's in the West, 332.

Hart, Charlotte, bequest of, to St. Bartholomew the Great, 41; memorial to, 50.

Hart, Sir John, purchased advowson of St. Swithin by London Stone, 294; buried there, 294, 295.

Hart, Philip, organist at St. Andrew Undershaft, 30.

Harvey, Benjamin, monument in St. Alban, Wood Street, to, 115.

Harvist, Edward, monument to, in St. Giles, Cripplegate, 66.

Hatton, Lady Elizabeth, married to Sir Edward Coke at St. Andrew's, Holborn, 130.

Hawkins, Sir John, monument to, in St. Dunstan's in the East, destroyed by the Fire, 164; acquainted with Ferrar, 289.

Hawksmoor, Nicholas, architect of St. Mary Woolnoth, 6, 345.

Haynes, William, benefactor to St. Dunstan's in the East, 168.

Hayward, Sir Rowland, monument to, in St. Alphage, 313.

Hazlitt, William, married at St. Andrew's, Holborn, 131, 210.

Heath, James, buried at St. Bartholomew the Less, 315.

Helena, Empress, mother of Constantine, St. Helen's Church dedicated to, 73.

Heminge, John, buried at St. Mary, Aldermanbury, 228.
Henry I., King, his interest in Rahere, 37; 55, 94, 191, 272, 287, 344.
Henry III., King, 149, 209; charter granted to the Hanse merchants by, 263; St. Dunstan's in the West granted by Abbot of Westminster to, 331; St. Sepulchre's confirmed to Priory of St. Bartholomew by charter of, 352.
Henry VI., King, temporary restoration of, by Earl of Warwick, 16; 216, 285, 287, 345, 352.
Henry VII., King, 89, 90, 133: his obligations to Morton, 165; Lord Stanley created Earl of Derby by, 183; 262, 269; Collegiate Church of St. Martin-le-Grand given to Abbey of Westminster by, 278, 311, 317; 343.
Henry VIII., King, Church of the Grey Friars made parochial by, 2; advowson of All Hallows Barking granted to see of Canterbury by, 16; 21, 22, 23; Holbein his painter, 35; dissolution of Priory of St. Bartholomew by, 38; John Larke executed for denying the ecclesiastical supremacy of, 54; St. Helen's Priory surrendered to, 74; Pickering employed by, 86; 90; plot against, 97, 322; Priory of Holy Trinity, Aldgate, and advowson of St. Katherine Cree granted to Lord Audley by, 99; 109; his palace of St. James's, 113; Convent of Bermondsey dissolved by, 126; advowson of St. Andrew's, Holborn, bestowed on Earl of Southampton by, 129; advowson of St. Bride's, Fleet Street, granted to deanery of Westminster by, 142; frequently resided at Bridewell, 149; Christ Church, Newgate Street, founded by, 152; Priory of Butley dissolved by, 208; Hospital of St. Thomas of Acon sold to the Mercers' Company by, 211; 212; Elsing's Hospital surrendered to, 228, 311; Whittington's College dissolved by, 259; advowson of All Hallows the Great granted to see of Canterbury by, 262; 269, 289; advowson of St. Swithin by London Stone granted to Earl of Oxford by, 294; Leland commissioned to search for records by, 301; advowson of St. Matthew, Friday Street, transferred to bishopric of Westminster by, 302; advowson of St. Peter, West Cheap, granted to Earl of Southampton by, 303; Priory of the Holy Trinity, Aldgate, surrendered to, 321; Convent of Alnwick dissolved by, 331; Abbey of the Minoresses surrendered to, 338; advowson of St. Mary Woolnoth granted to Sir Martin Bowes by, 343.
Henry, Prince of Wales, Life of, by Birch, 214.
Henslowe, Philip, Alleyn's partner, 60.
Herbert, George, figure of, in stained glass, at St. Dunstan's in the West, 337.
Herdson, Henry, benefactor to St. Dunstan's in the East, 168.
Heriot, Alison, wife of "Jingling Geordie," buried at St. Gregory by St. Paul's, 221.

Heriott, Sir William, benefactor to St. Dunstan's in the East, 168.
Herne, Sir Nathaniel, ancestor of the Earls of Jersey, 193.
Herrick, Robert, baptized at St. Vedast's, 300.
Hertford, Marquis of, giants at St. Dunstan's in the West purchased by, 333.
Hewet, Dr. John, execution of, 221, 222.
Hewit, Anna, wife of Sir Edward Osborne, 160.
Hewit, Sir William, buried at St. Martin Orgar, 160.
Hickes, Dr. George, vicar of All Hallows Barking, 26; his Jacobitism, 27; read the burial service over Pepys, 107.
Hicks, Sir Baptist, Viscount Campden, ancestor of the Earls of Gainsborough, 193.
Hill, Messrs., organ at St. Andrew's, Holborn, by, 129; organ at St. Mary-at-Hill by, 239.
Hilton, William, R.A., picture by, in St. Michael Paternoster Royal, 260.
Hoadly, Benjamin, afterwards Bishop of Winchester, rector of St. Peter-le-Poer, 349.
Hoare, Sir Richard, monument to, in St. Dunstan's in the West, 336.
Hoare, Sir Richard, the younger, monument to, in St. Dunstan's in the West, 336.
Hodges, Nathaniel, tablet to, in St. Stephen, Walbrook, 292.
Hodgson, John, memorial window to, in St. Helen, Bishopsgate, 92.

Hodgson, Sir Thomas, window given by, to St. Andrew's, Holborn, 128.
Hogarth, William, baptized at St. Bartholomew the Great, 50.
Holbein, Hans, tablet to, in St. Andrew Undershaft, 35; said to have been buried at St. Katherine Cree, 97, 98.
Holden, —, mentioned by Pepys, 143.
Holdsworth, Richard, rector of St. Peter-le-Poer, 348, 349.
Holinshed, Raphael, his chronicle, 21.
Holland, Sir Nathaniel Dance, picture by, in All Hallows on the Wall, 308.
Holleis, Dame Elizabeth, Sir Andrew Judde her executor, 84.
Hollis, Sir William, buried at St. Helen, Bishopsgate, 84.
Holman, George, munificence of, to St. Benet Fink, 351.
Hooker, Richard, figure of, in stained glass, at St. Dunstan's in the West, 337.
Horne, —, architect of St. Katherine Coleman, 340.
Hotham, Captain, buried at All Hallows Barking, 20.
Hotham, Sir John, buried at All Hallows Barking, 20.
Hothersall, Henry, font at St. Bride's, Fleet Street, presented by, 143.
Heward, Lady Elizabeth, married to Dryden at St. Swithin by London Stone, 295.
Howley, William, Archbishop of Canterbury, his arms in St. Dunstan's in the East, 168.
Hughes, John, the poet, burial of,

recorded in register of St. Andrew's, Holborn, 130.

Hume, David, criticisms of, answered by Douglas, 138.

Hungerford, Dame Margaret, re-erected the Halliday monument, 194.

Hunt, Sir Thomas, benefactor to St. Dunstan's in the East, 169.

Hutchinson, Colonel John, married at St. Andrew's, Holborn, 131.

Hyde, Sir Bernard, benefactor to St. Dunstan's in the East, 169; monument erected by, 173.

Inverness, Duchess of, 174.

Ireland, John and Elizabeth, grandparents of Sir Nicholas Crispe, buried in St. Mildred, Bread Street, 271.

Ironside, Gilbert, Bishop of Hereford, buried at St. Mary Somerset, 278.

Isabella, queen of Edward II., hired a house from Priory of St. Helen's, 74; buried in the Grey Friars' Church, 151.

Islip, Simon, Archbishop of Canterbury, patronage of St. Dunstan's in the East, granted to, 164.

James I., King, portrait of, in stained glass, at St. Andrew Undershaft, 29; Stow's petition to, 32; 36, 67; Caesar advanced by, 85; Earl of Southampton restored to his honours by, 129; account of his progresses, etc., by Nichols, 147; 159, 214, 221; Hugh Myddelton created a baronet by, 303; 315; Sir Paul Pindar sent ambassador to Turkey by, 326; advowson of St. Sepulchre's granted to Francis Philips by, 356.

James II., King, Hickes made a bishop by, 27; affection felt by Pepys for, 106; 148; Parliament of, 172; parishioners of St. Nicholas Cole Abbey touched for the king's evil by, 276; President and Fellows of Magdalene College, Oxford, ejected by, 278.

James IV., King of Scotland, story told by Stow about the head of, 265, 266.

James, Sir Bartholomew, benefactor to St. Dunstan's in the East, 168, 169.

James, Roger, brass to, at All Hallows Barking, 23.

Jeffreys, Judge, decided in favour of Father Smith's organ, 128; buried at St. Mary, Aldermanbury, 231.

Jeffreys, John, second Baron, buried at St. Mary, Aldermanbury, 231.

Jennings, Sir Stephen, rebuilder of St. Andrew Undershaft, 29.

Jewell, John, Bishop of Salisbury, book by, at St. Andrew Undershaft, 36.

Joan of the Tower, Queen of Scots, buried in the Grey Friars' Church, 151.

John, King, Priory of St. Helen founded in his reign, 73.

John of Gaunt, parliament packed by, 183.

Johnes-Knight, Rev. Samuel, vicar of All Hallows Barking, 27.

Johnson, Dr. Samuel, his "Life of Savage," 131; his friendship for Richardson, 147; his praise of Sir Nicholas Crispe, 271.

Jolles, Sir John, buried at All Hallows Barking, 25.
Jones, Inigo, his work at St. Helen, Bishopsgate, 75, 76; said to have designed St. Katherine Cree, 95; said to have rebuilt St. Alban, Wood Street, 114; buried at St. Benet, Paul's Wharf, 139, 140; pulled down part of St. Gregory by St. Paul's, 221; baptized at St. Bartholomew the Less, 315.
Jonson, Ben, edition of his works by Whalley, 214; son of, buried at St. Botolph, Bishopsgate, 325.
Jordan, Abraham, organ of St. Magnus built by, 201; font presented to St. Michael Paternoster Royal by, 261.
Jortin, Dr. John, rector of St. Dunstan's in the East, 173, 174.
Judde, Sir Andrew, screen in memory of, at St. Helen's, Bishopsgate, 77; monument to, 83, 84.
Judkin, Hobson, tablet to, in St. Dunstan's in the West, 336.

Keate, Gilbert, benefactor to St. Dunstan's in the East, 169.
Keats, John, baptized at St. Botolph, Bishopsgate, 329.
Keble, Sir Henry, St. Mary Aldermary rebuilt by, 232, 233, 235.
Kemp, Thomas, Bishop of London, vicarage ordained at St. Stephen's, Coleman Street, by, 285.
Kempthorne, Dame Joanna, monument to, at All Hallows Barking, 24.
Ken, Thomas, Bishop of Bath and Wells, figure of, in stained glass, at St. Dunstan's in the West, 337.

Kennett, White, afterwards Bishop of Peterborough, incumbent of St. Botolph, Aldgate, 323, 324.
Kettlewell, John, monument to, in All Hallows Barking, 24, 25.
King, Daniel, subscriber towards rebuilding Holy Trinity, Minories, 338.
Kirton, —, Pepys's bookseller, 136.
Kirwin, Benjamin, Magdalene, and William, monument to, in St. Helen, Bishopsgate, 80.
Knight, Alderman Henry Edmund, arms of, in St. Giles, Cripplegate, 69.
Knollys, Sir Francis, married at All Hallows on the Wall, 307.
Knowles, or Knoles, Thomas, rebuilder of St. Antholin's, buried there, 236; patron of All Hallows, Honey Lane, 245.

Laing, David, architect of St. Dunstan's in the East, 167.
Lake, John, ancestor of Oliver Cromwell, 289.
Lamb, Charles, best man at Hazlitt's wedding, 131; school days of, at Christ's Hospital, 156; at St. Mildred's in the Poultry, 210.
Lamb, Mary, bridesmaid at Hazlitt's wedding, 131.
Lambarde, John, father of William, buried at St. Michael, Wood Street, 265.
Lambarde, William, his account of Sevenoake, 216, 217; his works, 265.
Lancaster, Edmund, Earl of, founded Abbey of the Minoresses, 338.

Index of Proper Names.

Langham, Sir John, benefactor to St. Michael, Cornhill, 255.

Langley, Charles, monument to, in St. Giles, Cripplegate, 61, 67.

Large, Robert, benefactor to St. Margaret, Lothbury, 205; buried at St. Olave Jewry, 208.

Larke, John, rector of St. Ethelburga, Bishopsgate Street, 54.

Latimer, Lord, condemned for defrauding the Treasury, 183.

Laud, William, Archbishop of Canterbury, temporarily interred at All Hallows Barking, 20; Snayth's affection for, 23, 24; uncle of Layfield, 26; his consecration of St. Katherine Cree, 94, 95; last of the ecclesiastical statesmen, 163.

Lauder, William, literary frauds of, detected by Douglas, 138.

Lawrence, Dame Abigail, tablet to, in St. Helen, Bishopsgate, 91.

Lawrence, Sir John, arms of, in St. Helen, Bishopsgate, 88; Lord Mayor during the Plague, 91.

Lawson, Sir John, buried at St. Dunstan's in the East, 164.

Layfield, Dr. Edward, vicar of All Hallows Barking, 26.

Layton, Alexander, tablet to, in St. Dunstan's in the West, 335.

Leach, —, model presented by, to St. Dunstan's in the East, 170.

Lee, Lady Elizabeth, married to Young, the poet, at St. Mary-at-Hill, 240.

Lee, Sir Richard, patron of St. Stephen, Walbrook, 287.

Legge, George, first Lord Dartmouth, monument to, in Holy Trinity, Minories, 339.

Legge, Colonel William, monument to, in Holy Trinity, Minories, 338, 339.

Legh, Gerard, monument to, in St. Dunstan's in the West, 335.

Leicester, Earl of, patron of St. Andrew by the Wardrobe, 122.

Leland, John, buried at St. Michael-le-Querne, 301, 302.

Le Sœur, Hubert, monument at St. Bartholomew the Great ascribed to, 46.

Leventhorpe, John, brass to, in St. Helen, Bishopsgate, 90.

Levison, Nicholas, brass to, in St. Andrew Undershaft, 34, 35.

Lilbourn, John, monument to, in St. Stephen, Walbrook, 292.

Lilburne, John, buried in the burying-ground in Petty France, 326.

Lloyd, Robert, buried at St. Bride's, Fleet Street, 147.

Loftie, Rev. J. W., his explanation of "Colechurch," 211; his conjecture as to "Cole Abbey," 275.

Longfellow, Henry Wadsworth, King Olaf commemorated by, 100.

Lovekin, John, buried at St. Michael, Crooked Lane, 203; Walworth apprenticed to, 204.

Lovelace, Richard, said to have been buried at St. Bride's, Fleet Street, 146, 147.

Lowell, James Russell, monument to Pepys unveiled by, 107.

Lucas, Alderman Matthias Prime, lithograph presented by, to St. Dunstan's in the East, 170.

Lucie, Thomas, buried at St. Giles, Cripplegate, 63.

Lucius, legendary King of Britain, St. Peter's, Cornhill, said to have been founded by, 280, 281, 283.

Lucy, Margaret, monument to, in St. Giles, Cripplegate, 63.

Lucy, Sir Thomas, received Fox into his house, 63.

Luke, Sir Samuel, a parishioner of St. Anne, Blackfriars, 123.

Lydgate, John, his works collected by Shirley, 315.

Lyons, Richard, buried at St. James, Garlickhithe, 183.

Macaulay, Lord, his opinion of Kettlewell, 24, 25; lines by, quoted on Frobisher's monument, 64; his account of Sherlock, 181.

Macdougall, Alexander, memorial window to, in St. Helen, Bishopsgate, 92.

Madden, Thomas, monument in St. Andrew Undershaft by, 33.

Magnus, St., Newcourt's account of, 197.

Maiden, Thomas, London Stone preserved through the exertions of, 297.

Maitland, William, story told about Stow's remains by, 32, 33.

Man, Henry, Bishop of Man, buried at St. Andrew Undershaft, 35.

Manley, Mrs., buried at St. Benet, Paul's Wharf, 141.

Manning, Samuel, monument in St. Andrew by the Wardrobe by, 125.

Maratti, Carlo, picture in St. Margaret Pattens attributed to, **213**.

Margaret, queen of Edward I., commenced choir of Grey Friars' Church, buried there, 150, 151.

Margaret, The Lady, mother of Henry VII., 183; her patronage of Oldham, 269.

Markeby, William, brass in St. Bartholomew the Less to, 315.

Marriott, Robert, monument to, in St. Stephen, Walbrook, 292.

Martin, Messrs., bank of, 202.

Mary, Queen, 23, 62, 85, 86, 103, 123; advowson of St. Anne and St. Agnes granted to see of London by, 133; Derby House granted for Heralds' College by, 139, 184; abbot and convent of Westminster re-established by, 142; advowson of St. Clement, Eastcheap, granted to see of London by, 159; also that of St. James, Garlickhithe, 186; and those of St. Magnus and St. Margaret, New Fish Street, 198; Coverdale deprived of his bishopric by, 198, 207; 225, 250, 260; advowson of St. Alphage granted to see of London by, 311; and that of St. Katherine Coleman, 341; 356.

Mason, Roger, tablet to, in St. Giles, Cripplegate, 66.

Master, Ann, tablet to, in St. Bartholomew the Great, 49.

Master, Streynsham, gallant exploit of, 49.

Masters, Dame Ann, monument to, in All Hallows Barking, 25.

Matilda, queen of Henry I., Priory of Holy Trinity, Aldgate, founded by, 2, 94, 321; Guild at St. Giles, Cripplegate, established by, 55.

Maydenstone, Radulphus de, Bishop of Hereford, said to have purchased advowson of St. Mary Mounthaw, 278.

Melker, William, builder of St. Leonard, Eastcheap, 120.

Mendelssohn, Felix, played organ at St. Peter, Cornhill, 283.

Mennis, Sir John, tablet to, in St. Olave's, Hart Street, 108.

Micklethwait, Sir John, monument to, in St. Botolph, Aldersgate, 318.

Middlemore, Samuel, memorial to, in St. Clement, Eastcheap, 162.

Milbourn, Luke, rector of St. Ethelburga, Bishopsgate Street, 54.

Mildmay, H. B., Sir Walter Mildmay's monument repaired by, 45.

Mildmay, Sir Walter, monument to, in St. Bartholomew the Great, 43, 45, 46, 47.

Mildred, St., 209.

Milles, Dr. Jeremiah, Dean of Exeter, rector of St. Edmund and St. Nicholas Acon, monument to, in St. Edmund the King and Martyr, 178.

Millet, Captain John, monument to, in St. Bartholomew the Great, 47.

Mills, Dr. Daniel, rector of St. Olave's, Hart Street, criticised by Pepys, 105; buried in the church, 108.

Milman, Henry Hart, Dean of St. Paul's, narrative of the Great Fire quoted by, 136.

Milton, John, buried in St. Giles, Cripplegate, 65; monument to, 65, 66; his "Comus," 69; his houses in Aldersgate Street and the Barbican, 70; vindicated by Douglas, 138; his lodging in St. Bride's Churchyard, 148, 149; edition of his prose works by Birch, 214; married his second wife at St. Mary, Aldermanbury, 228; his third wife at St. Mary Aldermary, 232; editions of his poems by Bishop Newton, 249; baptized at All Hallows, Bread Street, 251.

Milton, John, the elder, buried in St. Giles, Cripplegate, 65; mention of, on his son's monument, 66; place of his death, 70.

Minshull, Elizabeth, married to Milton at St. Mary Aldermary, 232.

Molins, Dr. James, tablet to, in St. Bride's, Fleet Street, 148.

Monmouth, Duke of, his connection with Thomas Thynne referred to by Dryden, 21.

Moore, Sir John, benefactor to St. Dunstan's in the East, 169; monument to, 170, 171; writing school of Christ's Hospital built by, 172.

Moore, Dame Mary, tablet to, in St. Dunstan's in the East, 171.

More, Sir Thomas, execution of, 20; John Larke his friend, 54.

Morgan, Dr. John, organist at St. Andrew Undershaft, 30.

Morley, Thomas, brass plate to, in St. Olave's, Hart Street, 102.

Mortimer, Roger, Earl of March, buried in the Grey Friars' Church, 151.

Morton, John, afterwards Archbishop of Canterbury, rector of St. Dunstan's in the East, 165.

Motteux, Peter Anthony, buried at St. Andrew Undershaft, 36.

Mounson, Sir John, benefactor to St. Michael, Cornhill, 255.

Mountain, Thomas, rector of St. Michael Paternoster Royal, 260.
Munday, Anthony, buried at St. Stephen, Coleman Street, 285, 286; story of a Persian interment told by, 325, 326; his account of St. Katherine Coleman, 340.
Murray, Rev. Thomas Boyles, memorial window to, in St. Dunstan's in the East, 169.
Muss, —, window in St. Bride's, Fleet Street by, 145.
Myddelton, Sir Hugh, buried at St. Matthew, Friday Street, 302, 303.

Nares, Rev. Robert, rector of All Hallows on the Wall, 309.
Needler, Henry, benefactor to the poor of Christ Church, Newgate Street, 154.
Newcourt, Richard, his account of St. Augustine, 135; of St. Magnus, 197; his opinion of St. Mary Aldermary; 235; his account of St. Stephen, Coleman Street, 285; of St. Mary Woolnoth, 343; of St. Mary Woolchurch Haw, 344; of Dr. Holdsworth, 349.
Newton, Sir Isaac, at Holy Trinity, Minories, 339.
Newton, Rev. John, tablet to, in St. Mary Woolnoth, 346.
Newton, Thomas, Bishop of Bristol, monument to, in St. Mary-le-Bow, 249.
Nichol, Mary, Boydell's monument erected by, 209.
Nichols, John, brass plate in St. Bride's, Fleet Street, to wife and children of, 147.

Norman, John, buried at All Hallows, Honey Lane, 245.
North, Elizabeth, monument to, in St. Dunstan's in the West, 335.
North, Roger, monument to, in St. Dunstan's in the West, 335.
Northampton, Marquis of, monument of Sir John Spencer repaired by, 91.
Offa, King, connected with St. Alban, Wood Street, 113.
Offley, Sir Thomas, monument to, in St. Andrew Undershaft, 33, 34.
Oglethorpe, —, Bishop of Carlisle, buried at St. Dunstan's in the West, 332.
Olaf, King of Norway, St. Olave's dedicated to, 100.
Oldham, Hugh, afterwards Bishop of Exeter, rector of St. Mildred, Bread Street, 269.
Oldys, William, buried at St. Benet, Paul's Wharf, 141.
Oliver, Alderman Richard, a champion of the liberty of the press, 27.
Orgene, John, tablet to, in St. Olave's, Hart Street, 103.
Osborne, Sir Edward, story of his rescue of Anna Hewit, 160; ancestor of the Dukes of Leeds, 160, 193.
Osyth, St., St. Benet Sherehog originally dedicated to, 288.
Oteswich, John, monument to, in St. Helen, Bishopsgate, 88, 89.
Overbeck, Friedrich, copy from painting by, in St. Dunstan's in the East, 168.
Oxford, Edward, Earl of, sold advowson of St. Swithin by London Stone to Sir John Hart, 294.

Oxford, John, Earl of, advowson of St. Swithin by London Stone granted by Henry VIII. to, 294.

Packington, Dame Anne, monument to, in St. Botolph, Aldersgate, 318.
Palmer, Matthew, monument to, in St. Giles, Cripplegate, 67.
Pancras, St., martyrdom of, 244, 245.
Papworth, J. B., St. Bride's Avenue designed by, 144.
Paravicini, Sir Peter, daughter of, buried at St. Andrew Undershaft, 35; became bail for Pepys, 36; tablet to, in St. Dunstan's in the East, 173.
Parker, Matthew, Archbishop of Canterbury, induced Elizabeth to give advowson of St. Mary Abchurch to Corpus Christi College, Cambridge, 223.
Patience, Joseph, monument to, in All Hallows on the Wall, 308.
Paul, James, font of St. Michael, Cornhill, presented by, 255.
Peake, Sir Robert, buried at St. Sepulchre's, 355.
Pearson, John, Bishop of Chester, memorial to, at St. Clement, Eastcheap, 161, 162; rector of St. Christopher-le-Stocks, 207; Cleveland's funeral sermon preached by, 260.
Pearson, John L., R.A., his work at St. Helen, Bishopsgate, 78.
Peckard, Peter, Dean of Peterborough, his life of Nicholas Ferrar, 288.
Peck, Sir Henry, patron of St. Andrew Hubbard, 239.

Pemberton, Hugh, monument to, in St. Helen, Bishopsgate, 79, 92.
Penn, William, baptized at All Hallows Barking, 27.
Pennant, Sir Samuel, monument to, in St. Michael Paternoster Royal, 261.
Pepys, Elizabeth, monument to, in St. Olave's, Hart Street, 106, 107.
Pepys, Samuel, his account of the Great Fire, 17, 18, 136; Sir John Kempthorne mentioned by, 24; accused of treasonable correspondence with France, 36; details respecting, 105, 106; buried in St. Olave's, Hart Street, 107; monument to, 108; his "bever," 143; 173.
Pepys, Tom, buried in St. Olave's, Hart Street, 106, 107.
Perkins, William, volume of sermons by, at St. Andrew Undershaft, 36.
Peverell, Ralph, patron of St. Martin in the Vintry, 262.
Peyton, Sir John de, patron of St. Mary Somerset, 279.
Philippa, queen of Edward III., benefactress to the Grey Friars' Church, 151.
Philips, Edward, his account of Milton, 148, 149.
Philips, Katharine, the "matchless Orinda," buried at St. Benet Sherehog, 289.
Phillips, Rev. F. P., benefactions of, to St. Bartholomew the Great, 41.
Pickering, Sir William, monument to, in St. Helen, Bishopsgate, 86, 87.
Pickering, Sir William, the elder, tablet to, in St. Helen, Bishopsgate, 87.

Pierson, Richard, bequest of, to St. Mary Aldermary, 232.

Pindar, Sir Paul, his loyalty and liberality, 326; monument to, in St. Botolph, Bishopsgate, 327, 329.

Pope, Alexander, references by, to Milbourn, 54; Denham praised by, 147; allusion of, to Duncombe, 201.

Pope, Alexander, the elder, 351.

Pope, Magdalen, buried at St. Benet Fink, 351.

Pope, Sir Thomas, buried at St. Stephen, Walbrook, 288.

Pophame, —, rebuilder of St. Sepulchre's, 352, 353.

Porteous, Beilby, Bishop of London, St. Peter-le-Poer consecrated by, 349.

Potter, John, Archbishop of Canterbury, father-in-law of Dr. Milles, 178.

Poultney, Sir John, St. Lawrence Poultney named after, 2; his College of Corpus Christi, 223, 225; said to have built All Hallows the Less, 262.

Pound, Mrs., benefactions of, to St. Katherine Cree, 96.

Poynings, Joan, brass to, at St. Helen, Bishopsgate, now lost, 90.

Prentice, —, window presented by, to St. Helen, Bishopsgate, 92.

Price, Joshua, window by, in St. Andrew's, Holborn, 127.

Pridden, Rev. John, tablet to, in St. Bride's, Fleet Street, 145.

Prince of Wales at St. Bartholomew the Great, 41.

Pritchard, Lady, subscriber towards rebuilding Holy Trinity, Minories, 338

Prynne, William, Laud attacked by, 95; set in the pillory, 302.

Pulteney, William, Earl of Bath, patron of Bishop Newton, 249.

Purcell, Henry, played for Father Smith, 128; organist at St. Clement, Eastcheap, 162.

Purchas, Samuel, the writer of travels, rector of St. Martin, Ludgate, 219, 220.

Purchas, Samuel, font of St. Peter, Cornhill, presented by, 283.

Purchase, William, buried at St. Lawrence Jewry, 190.

Racket, Mrs., Pope's half-sister, 351.

Radcliffe, Dame Anne, monument to, in St. Olave's, Hart Street, 102.

Radcliffe, Sir John, monument to, in St. Olave's, Hart Street, 102.

Rahere, founder of Priory and Hospital of St. Bartholomew, 37, 38, 39, 41; his tomb, 43, 45; pictures of, by Hogarth, 50; Alfune said to have been his friend, 55.

Raleigh, Sir Walter, copy of his "History of the World" at St. Andrew Undershaft, 36; life of, by Oldys, 141; edition of his works by Birch, 214; acquainted with Ferrar, 289.

Ramsey, Dame Mary, benefactress to Christ's Hospital, 152; tablet to, in Christ Church, Newgate Street, 153; 344.

Ramsey, Sir Thomas, husband of Dame Mary, 152; buried at St. Mary Woolnoth, 344.

Rawlins, Sir William, tomb of, in churchyard of St. Botolph, Bishops-

Index of Proper Names.

gate, 329 ; charitable bequest of, 330.

Rawson, Christopher, brass to, in All Hallows Barking, 22 ; his family, 22, 23.

Reynolds, Edward, afterwards Bishop of Norwich, vicar of St. Lawrence Jewry, 194.

Ria, Hubert de, St. Mary Woolchurch Haw built by, 344.

Riccard, Sir Andrew, monument to, in St. Olave's, Hart Street, 105 ; benefactor to St. Michael, Cornhill, 255.

Rich, Sir Richard, bought Priory of St. Bartholomew from Henry VIII., 38 ; created a peer and Lord Chancellor, 189, 190.

Rich, Richard, buried at St. Lawrence Jewry, 189; memorial window to, 193.

Richard I., King, benefactions of, to All Hallows Barking, 15 ; story about the burial of his heart, 15, 16.

Richard II., King, new buildings of, at Westminster Hall, 197 ; 217, 272, 289 ; rectory of St. Botolph, Aldersgate, appropriated by, to St. Martin's-le-Grand, 317.

Richard III., King, college of, at All Hallows Barking, 16 ; resided at Crosby Place, 87 ; 184 ; Rotherham imprisoned by, 301.

Richardson, Dame Elizabeth, monument to, in St. Botolph's, Aldersgate, 318.

Richardson, John, gift by, to All Hallows Barking, 18.

Richardson, Samuel, buried at St. Bride's, Fleet Street, 147 ; grandfather of Rev. Samuel Crowther, 155.

Riculphus, patron of All Hallows Barking, 15.

Ridley, Nicholas, Bishop of London, preached in favour of the establishment of Christ's Hospital, 152.

Rivers, James, monument to, in St. Bartholomew the Great, 46.

Robert of Gloucester, quoted by Weever, 216.

Robinson, John, monument to, in St. Helen, Bishopsgate, 78, 79.

Rochester, Robert, brass to, in St. Helen, Bishopsgate, 90.

Rodoway, William, bequest of, to St. Mary Aldermary, 232.

Roe, Sir William, buried at St. Lawrence Jewry, 190.

Roger, Bishop of Salisbury, bestowed St. Sepulchre's on the Priory of St. Bartholomew, 352.

Rogers, Henry, St. Mary Aldermary rebuilt from legacy left by, 233 ; memorials to, in the church, 234.

Rogers, John, the martyr, rector of St. Margaret Moses, 272 ; vicar of St. Sepulchre's, 356.

Rogers, Robert, gift by, to St. Mary, Aldermanbury, 231.

Rogers, Thomas, carvings by, at St. Michael, Cornhill, 255.

Rogers, W. Gibbs, carvings by, at St. Mary-at-Hill, 239.

Romaine, Rev. William, monument to, in St. Andrew by the Wardrobe, 124, 125 ; lecturer at St. Dunstan's in the West, 332.

Romilly, Isaac, tablet to, in St. Bride's, Fleet Street, 148.

Rose, Alderman William Anderson,

protested against the destruction of St. Mary Woolnoth, 347.

Rotherham, Thomas, afterwards Archbishop of York, rector of St. Vedast, 301.

Rothing, Richard, said to have rebuilt St. James, Garlickhithe, 183.

Roubiliac, Louis François, bust by, in St. Botolph, Aldersgate, 318.

Roycroft, Samuel, benefactor to the parish of St. Bartholomew the Great, 48.

Roycroft, Thomas, monument to, in St. Bartholomew the Great, 47, 48.

Rubens, Peter Paul, window copied from his "Descent from the Cross," formerly in St. Bride's, Fleet Street, 145.

Rus, William, benefactor to St. Michael, Cornhill, 256.

Rusche, John, brass to, in All Hallows Barking, 22.

Russell, Robert, tablet to, in St. Dunstan's in the East, 172.

Russell, Sir William, benefactor to St. Dunstan's in the East, 169; monument to, 172.

Rykedon, Robert, patron of St. Margaret Pattens and St. Peter, Cornhill, 281.

Rysbrack, John Michael, monument by, in St. Margaret Pattens, 215.

Sacheverell, Dr. Henry, rector of St. Andrew's, Holborn, 129, 130.

St. Michel, Alexander Marchant, Sieur de, father of Mrs. Pepys, 106.

Sancroft, William, Archbishop of Canterbury, his recommendation of Hickes, 27.

Sanderson, Robert, Bishop of Lincoln, figure of, in stained glass, at St. Dunstan in the West, 337.

Saunders, Rev. Isaac, monument to, in St. Andrew by the Wardrobe, 124, 125.

Saunders, Lawrence, rector of All Hallows, Bread Street, martyrdom of, 250.

Savage, Richard, baptism of, recorded in register of St. Andrew's, Holborn, 131.

Scheemakers, Peter, monuments by, 25.

Scott, Sir Gilbert, reredos at St. Olave's, Hart Street, designed by, 101; alterations at St. Michael, Cornhill, by, 254.

Scott, Sarah, monument to, in St. Lawrence Jewry, 196.

Scott, Sir Walter, his description of the Earl of Oxford, 294.

Scottow, Mary, benefactress to St. Michael, Cornhill, 255.

Seaman, Dutton, font at St. Mary Aldermary presented by, 234.

Sevenoaks, or Sevenoake, William, benefactor to St. Dunstan's in the East, 168, 169; account of, by Lambarde, 216, 217; by Stow, 217.

Seymour, Sir Thomas, commemorated at St. Lawrence Jewry, 193.

Shadworth, Sir John, buried at St. Mildred, Bread Street, 269; commemorated by a tablet, 273, 274.

Shakespeare, William, monument of, in Westminster Abbey, 25; connection of, with Sir Thomas Lucy, 63;

Crosby Place mentioned by, 88; supposed to have been a parishioner of St. Helen, Bishopsgate, 92; patronized by Earl of Southampton, 129; criticism on, by Whalley, 214, 215; first edition of his plays, 228; London Stone noticed by, 297.

Shaughsware, a Persian, account of the interment of, 326.

Shaw, John, architect of St. Dunstan in the West, 333; tablet recording his death, 336.

Shelley, Percy Bysshe, married Mary Wolstonecraft Godwin at St. Mildred, Bread Street, 274.

Sherehog, Benedict, St. Benet Sherehog named after, 288.

Sherlock, William, Dean of St. Paul's, rector of St. George, Botolph Lane, 181; Benjamin Calamy's funeral sermon preached by, 229.

Sherwood, Edward, monument to, in St. Mary Abchurch, 226.

Shirley, John, buried at St. Bartholomew the Less, 315.

Shorter, Sir John, ancestor of the Marquises of Hertford, 193.

Shrewsbury, Earl of, mansion of Cold Harbour pulled down by, 262.

Shute, John, buried at St. Edmund the King and Martyr, 176.

Sidney, Sir Philip, esteem of, for Albericus Gentilis, 82.

Silber, A. M., fountain given by, 115.

Slingsby, Sir Harry, execution of, 222.

Smallwood, George, rector of St. Mary-le-Bow, 246.

Smalpace, Percival, monument to, in St. Bartholomew the Great, 46.

Smethergill, —, organist at All Hallows Barking, 19.

Smith, Elizabeth, monument to, in St. Botolph, Aldersgate, 318.

Smith, Father, rival of Harris, 19; organ for the Temple built by, 128; organ of St. Dunstan in the East built by, 170; organ of St. James, Garlickhithe, built by, 185; organ of St. Peter, Cornhill, built by, 283; organ of St. Mary Woolnoth built by, 346.

Smith, Gerard, organ of All Hallows Barking repaired by, 19.

Smith, Dame Jane, altar-piece presented by, to St. Mary Aldermary, 234.

Smith, Captain John, buried at St. Sepulchre's, 354; his epitaph, 354, 355.

Smith, Lieutenant John, monument to, in St. Mary, Aldermanbury, 230, 231.

Smith, Sir John, buried at St. Mary Aldermary, 234.

Smith, Robert, godfather of Stow, buried at St. Michael, Cornhill, 257.

Snayth, George, brass plate to, in All Hallows Barking, 23, 24.

Southampton, Thomas Wriothesley, first Earl of, 70; advowson of St. Andrew, Holborn, granted by Henry VIII. to, 129; also that of St. Peter, West Cheap, 303.

Southey, Robert, letter of Lamb to, 131.

Speed, John, monument to, in St. Giles, Cripplegate, 64, 65.

Spencer, Sir John, screen in memory

of, at St. Helen, Bishopsgate, 77, 78; monument to, 90, 91.

Spenser, Edmund, edition of his "Faery Queen," by Birch, 214.

Stagg, Thomas, tablet to, in St. Giles, Cripplegate, 67.

Stainer, Sir Samuel, gift of, to St. Katherine Cree, 96.

Staines, John, monument to, in St. Giles, Cripplegate, 68.

Staines, Sir William, monument to, in St. Giles, Cripplegate, 68; arms of, in the church, 69; engraving of, 71; St. Bride's steeple repaired by, 143; Bow steeple repaired by, 247; St. Alphage rebuilt by, 312.

Staper, Richard, monument to, in St. Helen, Bishopsgate, 90.

Starling, Sir Samuel, arms of, on a window at All Hallows Barking, 18.

Steele, Sir Richard, account of the service at St. James, Garlickhithe, by, 186, 187.

Stillingfleet, Edward, afterwards Bishop of Worcester, rector of St. Andrew's, Holborn, 129.

Stock, John, tablet to, in Christ Church, Newgate Street, 156.

Stockton, Sir John, knighted by Edward IV., 87.

Stoddart, Sarah, married to Hazlitt at St. Andrew's, Holborn, 131.

Stone, Nicholas, monument of Sir Julius Cæsar by, 86.

Stow, John, his account of the foundation of the Priory of the Holy Trinity, Aldgate, 2; his story about Richard I.'s heart, 15; his account of the rebuilding of St. Andrew Undershaft, 28, 29; his monument there, 30, 31; his history and great merit, 31, 32, 33; his account of Sir Thomas Offley's bequest, 34; his derivation of Cripplegate, 55; his resemblance to Speed, 64, 65; his account of Garter House, 69, 70; of Crosby Place, 81, 90; of St. Helen, Bishopsgate, 83, 84; of St. Martin Outwich, 89; of St. Katherine Cree, 94, 95; Holbein's burial-place not mentioned by, 98; his account of St. Olave's, Hart Street, 100; of All Hallows Staining, 109; of St. James's Hospital, 113; of All Hallows, Lombard Street, 116; of St. Leonard, Eastcheap, 120; of St. Anne, Blackfriars, 123; of St. Faith's, 135; of St. Benet, Paul's Wharf, 139; of the Grey Friars' Church, 151; of Christ Church, Newgate Street, 152; of St. Clement, Eastcheap, 159; of St. Dunstan's in the East, 163; of St. Edmund the King and Martyr, 176; of St. Nicholas Acon, 177; of St. James, Garlickhithe, 183; of St. Michael, Queenhithe, 187; of Venele's monument, 197; of St. Margaret, Lothbury, 205; of St. Olave Jewry, 208; of St. Martin Pomary, 209; of St. Mary Colechurch, 211; of the Hospital of St. Thomas of Acon, 211; of St. Margaret Pattens, 212; of St. Martin, Ludgate, 216; of William Sevenoake, 217; of St. Mary Aldermary, 232; of St. Antholin's, 236; of St. Mary-le-Bow, 242-244; of Honey Lane, 245; of the shed by Bow

Church, 247, 248; of St. Michael, Cornhill, 254; his opinion of Fabian's "Chronicle," 256; born in the parish of St. Michael, Cornhill, 256; his father, grandfather, and godparents buried there, 256, 257; his account of St. Michael, Wood Street, 265; his story about James IV.'s head, 265, 266; his account of St. Mildred's, Bread Street, 269; of St. Mary Somerset, 277; of St. Mary Mounthaw, 278; of St. Peter, Cornhill, 280, 281; of St. Stephen, Coleman Street, 285; of St. Benet Sherehog, 288; of London Stone, 297; of St. Vedast's, 299; of St. Alphage, 311, 312; of John Shirley, 315; of St. Botolph, Aldgate, 321; of St. Botolph, Bishopsgate, 325; of St. Katherine Coleman, 340; of St. Mary Woolnoth, 343; of St. Mary Woolchurch Haw, 344; of St. Peter-le-Poer, 348; of St. Sepulchre's, 352, 353.

Strafford, Thomas Wentworth, Earl of, baptized at St. Dunstan's in the West, 332.

Strange, George, Lord, buried at St. James, Garlickhithe, 184.

Street, George Edmund, R.A., crypt discovered by, at St. Dionis Backchurch, 121.

Stretchley, Thomas, benefactor to the poor of Christ Church, Newgate Street, 154.

Strong, Edward, Wren's master-mason, 260.

Strype, John, his reflections on Stow's treatment, 31; mentions cause of Stow's death, 32; his account of St. Giles, Cripplegate, 56, 57; of Crowder's Well, 72; of St. Katherine Cree, 96-98; of Sir Andrew Riccard's monument, 105; of Bride Lane, 149; of Christ Church, Newgate Street, 153; of Sir William Russell's monument, 172; of a monument in St. Mary Magdalene, Old Fish Street, 210; of All Hallows, Bread Street, 230; of St. Mary Woolnoth, 345.

Stubbs, Rev. Philip, rector of St. James, Garlickhithe, reading of, praised by Steele, 187.

Suffolk, Henry Grey, Duke of, 20; at the monastery of Shene, 266; head at Holy Trinity, Minories, said to be his, 339.

Sumner, John Bird, Archbishop of Canterbury, arms of, in St. Dunstan's in the East, 168, 169.

Surrey, Henry Howard, Earl of, temporarily interred at All Hallows Barking, 20.

Sutton, Charles Manners, Archbishop of Canterbury, first stone of new church of St. Dunstan in the East laid by, 167; his arms in the church, 168.

Swift, Jonathan, advocated the claims of Sacheverell, 129.

Taswell, Dr., his narrative of the Great Fire, 136.

Tate, Sir Richard, buried at All Hallows Staining, 109.

Taylor, alias Cardmaker, John, vicar of St. Bride's, Fleet Street, martyrdom of, 145.

Tenison, Thomas, Archbishop of Can-

terbury, arms of, in St. Dunstan's in the East, 169.
Thavie, John, bequest by, to St. Andrew's, Holborn, 128.
Thesiger, Frederick, Lord Chelmsford, baptized at St. Dunstan's in the East, 175.
Thimbleby, Rev. —, Benjamin Disraeli baptized by, 132.
Thomas of St. Osyth, successor of Rahere, 39, 43.
Thornhill, Sir James, figures of Moses and Aaron at St. Michael, Queenhithe, retouched by, 188; vestry-room ceiling of St. Lawrence Jewry painted by, 192; cupola of St. Mary Abchurch painted by, 225.
Thorpe, Samuel, monument to, in St. Katherine Cree, 98.
Throckmorton, Sir Nicholas, monument to, in St. Katherine Cree, 97.
Thynne, William, brass to, in All Hallows Barking, 21; his edition of Chaucer, and family, 21.
Tillotson, John, raised to the primacy, 181; monument to, at St. Lawrence Jewry, 195; life of, by Birch, 214; refused living of St. Mary, Aldermanbury, 229.
Tite, Sir William, assistant architect of St. Dunstan's in the East, 167.
Tombes, Henry, decorated St. Andrew Undershaft, 29.
Tomkins, Nathaniel, buried at St. Andrew's, Holborn, 130.
Torriano, Charles and Rebecca, brass plate to, in St. Andrew Undershaft, 35.
Townley, Rev. G. S., tablet to, in St. Stephen, Walbrook, 293.

Trapp, Rev. Joseph, monument to, in Christ Church, Newgate Street, 156.
Travers, John, house hired by the Grey Friars from, 150.
Trenchaunt, Lord, buried at St. Mildred, Bread Street, 269; commemorated by a tablet, 273, 274.
Tricket, Ralph, patron of St. Martin Pomary, 209.
Trindle, Edmond, godfather of Stow, buried at St. Michael, Cornhill, 257.
Trott, Sir John, benefactor to the poor of St. Leonard's, Foster Lane, 154.
Turner, Peter, monument to, in St. Olave's, Hart Street, 103.
Turner, Samuel, tablet to, in St. Dunstan's in the East, 174.
Turner, Thomas, tablet to, in St. Dunstan's in the East, 174.
Turner, William, Dean of Wells, tablet to, in St. Olave's, Hart Street, 102, 103.
Tusser, Thomas, buried at St. Mildred in the Poultry, 210.
Tyler, Wat, Lyons put to death by, 183; slain by Walworth, 204.
Tyndale, William, preached at St. Dunstan's in the West, 332; carved head of, 334.
Tyson, Dr. Edward, monument to, in All Hallows, Lombard Street, 121.

Vanbrugh, Sir John, buried at St. Stephen, Walbrook, 293.
Vandeput, Sir Peter, monument erected by, in St. Margaret Pattens, 215.
Vandyck, Sir Anthony, a parishioner of St. Anne, Blackfriars, 123.

Index of Proper Names.

Vernon, Henry, monument to, in St. Stephen, Coleman Street, 286.
Vernon, John, monument to, in St. Michael, Cornhill, 257.
Veronese, Paul, copy of painting by, in St. Dunstan's in the East, 168.
Victoria, Queen, fountain erected in St. Giles, Cripplegate, churchyard, in commemoration of jubilee of, 71.
Vine, Rev. Marshall Hall, tablet to, in St. Mary-le-Bow, 249, 250.
Virby, Thomas, brass to, in All Hallows Barking, 22.
Vyner, Sir Robert, munificence of, towards St. Mary Woolnoth, 345.

Wagstaffe, Thomas, memorial to, at St. Margaret Pattens, 214.
Waithman, Alderman Robert, tablet to, in St. Bride's, Fleet Street, 148.
Waller, Edmund, plot of, 130.
Walsingham, Sir Francis, house of, in Seething Lane, 109.
Walton, Bryan, Bishop of Chester, memorial to, in St. Clement, Eastcheap, 161, 162.
Walton, Izaak, memorial window to, at St. Dunstan's in the West, 336, 337.
Walworth, Sir William, first mayoralty of, 183; buried at St. Michael, Crooked Lane, 204.
Ward, Sir Patience, monument to, in St. Mary Abchurch, 226.
Ward, Seth, afterwards Bishop of Salisbury, vicar of St. Lawrence Jewry, 194.
Warkenethby, Hugo de, last rector of St. Lawrence Jewry, 189.

Warren, Sir Ralph, great-grandfather of Oliver Cromwell, buried at St. Benet Sherehog, 289.
Warwick, Richard Nevil, Earl of, Henry VI. temporarily restored by, 16; patron of All Hallows the Great, 262.
Warwick, Countess of, married to Addison at St. Edmund the King and Martyr, 179.
Watkins, —, purchased advowson of St. Swithin by London Stone. 204.
Waugh, John, Bishop of Carlisle, rector of St. Peter, Cornhill, 283, 284.
Webb, Aston, restoration of St. Bartholomew the Great conducted by, 40.
Webster, John, said to have been buried at St. Andrew's, Holborn, 130.
Weever, John, his account of St. Martin, Ludgate, 216.
Wesley, John and Charles, grandsons of Samuel Annesley, 70.
West, Benjamin, picture by, in St. Stephen, Walbrook, 291.
Weybridge, Rev. John, monument to, in St. Giles, Cripplegate, 68.
Whalley, Peter, rector of St. Margaret Pattens, 214, 215.
Wharton, Dr. Thomas, tablet to, in St. Michael Bassishaw, 252, 253.
Wheeler, Daniel, tablet to, in St. Bartholomew the Great, 49, 50.
Whichcote, Dr. Benjamin, vicar of St. Lawrence Jewry, 195, 196.
Whitbread, Samuel, bust of Milton set up by, 65, 66.
White, Francis, afterwards Bishop of Ely, preacher at St. Benet Sherehog, 288, 289.

White, Dame Joan, great-grandmother of Oliver Cromwell, buried at St. Benet Sherehog, 289.

White, Sir Thomas, founder of St. John's College, Oxford, 289.

White, Thomas, afterwards Bishop of Peterborough, rector of All Hallows the Great, 264.

White, Dr. Thomas, vicar of St. Dunstan's in the West, 332.

White, William, benefactor to St. Katherine Coleman, 340.

Whitelocke, Sir Bulstrode, baptized at St. Dunstan's in the West, 332.

Whiting, John and Margaret, tablet to, in St. Bartholomew the Great, 48, 49.

Whiting, John, jun., tablet to, in St. Bartholomew the Great, 48; schools founded by, 48, 49.

Whitney, Constance, monument to, in St. Giles, Cripplegate, 63, 67.

Whittingham, Sir Robert, patron of St. Stephen, Walbrook, 287.

Whittington, Sir Richard, library built for the Grey Friars by, 151; advowson of St. Margaret Pattens given to the mayor and commonalty of London by, 212; story of Bow Bells, 242; rebuilt St. Michael Paternoster Royal, and founded a college there, 259; buried there, 260; memorial window to, 261; advowson of St. Peter, Cornhill, given to the mayor and commonalty of London by, 281, 282.

Whitwell, John, benefactor to St. Michael, Cornhill, 256.

Wickenbroke, Hugo de, gave advowson of St. Lawrence Jewry to Balliol College, Oxford, 189.

Wilkes, John, his defence of the freedom of the press, 27; obelisk to, in Ludgate Circus, 148.

Wilkins, John, Bishop of Chester, preceded Pearson, 161; vicar of St. Lawrence Jewry, 194; buried there, 195; succeeded there by Whichcote, 196.

Willement, —, window by, in St. Stephen, Walbrook, 291.

William, the Conqueror, King, 242, 250, 262; St. Alphage confirmed to St. Martin-le-Grand by, 311; 321.

William Rufus, King, privileges of the Knighten guild confirmed by, 321.

William III., King, 24, 160; Namur besieged by, 296.

William, son of William the goldsmith, Priory of St. Helen founded by, 73.

Williams, John, Archbishop of York, and Lord Keeper, life of, by Hacket, 129.

Williams, Sir Richard, convent buildings of St. Helen's bestowed by Henry VIII. on, 74.

Williams, Thomas, brass to, in St. Helen, Bishopsgate, 90.

Williams, William Meade, memorial window presented to St. Helen, Bishopsgate, by, 92.

Williamson, Dame Dyonis, munificence of, towards St. Dunstan's in the East, 165, 169; tablet to her grandfather set up by the parishioners, 172, 173 munificence of, to St. Mary-le-Bow, 245, 246.

Willow, Andrew, monument to, in St. Botolph, Bishopsgate, 329.

Index of Proper Names.

Wilson, Alderman Colonel, window presented by, to St. Helen's, Bishopsgate, 92.

Wilson, Dr. Thomas, picture presented to St. Stephen, Walbrook, by, 291; tablet to, 293.

Winwood, Sir Ralph, buried at St. Bartholomew the Less, 315.

Withers, H. T., organ-case presented to St. Bartholomew the Great by, 41.

Wood, Sir Matthew, arms of, in St. Giles, Cripplegate, 69; portrait of, 71.

Woodcocke, Katherine, married to Milton at St. Mary, Aldermanbury, 228.

Woodthorpe, Edmund, Milton's cenotaph designed by, 65.

Worcester, John Tiptoft, Earl of, brotherhood established at All Hallows Barking by, 16.

Worde, Wynkyn de, buried in St. Bride's, Fleet Street, 146.

Wotton, Sir Henry, figure of, in stained glass, at St. Dunstan's in the West, 337.

Wotton, Nicholas, brass to, in St. Helen, Bishopsgate, 90.

Wray, Daniel, tablet to, in St. Botolph, Aldersgate, 319.

Wren, Sir Christopher, the great rebuilder of city churches, his genius, and method of work, 3-5; demolition of some of his churches, 7; catalogue of his churches, 8-11; rebuilt St. Alban, Wood Street, 113-115; All Hallows, Lombard Street, 116-121; St. Andrew by the Wardrobe, 122-125; body of St. Andrew, Holborn, 126-132; St. Anne and St. Agnes, 133, 134; St. Augustine's, 135-138; St. Benet, Paul's Wharf, 139-141; St. Bride's, 142-149; Christ Church, Newgate Street, 150-157; St. Clement, Eastcheap, 159-162; St. Dunstan in the East, 163-175; designed writing school of Christ's Hospital, 172; rebuilt St. Edmund the King and Martyr, 176-179; St. George, Botolph Lane, 181, 182; St. James, Garlickhithe, 183-188; St. Michael, Queenhithe, 187, 188; St. Lawrence Jewry, 189-196; St. Magnus, 197-204; St. Michael, Crooked Lane, 204; St. Margaret, Lothbury, 205-211; St. Christopher-le-Stocks, 207; St. Bartholomew by the Exchange, 207; St. Olave Jewry, 209; St. Mildred in the Poultry, 210; St. Margaret Pattens, 212-215; St. Martin, Ludgate, 216-222; St. Mary Magdalene, Old Fish Street, 220-222; St. Mary Abchurch, 223-227; St. Mary, Aldermanbury, 228-231; St. Mary Aldermary, 232-237; St. Antholin's, 236; St. Mary-at-Hill, 238-241; St. Mary-le-Bow, 242-251; All Hallows, Bread Street, 250; St. Michael Bassishaw, 252, 253; St. Michael, Cornhill, 254-258; St. Michael Paternoster Royal, 259-264; All Hallows the Great, 263; St. Michael, Wood Street, 265-268; St. Mildred, Bread Street, 269-274; St. Nicholas Cole Abbey, 275-279; St. Mary Somerset, 277, 278; St. Peter, Cornhill, 280-284; St. Stephen

Coleman Street, 285, 286; St. Stephen, Walbrook, 287-293; St. Swithin by London Stone, 294-298; St. Vedast's, 299-303; St. Matthew, Friday Street, 302; repaired St. Mary Woolnoth, 345; rebuilt St. Benet Fink, 351; uncertain whether he rebuilt St. Sepulchre's, 353.

Wren, Jane, daughter of Sir Christopher, 166.

Wrench, Rev. Thomas Robert, monument to, in St. Michael, Cornhill, 258.

Wrench, Rev. Thomas William, tablet to, in St. Michael, Cornhill, 258.

Wrenne, Geoffrey, rector of St. Margaret, New Fish Street, 198, 199.

Wright, Robert, afterwards Bishop of Lichfield, rector of St. Katherine Coleman, 340.

Wright, Samuel, monument to, in St. Alphage, 313.

Wynne, Richard, monument to, in St. Alban, Wood Street, 115.

Yenele, or de Yeveley, Henry, buried at St. Magnus, 197.

Young, Charles, organist at All Hallows Barking, 19.

Young, Edward, the poet, married at St. Mary-at-Hill, 240.

Young, Launcelot, said to have brought James IV.'s head from Shene to Wood Street, 266.

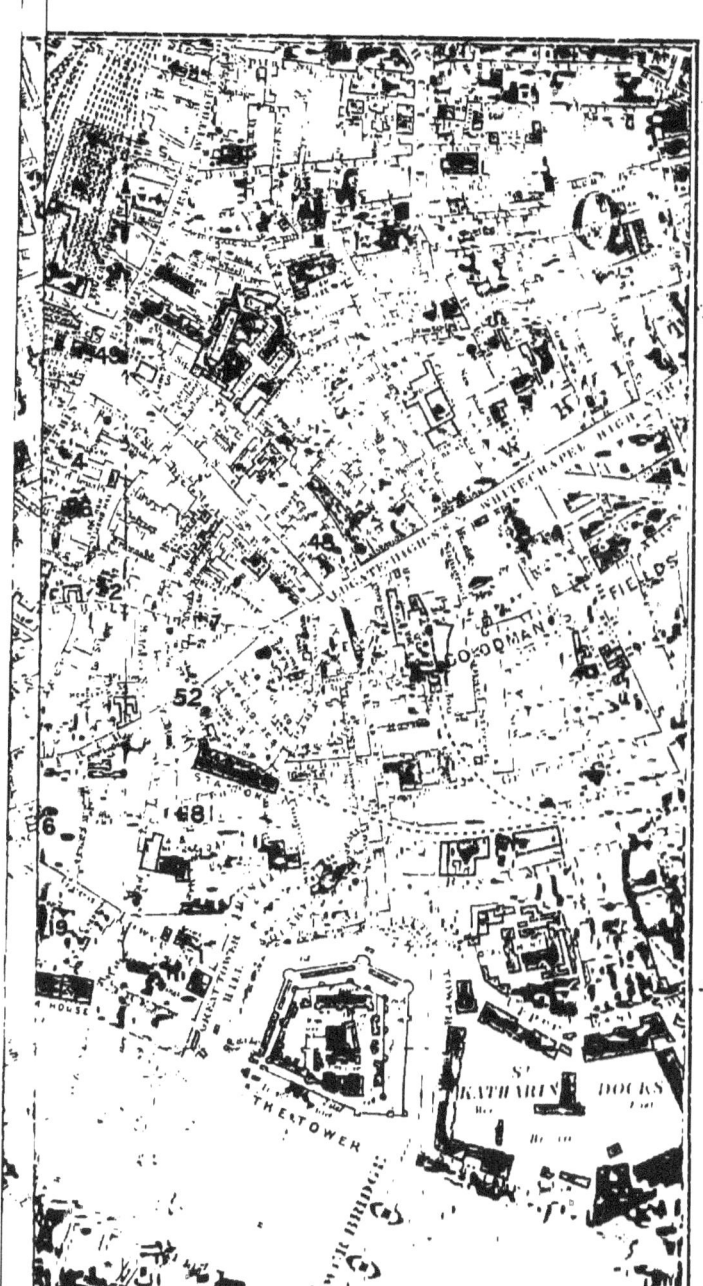

LONDON CITY CHURCHES

Wren's Churches marked thus ...... ■